Joseph Priestley

Discourses relating to the evidences of revealed religion:

Delivered in the Church of the Universalists, at Philadelphia, 1796 - Vol. 1

Joseph Priestley

Discourses relating to the evidences of revealed religion:
Delivered in the Church of the Universalists, at Philadelphia, 1796 - Vol. 1

ISBN/EAN: 9783337718527

Printed in Europe, USA, Canada, Australia, Japan

Cover: Foto ©Lupo / pixelio.de

More available books at **www.hansebooks.com**

DISCOURSES

RELATING TO

The Evidences of Revealed Religion,

DELIVERED IN THE

CHURCH OF THE UNIVERSALISTS,
AT PHILADELPHIA, 1796.

AND

PUBLISHED AT THE REQUEST OF MANY OF THE
HEARERS.

BY *JOSEPH PRIESTLEY*, LL.D. F.R.S.
&c. &c.

Be ready always to give an anſwer to every man that aſketh you a reaſon of the hope that is in you.

1 PET. iii. 15.

PHILADELPHIA,
PRINTED FOR T. DOBSON, BY JOHN THOMPSON.
1796.

Copy Right ſecured according to Law.

THE DEDICATION.

To JOHN ADAMS,

VICE-PRESIDENT OF THE UNITED STATES OF AMERICA.

DEAR SIR,

THE happiness I have had of your acquaintance and correspondence ever since your embassy to England, our common friendship for Dr. Price, the ardent friend of liberty and of America, your steady attachment to the cause of christianity, the favourable attention you gave to the following Discourses, when they were delivered, and the wish you expressed that they might be published, induce me to take the liberty to dedicate them to you.

Statesmen who have the firmness of mind to profess themselves Christians, and who have a just sense of the importance of christianity, are not numerous; and those of them who adopt a rational christianity, the evidences and doctrines of which will bear to be submitted to the test of reason, in this age, in which, while many are carried away by the prevailing tide of infidelity, others oppose it by an enthusiasm which disclaims the aid of reason, are still fewer; and are therefore entitled to the greater esteem of those who entertain the same sentiments.

THE DEDICATION.

We shall, no doubt, ourselves be ranked with enthusiasts by those unbelievers (and by far the greater part of them are of this class) who have become so without any just knowledge of the subject, or investigation of the evidence of revelation. But the contempt of such persons, whatever rank they may hold in the political or the learned world, is itself contemptible. Every serious inquirer after truth, will respect other serious inquirers, though their opinions should differ ever so much. But the censures of men, whether well or ill informed, will appear of little moment to those who look to the decision of the impartial Judge of all. And, mindful of his solemn warning, we must not be ashamed of him, or of his cause, *in any circumstances, however unfavourable, lest he should be ashamed of us at a time when his favour will be of infinitely greater moment to us than any thing else.*

You and I, Sir, are advancing to a period of life in which these views naturally open more and more upon us. We find this world receding, and another fast approaching, and we feel the importance of having something to look to when the present scene of things shall be closed. And whatever we value for ourselves, it behoves us to recommend to others. You will, therefore, rejoice if an exhibition of the evidences of revealed religion, such as is contained

tained in these Discourses, should produce any effect.

It is happy that, in this country, religion has no connection with civil power, a circumstance which gives the cause of truth all the advantage that its best friends can desire. But religion is of as much use to Statesmen as to any individuals whatever. Christian principles will best enable men to devote their time, their talents, their lives, and what is often a greater sacrifice still, their characters, to the public good; and in public life this will often be, in a great measure, necessary.

Let a man attain to eminence, of any kind, and by whatever means, even the most honourable, he will be exposed to envy and jealousy, and of course he must expect to meet with calumny and abuse. It was the lot of our Saviour himself, and it is a part of the wise order of providence that it should always be so. For, besides that it is of the greatest importance to the community, that every person in a public station, should have the strongest motive for the greatest circumspection, unmixed praise is what no human mind can bear without injury. An undue elation, which would soon be found to be as hurtful to himself as unpleasant to others, would be the necessary consequence

sequence of it. And what principles can enable a man to consult the real good of his fellow citizens, without being diverted from his generous purpose by a regard to their opinion concerning him, like those of the Christian, who can be satisfied with the approbation of his own mind (which of course draws after it that of his Maker) and who, though not insensible to due praise, can despise calumny, and steadily overlooking every thing that is intermediate, patiently wait for the day of final retribution? As these principles enabled the apostles to rejoice in tribulation, and persecution of every kind, so the virtuous statesman will not complain of that abuse which operates so favourably both with respect to his own mind, and the interests of his country. They are Christian principles that best enable a man to bear this necessary and excellent discipline, and form the truly disinterested and magnanimous patriot.

I cannot conclude this address without expressing the satisfaction I feel in the government which has afforded me an asylum from the persecution which obliged me to leave England, persuaded that, its principles being fundamentally good, instead of tending, like the old governments of Europe, to greater abuse, it will tend to continual melioration. Still, however, my utmost wish is to live as a stranger

ger among you, with liberty to attend without interruption to my favourite purſuits; wiſhing well to my native country, as I do to all the world, and hoping that its intereſts, and thoſe of this country, will be inſeparable, and conſequently that peace between them will be perpetual.

I am, with the greateſt eſteem,

Dear Sir,

PHILADELPHIA,
May, 1796.

Yours ſincerely,

J. PRIESTLEY.

THE PREFACE.

THE Difcourfes contained in this volume may be confidered as fupplemental to thofe which I delivered in England relating to the fame fubject, juft before I left that country, and which have been re-printed in this. Being requefted to preach in this city, I thought I could not make choice of any fubjects more unexceptionable, or more ufeful, than of fuch as relate to the *evidences of revealed religion,* in an age abounding with unbelievers, many of whom have become fo merely for want of better information. Being unwilling to go over the fame ground that I had been upon before, I have made thefe difcourfes interfere as little as poffible with the former. Some of the fame obfervations will, no doubt, be found in both; but they are not many, and of fuch particular importance, that they cannot be too much impreffed on the minds of chriftians.

As

As I had no intention of publishing these discourses, at least at this time, I did not note the authorities I have made use of in them, as there could not have been any propriety, or use, in reciting them from the pulpit; and being at a distance from my library, I cannot add them now. But they are such as, I am confident, no person at all acquainted with the subjects will call in question. They were by no means originally collected by myself. The far greater part of them have been frequently quoted, and their accuracy never disputed. I had little to do besides collecting, arranging, and applying them, in a manner somewhat more adapted to my present purpose. The greater part of them will be found in *Leland's Necessity of Revelation*, *Young's Discourses on Revelation the Cure of superstition*, and the *Letters of some Jews to Voltaire*, all which works I would recommend to the attentive perusal of my readers. The doctrines of the heathen philosophers were almost all copied *verbatim* from *Brucker's History of Philosophy abridged by Dr. Enfield*, a truly valuable, accurate, and well digested work. The account of the Grecian oracles, and various of their superstitions, will be found in *Potter's Antiquities of Greece*, a common, but most excellent work.

The

The *Second Part of Mr. Paine's Age of Reason* being published in this city during the delivery of these Discourses, I thought proper to animadvert upon such parts of it as appeared to me most deserving of notice. I had once thought of replying to this part of the work more at large, as I did to the first part; but I afterwards thought that assertions so extravagant and ill founded as Mr. Paine's generally are, may be safely left to have their full effect, as it can only be upon the minds of persons so extremely ignorant and prejudiced, that no refutation would be attended to by them, so that it would only be throwing *pearls before swine*.

So great is Mr. Paine's ignorance with respect to subjects of this nature, that he maintains, page 35, that the book of Job has " all the " circumstantial evidences of being an original " book of the Gentiles," principally because he finds in it the mention of *Orion, Arcturus,* and the *Pleiades,* which are Greek words; when these terms occur only in translations, those in the original being quite different. Surely he had access to some unbelievers, who could have informed him better.

Without deigning to reply to any thing that had been advanced against the first part of his work, Mr. Paine in this proceeds with an air of insolent triumph, as if all the advocates

for

of revelation lay proſtrate at his feet, whereas they are looking down upon him, and feel no emotions but thoſe of pity for himſelf, and his deluded followers, *the blind led by the blind*.

There are, however, unbelievers more ignorant than Mr. Paine. M. Volney, Laquinio, and others in France, ſay that there never was ſuch a perſon as Jeſus Chriſt, and therefore, though they may have heard that there are ſuch books as thoſe of the New Teſtament, I conclude that they cannot have read them. Surely ſuch ignorance as this does not mark the *Age of Reaſon*.

I have more than once obſerved that the diſbelief of revelation makes the belief of the being of God of no practical uſe, and that it has, in France, led to ſpeculative atheiſm. In a tract publiſhed at Paris in 1793, intitled *A Letter to a Senſible Woman*, is the following paragraph, p. 25.

" Theiſm is an opinion reſpectable for the
" genius, and the virtues, of men who have
" embraced it" (referring, in a note to Socrates
and Rouſſeau) " no leſs than for the advantage
" which this firſt ſtep towards reaſon, on
" abandoning the prejudices of infancy, has
" been of to mankind. But, after all, it is
" but a firſt ſtep, and no perſons would ſtop
" there, if they would frankly give way to the
                                                " impulſe

"impulse they have received. No person remains
"in this intermediate system but through want
"of reflection, timidity, passion, or obstinacy.
"Time, experience, and an impartial examina-
"tion of our ideas, will undeceive us. Voltaire,
"who was long the apostle of theism, professed
"to doubt towards the close of his life, and
"repented that he had been too confident.
"Many others have experienced the same."

If, then, any person be in a state of mind in which he is shocked at the idea of absolute *atheism*, let him pause before he abandon *revelation*, and give way to what this writer calls *the first impulse*. But on no account let any obstruction be laid in the way of free enquiry. With the apostle (1 Thess. v. 2.) let us *prove all things, and hold fast* only that which shall appear to be *good*.

I might have given a curious counterpart to the hypotheses of the antient philosophers in those of the most distinguished of the modern unbelievers. For many of their opinions concerning the origin of the universe, its subsequent revolutions, and other subjects connected with religion and morals, are not less wild, incoherent, and absurd; as every theory must be that excludes the belief of a God, and a superintending providence. This undertaking, however, has been executed with equal truth and ability in a French work

work, entitled *Les Helviennes, ou Lettres Provinciales Philosophiques,* in five volumes, 12 mo. 1784. They are called *Provincial Letters* in imitation of those of that title by the famous Pascal, in which he exposed the absurdities of the principles of the Jesuits, a work of genuine humour, to which this is, in many respects, not inferior. It is therefore adapted to afford equal entertainment and instruction.

From this excellent work it will be evident that the rejection of revealed religion will be attended with all that dissoluteness of morals for which the antient heathens were remarkable, there being no vice for which some of the most eminent of modern philosophical unbelievers have not been advocates; and therefore that, in an advanced state of society, human reason has never proved a sufficient barrier against vice. It will also be evident that a propensity to the unrestrained indulgence of all the passions has been the principal cause of the prevaling disposition to throw off the salutary restraints of religion.

Not only are the great Christian virtues of humility, the forgiveness of injuries, and the loving of enemies, excluded from the class of virtues, and a spirit of pride and revenge encouraged; not only is all virtue reduced to mere self-love, the great end of human life represented to to be the purfuit of pleafure in the loweft fenfe of the word, and fuicide recommended when this object is no longer attainable; but the very barrier between men and brutes has been thrown down by many eminent unbelievers.

All the antient legiflators even among the heathens, confidered the laws of *marriage* as the firft ftep towards civilization, and the conjugal and parental relations as, what no doubt they are, the chief fource of the fweets of focial life. But many modern unbelievers openly plead not only for an unbounded liberty of divorce, but a community of women, and make very light of the vices moft contrary to nature. What is this but reducing men even lower than the ftate of brutes? And what can we expect from the natural operation of thefe principles, but the prevalence of thofe vices, which the apoftle in his fecond epiftle to Timothy enumerates as a fymptom of the approach of the *laft times*, which are elfewhere defcribed as exceedingly calamitous, 2 Tim. iii. 1. *This know, that in the laft days perilous times fhall come. For men fhall be lovers of their own felves, &c.* The apoftle Peter alfo fays, 2 Pet. iii. 3. *Knowing this that there fhall come in the laft days fcoffers, walking after their own lufts, and faying, Where is the promife of his coming, &c.* Reflecting on thefe things, we may well fay with the evangelifts, after they had related our

Saviour's

Saviour's predictions concerning the destruction of Jerusalem, and the various signs of its approach, *Let him that readeth, understand,* Math. xxiv. 15. Mark xiii. 14.

Unbelievers often complain of the difference of opinion among Christians, but their own opinions, even on the subject of christianity are as various. The celebrated Mr. D'Alembert, in his *Letters to the late king of Prussia* (Œuvres Posthumes, tom. 14. p. 105.) says, " It appears
" evident to me, as it does to your majesty, that
" christianity in its origin was nothing but pure
" deism, that Jesus Christ, the author of it,
" was only a kind of philosopher, the enemy of
" superstition, of persecution, and of priests;
" who preached benevolence and justice, and
" reduced the whole law to the love of our
" neighbour, and the worship of God in spirit
" and in truth, and that afterwards, St. Paul,
" then the fathers of the church, and lastly the
" councils, unhappily supported by the sovereigns,
" changed this religion. I therefore think it would
" be doing great service to mankind to reduce
" christianity to its primitive state, confining it
" to preaching to the people the doctrine of a
" God rewarding virtue, and punishing vice,
" who abhors superstition, detests intolerance,
" and who requires of men no other worship
" than that of loving and assisting one another."

The

The scheme of reducing christianity to its primitive state, is, no doubt, excellent, and this writer's idea of that state is not far from the truth. But his assertion that Jesus Christ taught *pure deism*, is altogether unfounded. If there be any truth in his history, he taught the doctrine of a *resurrection*, and supported it by miracles; and Paul was far from making any addition to the doctrine of his master. He had too many enemies among christians to have had that in his power. How christianity was corrupted afterwards is well known, and I have shewn the progress of it in my *History of the Corruptions of Christianity*.

Since the writing of this Preface, I have been favoured with a sight of the third volume of ' Asiatic Antiquities,' a work which promises to throw great light on the mythology, and early history, of several antient nations; and one passage in it, containing a quotation from an antient Hindoo writer, perhaps nearly as old as Moses, is so curious in itself, and such a confirmation of one part of his history, that I am persuaded my readers will be pleased with the communication of it. The work is intitled *Padma-puran*, and the translation of it is by Sir William Jones. Though the narrative is in substance the same with that of Moses, they differ in so many circumstances, that it is evident the writers did not copy from one another.

' To

"To Satyavarman, that sovereign of the whole earth, were born three sons, the eldest Sherma, then Charma*, and thirdly Jyapeti by name. They were all men of good morals, excellent in virtue, and virtuous deeds, skilled in the use of weapons, to strike with, or to be thrown, brave men, eager for victory in battle. But Satyavarman being continually delighted with devout meditation, and seeing his sons fit for dominion, laid upon them the burden of government.

"Whilst he remained honouring and satisfying the gods, and priests, and kine; one day, by the act of destiny, the king, having drank mead, became senseless, and lay asleep naked. Then was he seen by Charma, and by him were his two brothers called. To whom he said, "What now has befallen. In what state is this our sire? By those two was he hidden with clothes, and called to his senses again and again.

"Having recovered his intellect, and perfectly knowing what had passed, he cursed Charma, saying, Thou shalt be the servant of servants, And since thou wast a laughter in their presence, from laughter shalt thou acquire a name. Then he gave to Sharma the wide "domain

---

* Colonel Wilford observes, that in the vulgar dialects *Charma* is usually pronounced *Cham*, and *Sharma*, *Sham*.

"domain on the south of the snowy mountain. And to Jyapeti he gave all on the north of the snowy mountain; but he, by the power of religious contemplation, attained supreme blifs."

Sir William Jones had before advanced a conjecture that the *Afghans* might be of Hebrew extraction, and part of the ten tribes that were carried into captivity by the Assyrians. In his 'Anniverfary difcourfe,' prefixed to this volume, he fays, p. 6. "There is folid ground for believing that the Afghans are defcended from the Jews, becaufe they fometimes in confidence avow that unpopular origin, which in general they feduloufly conceal, and which other muffelmen perpetually affert; becaufe *Hazaret*, which appears to be the *Afereth* of Efdras, is one of their territories, and principally becaufe their language is evidently a dialect of the fcriptural Chaldaic."

Laftly, after reciting the unfavourable character given of the Jews by their enemies, and acceding to it, for which I am far from feeing fufficient reafon, he fays, p. 15, "They had the peculiar merit, among all the races of men under heaven, of preferving a rational and pure fyftem of devotion, in the midft of a wild polytheifm, inhuman or obfcene rites, and a dark labyrinth of errors, produced by ignorance, and fupported by interefted fraud. Theological inquries," he adds, "are no part of "of my prefent fubject, but I cannot refrain from adding, that the collection of tracts which from their excellence, we call *the fcriptures*, contain, independently of a divine origin, more true fublimity, more exquifite beauty, purer morality, more important hiftory, and finer ftrains both of poetry and eloquence, than could be collected within the fame compafs from all other books that were ever compofed in any age, or in any idiom. The two parts of which the fcriptures confift, are connected by a chain of compofitions" (meaning the prophetical books) "which bear no refemblance in form or ftyle to any that can be produced from the ftores of Grecian, Indian, Perfian, or even Arabian, learning. The antiquity of thefe compofitions no man doubts, and the unftrained application of them to events long fubfequent to their publication, is a folid ground of belief, that they were genuine productions, and confequently infpired."

When I compare the decided opinion of fuch a man as Sir William Jones, in which all men of learning will concur, with the confident affertions of Mr. Paine, who fays that the books of fcripture are but modern compofitions, I think of a man either really blind, or willfully fhutting his eyes, and declaring that *there is nothing to be feen*

CONTENTS.

DISCOURSE. PAGE.
I. *The Importance of Religion* - 1
II. *Of the superior Value of Revealed Religion* 27
III. *A View of Heathen Worship* - - 56
IV. *The same continued* - - 86
V. *The excellence of the Mosaic Institutions* 114
VI. *The same continued* - - 145
VII. *The Principles of the Heathen Philosophy compared with those of Revelation* - - - 176
VIII. *The same continued* - - 201
XI. *The evidence of the Mosaic and Christian Religions* - - 237
X. *The same continued* - - - 269
XI. *The Proof of Revealed Religion from Prophecy* - - 313
XII. *Internal Evidence of Jesus being no Impostor* - - 356
XIII. *The moral Influence of Christian Principles* - - - 395

ERRATA.

N. B. *(b)* signifies from the bottom of the page.

Page	line	for	read
41,	2,	*an,*	*our*
45,	7,	*wherever,*	*whenever*
51,	6 *(b)*	*a million,*	*two millions*
101,	1 *(b)*	*made*	*made it*
105,	7 *(b)*	*act,*	*art*
138,	14	*hear,*	*bear*
177,	9 *(b)*	*those,*	*these*
182,	13,	*not,*	*not that*
186,	13,	*Democrates,*	*Democritus*
232,	10,	*for,*	*and for*
243,	2 *(b)*	*cannot,*	*could not*
267,	2 *(b)*	*for*	*to*
271,	2,	*shall*	*shall now*
281,	1 *(b)*	*chargeable,*	*charged*
301,	7,	*an,*	*the best*
309,	2,	*that,*	*that though*
326,	1 *(b)*	*Jerusalem,*	*Jeroboam*
359,	5,	*is,*	*his*
363,	11 *(b)*	*erected,*	*erect*
370,	11,	*lewdest,*	*lowest*
402,	3,	*good,*	*goods*

A VIEW
OF THE
EVIDENCES OF REVEALED RELIGION.

DISCOURSE I.

The Importance of Religion.

The fear of the Lord is the beginning of wisdom; but fools hate knowledge and instruction.

PROVERBS, i. 7.

BY the *fear of God* we may very well understand *religion* in general, and there can be no doubt but that by religion Solomon meant such principles of it as he held to be the best founded, or the revelation by Moses. And as I propose, in a series of discourses, to give a view of the evidences of revealed religion, I shall in this show that the subject is of *importance*, that the knowledge we receive by means of it is of real

real value, tending to exalt the character, and add to the happinefs of man. Indeed if this be not the ufe of religion, it would not be worth our while to make any enquiry into its evidences; becaufe on that fuppofition, true or falfe, it would be an ufelefs and infignificant thing. The queftion is the more deferving of an attentive confideration, as many, I imagine, moft, unbelievers, maintain that religion is not merely an ufelefs, but a hurtful thing, debafing the mind of man, and adding to the miferies of his exiftence, fo that it is rendering him an effential fervice to free his mind from it.

Now, what is it that the friends of religion, fay is fo beneficial, and its adverfaries fo mifchievous, to man? The principles of religion are acknowledged to confift in the belief of the being, the perfections, and providence of God here, and of a future ftate of retribution hereafter. The man who believes thefe things is faid to have religion, and the man who difbelieves them, who thinks that there is no God,

God, no providence, or no future state, whatever he be in other respects, whether he be virtuous or vicious, cannot be said to have any *religion*, properly so called. Let us, then, consider the nature of these principles, and what effect they *must* have on those who seriously believe them. That principles, or opinions, of some kind or other, have real influence on the general character, and on the conduct and happiness of human life, cannot be denied. Man is a thinking being. All his actions proceed from some thought or design, and his actions and conduct are certainly of importance, issuing in a better or worse state of his circumstances. If the maxims he acts upon, and the objects of his pursuit, be just, and if his measures be well laid, he improves his condition; whereas if his maxims of conduct be false and fallacious, if the objects of his pursuit be unworthy of him, or his conduct be ill directed, he must expect to suffer in consequence.

It also cannot be denied that what is called *virtue*, or the right government of the paſſions, adds to the dignity of man, and to the happineſs both of individuals and of ſociety; and religion certainly comes in aid of virtue. The man who follows the dictates of paſſion, and preſent inclination, without reflecting on the tendency and iſſue of his conduct, is ſure to involve himſelf in difficulties. The unreſtrained indulgence of the natural appetites, both ſhortens life, by introducing diſeaſes and premature death, and makes a ſhort life miſerable; whereas moderation and diſcretion is the ſource of the trueſt and moſt laſting enjoyment. Manhood conducted by mere paſſion and inclination, without foreſight of conſequences, is only a protracted childhood; and what father is there who thinks it wiſe to indulge a *child* in all its varying humours. It would ſoon deſtroy itſelf. And equally deſtructive and ruinous would be the conduct of a *man* who ſhould make no more uſe of his reaſon, but prefer his preſent gratification to future good, which is the general deſcription of *vice*.

Could

Could the moſt intemperate of men have a clear foreſight of all the diſorders and wretchedneſs that will be the ſure, or very probable, conſequence of his conduct, with reſpect to his health and life, and alſo of the poverty and contempt which generally attends that mode of life, whatever might be his fondneſs for any ſpecies of ſenſual indulgence, he would certainly reſtrain himſelf. Alſo, how greedy ſoever any perſon might be of riches, could he foreſee all the anxiety, and riſk, attending a courſe of fraudulent practices, and the little enjoyment men have of diſhoneſt gain, he would be content to be leſs rich and more happy. The ambition of Alexander, of Cæſar, or of Charles the twelfth of Sweden, would have been reſtrained, if they could have ſeen the whole progreſs and termination of their ſchemes.

1. Now religion, both extends the foreſight of man, and puts him under the direction of a being whoſe foreſight is greater than that of any man. When a man

man loses his natural parent, and guide, religion supplies him with another, superior in all respects to the former. By religion he puts himself under the direction of the Supreme Being, his true parent and best friend, on whose wisdom he may always rely, and in whose guidance he is sure to find happiness. Any rule of life and conduct drawn up by men like ourselves may be erroneous, being founded on imperfect views of things. The best parent may err in the management of his favourite child, whose welfare he has most at heart. But the great Being who made man can never err. The observance of his precepts must lead to happiness; and the full persuasion of this, which religion cannot fail to give us, puts an end to all doubt and uncertainty about what we ought to do, superseding our own judgment, and silencing all the evasions of passion and prejudice. And this alone is a circumstance of unspeakable advantage.

A person bent upon any particular gratification, however criminal, will make a thousand a thousand apologies for the innocence, and perhaps the public utility, of it, which his own reason, biassed, of course, by inclination, might never be able to see the fallacy of; which however the authority of an acknowledged master will silence at once. What has not the ingenuity of libertines pleaded in favour not only of fornication, but even of adultery; and by what specious names have those gross offences against the order, the decency, and peace of society been not only covered from ignominy, but even recommended, as indications of a man's spirit, as a source of real pleasure to some, and only an imaginary injury to others? How many persons have actually made their boast of actions of other kinds for which they deserved to be banished from all civilized society? How has murder itself, in the form of a duel, and in some countries in that of private assassination, been more than justified, from false notions of honour, the supposed dignity of revenge, and the meanness of submitting to insults and wrongs?

We

We see that men who have no belief in religion, actually commit these crimes, and indeed any other, without remorse. But this can never be the case where there is a principle of religion, where it is really believed that the authority of the Supreme Being has interposed, and expressly, as by a voice from heaven, absolutely forbidden the practices above mentioned, how ingeniously soever apologized for; saying to man, *Thou shalt not commit murder, thou shalt not commit adultery, thou shalt not steal,* &c. &c.

2. Many persons, influenced by regard to their reputation, will refrain with sufficient care from such actions as they know would dishonour them in the opinion of their fellow creatures; but without a sense of religion they would feel little or no remorse in committing any crime with respect to which they had no suspicion of being detected and exposed. Religion is a guard against even secret vices. The belief that nothing is concealed from the eye of God, that he sees what man cannot see,

see, discerning even the thoughts and inclinations of the heart, will make a man as careful not to offend in private as in public. When the eye of man is not upon him, he well knows there *is* an eye that always sees him, and that though he might escape the censure of man, he has no means of escaping the righteous judgment of God.

Not only public censure, but other punishments, often fail to be inflicted on the guilty in this world. A man, therefore, who has no belief in another, may be tempted to risk a great deal with a reasonable prospect of impunity. For of the many crimes that are committed in human society, only a few are actually punished. But this avails nothing to a believer in religion, and a future state. He knows that there is a day coming in which God will judge the world in righteousness, and that no vice, though undetected, and unpunished, here, will escape animadversion and punishment hereafter.

Many offenders efcape punifhment in this world by means of their power, as well as their addrefs. The rich and the great have, in too many cafes, little to fear from the moft flagrant violations of juftice with refpect to the poor, who are without money and without friends; and the kings and tyrants of the earth, to gratify their revenge, their luft of power, or mere caprice, ravage whole nations, and introduce an incalculable mafs of mifery among their fellow-creatures, without the moft diftant apprehenfions of fuffering in their own perfons in confequence of it. But all this ends with the prefent fcene. In the future the greateft monarchs will appear on a footing with the meaneft of rational beings. No wealth or power will be of any avail then, and the knowledge of this may well be fuppofed to reftrain men from thofe violences and oppreffions of which they now are the authors. Thus is religion a powerful auxiliary of virtue, and thereby contributes to the good order and peace of fociety, as well as to the regulation

regulation of the private paſſions, and the happineſs of individuals.

3. Religion is of no leſs uſe with reſpect to the troubles of life, than the duties of it. That, with a great preponderance of happineſs (which ſufficiently proves the goodneſs of God) there is a conſiderable mixture of miſery in the world, is what no perſon who is at all acquainted with it, will deny. We need not adopt the melancholy deſpairing language of Job, and ſay, *Man that is born of a woman is of few days and full of trouble*, or that *he is born to trouble as the ſparks fly upwards;* for this gives an idea of a preponderance of miſery, as the proper and intended lot of man. But certainly there is in the world ſickneſs as well as health, pain as well as pleaſure, and on many accounts grief as well as joy. Induſtry is not always ſucceſsful, marriages are not always happy, children are not always a bleſſing to their parents, and other connections in life, which are generally ſources of pleaſure, are not always ſo.

There

There are also many evils against which no human prudence can guard us, as famine from inclement seasons, and pestilential disorders, which we are as yet unable to investigate, or prevent. All countries are more or less subject to hurricanes, tempests, and earthquakes; and the happiest and longest life must terminate in death. It is in vain to say, with the Stoics, that what we suffer by these means are no evils, or that we do not feel them.

But when nature abandons us to grief and despair, religion steps in to our consolation, assuring us, that nothing can befal us, or others, without the will and appointment of God, our heavenly Father, and that whatever he wills is always wisest and best, whether, at the time, we can see it to be so or not. As the Psalmist says, *though clouds and darkness are round about him, righteousness and judgment are the habitation of his throne.* Religion assures us that, if by means of the evils of life, God chastises us, it is with the affection of a parent, and always for our good.

We

We can then say, with the apostle, that *all things will be made to work together for good to them that love God*, that, in this case, *life or death, things prosperous, or things adverse*, are equally *ours*, and will terminate in our advantage. With this persuasion we may bear all the evils of life, numerous and heavy as they sometimes are, not only with patience and resignation, but even with satisfaction and pleasure, *rejoicing*, as the apostles did, *in* all kinds of *tribulation*.

4. But religion is found to be of the greatest value at the close of life, opening to us a better prospect than that on which we then shut our eyes. Without religion all that the greatest philosopher can pretend to is that he has had enough of life, and that he obeys the call of nature without reluctance. But even this, if he has really enjoyed life, is more than he can say with truth. If he has enjoyed life, it must be sweet to him, and consequently he cannot but wish to prolong or resume it. A good man

man may, in one sense, have had enough of life, and, from the fatigues and uniformity of it, be as it were weary of it; but it is only such weariness as is felt at the close of an active well spent day, when we wish for rest, but with the hope of rising with renewed vigour and activity, and with the prospect of greater enjoyment, in the morning. That morning to a christian is the resurrection to a new and better life. Of this nature gives us no hope; but religion the greatest certainty.

According to the principles of religion, this world is only the infancy of our being. This life is only a school, in which we are training up for a better and immortal life, and all the events and discipline of it are calculated to prepare us for entering with advantage upon it; so that a good man, with the faith and hope of a christian, can bid adieu to this world not only with tranquility, but with satisfaction and triumph; singing the triumphant song, *O death where is thy sting, O grave where is thy victory*.

When

When chriftians lofe their friends and relations by death, they do not grieve as the heathen who have no hope; but commit them with confidence to the hands of their merciful creator, whofe views in calling them into being were not confined to this prefent life. He believes that this his feparation from his virtuous friends is but for a time, and a fhort time, and he has no doubt of meeting them again, and in more favourable circumftances for enjoying their fociety than ever. There the affectionate parent will meet his beloved children, and children their parents, not worn down by affliction, difeafe, or hard labour, incapable of enjoyment, which is often the cafe in this world, but with all their faculties in full vigour, and fuperior to what ever they where before; every thing valuable and amiable in them improved, and their imperfections done away; fo that their fociety, which we fhall never lofe again, will be more defirable than ever. Compared with this folid ground of confolation under the troubles

bles of life, and the fears of death, what has mere reason or philosophy to offer?

5. And it is a particular recommendation of religion, that both its teachings and consolations require no acuteness of intellect. They are level to the understandings of all men. As to the precepts of religion, they are thus summed up by the prophet, *What doth the Lord thy God require of thee, but to do justice, to love mercy, and to walk humbly with thy God.* In this short compass are comprized all the great duties of religion, and surely nothing can be more intelligible.

As to the consolations of religion, they are addressed to the common feelings and principles of human nature, such as men act upon every day. It is the expectation of distant good as a balance to present evil. Religion does not require men to give up their ease, their fortunes, or their lives, for nothing; but for a sufficient recompence. *Thou shalt be recompenced* said our Saviour, *at the resurrection of the just.* All that is requisite is a stretch of thought, and

and a comprehenſion of mind, which ſhall enable men to contemplate a thing certainly future, as if it was preſent: and by this means give it its proper value in compariſon with things preſent, which, in conſequence of being ſo, are poſſeſſed of an undue advantage over them. But what things that are future loſe in this reſpect, is balanced by their real magnitude, and importance. *The things that are ſeen,* ſays the apoſtle (2 Cor. iv. 18) *are temporal, but the things that are unſeen are eternal.* It is, therefore, the more eaſy, by a firm faith, and a ſteady contemplation, to give them their juſt degree of eſtimation, and to feel and act properly with reſpect to them; as thouſands and millions have actually done, who have cheerfully abandoned every thing in life, and life itſelf, when the retaining of them was incompatible with their great proſpects beyond the grave.

6. It is by habituating the mind to contemplate great and diſtant objects, that religion enlarges and ennobles the minds of men, advancing them farther beyond the

state of children, who are only affected by things immediately present to them, and from the great bulk of mankind, who do indeed look before them, but not far. They can sow and plant one year in hope of a return in the next, and they can expend their money in the purchase of goods with a view to sell them to advantage in a future and distant market. Also, when they labour under any disorder, they can take disgusting medicines in the hope of a cure. But this is far short of looking to a world beyond the grave, laying up treasure in heaven, making friends of the mammon of unrighteousness here, in order to be received into everlasting habitations hereafter. This is done by the help of religion, which by this means makes a man a superior kind of being to what he was before.

If *great thoughts*, as Lord Bacon says, *make great minds*, how much superior must be that man who is habitually employed in the contemplation of God, of a providence, and a future state, who sees the hand of of God in every thing, and receives all the dispensations of providence with a contented and thankful heart, whose faith is not shaken by all the distress and calamity of which he is a witness, and all that himself, his friends, his country, or the world, may suffer, and who when he comes to die can look back with satisfaction, and forward with hope and joy, to the man who is either wholly ignorant of these great principles, or an unbeliever in them, whose views are bounded by what he sees in this life, and who can only say, *Let us eat and drink for to-morrow we die.* To such persons life is indeed of little value. And it is no wonder that, under any particular pressure of trouble or disappointment, they throw it up, and put an end to their lives in despair.

7. Though I have represented the religious man as acting on plain and intelligible principles, and as overlooking present evils for the sake of future good, it by no means follows that he will be an interested character, and never love virtue for

for its own fake. It is by a rational felf interest that the most disinterested characters are formed. This admits of an easy illustration from what we know concerning the love of money. The greatest miser does not begin with the love of money as an ultimate object, or for its own fake, but only for the fake of the advantages it can procure him. And yet we fee that it is possible, in a course of time, for men to come to love money, and to employ all their powers, and all their time, in the acquisition of it, without giving the least attention to the use of it, and indeed without ever making any proper use of it at all; their ideas never going beyond the mere accumulation of it. Let any thing be pursued, though as a means, and in a course of time, it will come to be an end.

In like manner, let a man from any principle, habituate himself to respect the authority of God, to do good to others, and practise virtue in general, though at first with no other view than to his reward in a future state, and in time he will live

live virtuously, without giving any attention to his ultimate interest in it; and in this progress he will necessarily become as disinterestedly virtuous as it is possible, in the nature of things, for a man to be. He may begin with the mere *fear* of God, or a dread of his displeasure, but at length he will be actuated by the purest *love*, and an entire devotedness to his will, as such. He may begin with doing kind offices to others from any motive sufficient to produce the external action, but at length he will come with the apostle, *to love with a pure heart fervently*, taking the greatest pleasure in doing kind offices, without any idea, or expectation, of a return. He may at first abstain from sensual indulgence from a persuasion of what he may ultimately suffer in consequence of it, but in time he will have greater satisfaction in moderation than he ever had in excess, and he will readily and cheerfully do whatever he apprehends to be *right*, without asking *why*. The dictates of conscience will be with him a supreme rule of action.

This

This is that truly great and sublime character to which religion, and religion alone, can raise a man. Without the principles of religion, without *the fear of God*, which Solomon justly calls *the beginning of wisdom*, he wants the first necessary step in this progress. There must be a belief in the being and providence of God, and in a life of retribution to come, to give a man that comprehensive view of things, which alone can lead him to overlook temporary gratifications, and give him that due command of his passions which is essential to rational life. He must first look beyond the things that are seen, and temporal, to things unseen and eternal, or he might never see sufficient reason for the practice of those virtues which do not bring an immediate recompence. He would never respect the authority of God, unless he had a belief in his being and providence. All his works would be done to be seen of men; and if the only reward of virtue was in another world, which he believed to have no existence,

existence, he would have no sufficient reason to exercise it at all.

But having this *faith,* the foundation of right conduct, the superstructure is easily raised upon it. Possessed of this first principle, a seed is sown, which cannot fail in time to produce the noble and full grown plant, the excellent character above described. If the mind be thoroughly impressed with the fear of God, the two great principles, which comprise the whole of the moral law, the love of God, and of our neighbour, will in due time appear, and produce all *the fruits of righteousness,* without the least view to any reward whatever; and on this account will be intitled to, and will assuredly find, the greatest. This is to be most truly godlike, and the necessary consequence of being *like God,* of being *perfect* (or approaching as near to it as may be) as *God is perfect,* which our Saviour requires and encourages us to be, must be accompanied with a degree of happiness approaching the divine.

Such

Such being the obvious use and substantial value of religion, with respect to the conduct of life, the troubles we are exposed to in it, and at the hour of death, and to form the most exalted of human characters, it certainly behoves us to examine the evidence of it, and to do this not superficially, but with the greatest attention, as a question in the decision of which we are all most deeply interested. I may add that a virtuous and good man cannot but wish that the principles of religion may appear to be well founded, because it is his interest that they should be so; and if there be this bias on our minds in this enquiry, it is a reasonable and honourable bias, such as no person need be ashamed to avow.

At the same time, the greater is the object proposed to us, the more scrupulous we shall naturally be in our enquiries concerning it. When the apostles were first informed of the resurrection of their beloved master, it is said by the historian, that

that *they did not believe through joy*; and it was not without the moſt irreſiſtible evidence, that of their *ſenſes*, that they were at length ſatisfied with reſpect to it. Let us act the ſame part, and not receive a pleaſing tale merely becauſe it is pleaſing to us, but ſtrictly examine the evidence of it; and this is what I propoſe to lay before you, with the greateſt plainneſs, without concealing any difficulties that appear to me to be worthy of much notice. Chriſt and the apoſtles always appealed to the underſtanding of their hearers, and it can only be a ſpurious kind of *religion* that diſclaims the uſe of *reaſon*, that faculty by which alone we are capable of religion, and by which alone we are able to diſtinguiſh true religion from falſe, and that which is genuine, from the foreign and heterogeneous matter that has been added to it.

DISCOURSE II.

Of the superior Value of Revealed Religion.

He hath shewed thee, O man, what is good; and what doth the Lord require of thee, but to do justly, to love mercy, and to walk humbly with thy God.

MICAH, vi. 8.

PROPOSING to deliver a series of Discourses on the evidences of revealed religion, I have begun with shewing the real value of *religion in general*, consisting in a belief of the being and providence of God, and of a future state of retribution. Taking it, therefore, for granted, that this faith is of real value to men, both as individuals and as members of society, I shall now endeavour to shew that the plan of *communicating* this knowledge by occasional interpositions of the Supreme Being

ing is, in feveral refpects, preferable to that which unbelievers boaft of as fuperior to it, viz. the gradual acquifition of it by the mere ufe of reafon.

But I would previoufly obferve that, provided the great *end* be gained, viz. the improvement of the human character by the attainment of fuch knowledge, and the forming of fuch habits, as will qualify men to be moft happy in themfelves, and difpofe them to communicate the moft happinefs to others (which is the great object with God, the common parent of us all) the *means* are of no farther value. That fcheme, or fyftem, whatever it be, which beft promotes this great end, is, for that reafon the beft; and if the two fchemes be equally adapted to gain the fame end, they are exactly of equal value.

Religion itfelf is only a means, or inftrument, to make men virtuous, and thereby happy, in fuch a manner as rational beings are alone capable of being made happy: and the different kinds, forms,

forms, rites, or exercises, of religion are of no value but as they tend to make men religious, inspiring them with the fear of God, and a disposition conscientiously to observe whatever he is supposed to require of them. This great truth, which we ought ever to bear in mind, is clearly expressed in my text, *What doth the Lord require of thee, but to do justly, to love mercy, and to walk humbly with thy God,* i. e. to entertain just sentiments, and observe a right conduct, with respect to God and man; and every thing that God has *shewed* us, whether by the light of nature, or by occasional interpositions, has no other object than this. *He hath shewed thee, O man, what is good,* what tends to make him virtuous and happy.

Let no person, therefore, value himself on his religion as such, be the principles of it ever so true, his knowlegde of it ever so exact, and his faith in it ever so firm. He is thereby only possessed of a means to a certain end, and if that end be not attained, he is so far from being a
gainer

gainer by being poffeffed of the means that he is highly culpable for having fuch an inftrument, and making no proper ufe of it. For *better*, as the apoftle fays, (2. Pet. ii. 21.) *would it be never to have known the way of righteoufnefs* than, *after having known it*, to depart from it, i. e. by living a vicious life. Alfo, according to our Saviour's moft folemn declarations, whatever may have been a man's relation to himfelf, even though he may have worked miracles in his name, if he be a *worker of iniquity* he will at the laft day difclaim all knowledge of him, and order him to depart from him.

As the improvement of the human character in virtuous principles and habits is the end of all religion, we muft judge of the preferablenefs of *natural*, or *revealed* religion by their fuperior tendency to effect this great end. But, indeed, fo little of *religion* properly fo called have men ever derived from the light of nature, and fo little are thofe who reject revelation really influenced by any religious principle, that the

the true ſtate of the queſtion, in fact, is whether it be better for man to have the religion that is taught in the ſcriptures, or none at all. They who reject revelation may not abſolutely, and in words reject the belief of a God, and of a providence (though we ſee in the example of the French philoſophers, and many others, that this is generally the caſe) they are not influenced by that belief. Nor can we wonder at this, when they certainly have not, in fact, any expectation of a future ſtate, which, as I ſhall ſhew, was never taught to any uſeful purpoſe but by revelation.

Religion implies the belief of the being and providence of God, and ſuch a reſpect for the will of God, as will effectually controul a man's natural inclinations and direct his conduct, reſtraining him from irregularities to which he is naturally prone, and exciting him to actions to which he is naturally averſe. But as men in general are governed either by ſtrong natural appetites, or a view to their intereſt,

tereſt, it cannot be expected that *virtue alone*, without any hope of future reward or puniſhment, can have ſuch charms for them, that they will abandon their pleaſure, their eaſe, or their advantage, for the pure love of it. Suppoſing that men might arrive at a knowledge of the will of God with reſpect to their conduct in life, they would not feel any ſufficient *obligation* to conform to it, without the great ſanction of future rewards and puniſhments. Mere authority, as that of a parent, or of a magiſtrate, is little or nothing without the power of rewarding and puniſhing. Nothing, therefore, but a firm belief in a future ſtate of retribution, can be expected to reſtrain men from giving into thoſe indulgences to which they have a ſtrong propenſity.

1. With reſpect to every article of religion, the light of nature is far from being ſufficiently clear and diſtinct, ſo as to be inferred with certainty by the moſt intelligent of men. With reſpect to what is moſt eſſential to human happineſs, the wiſeſt of men

men do not appear to have been, in fact, superior to the bulk, having in a variety of respects, laid down the most erroneous rules for the conduct of men. Plain as the most important maxims of morality are, there is not one of them, but what the most enlightened not only of the ancient philosophers, but of modern unbelievers, have controverted. What we call *conscience*, and which we might expect to be a better guide in this respect, than even *reason*, is by no means the same uniform principle in all men. It is formed by various associations of ideas, depending on the circumstances of our education, so that things which absolutely shock some persons, are not felt as at all improper by others. There is, therefore, something wanted superior to the dictates of reason, or natural conscience, and this can only be *revealed religion*, or the authority of our maker, which must be obeyed without reasoning. Man will, no doubt, dispute even about the will of God, when it is most clearly revealed, as they do concerning the

the moſt expreſs laws that are ever made by men, but if this be done with reſpect to the articulate voice of God, it will be done to a much greater extent, and with much more plauſibility, to the inarticulate voice of nature, which every perſon will interpret as he is previouſly inclined.

If when men are hurried on by paſſion, or ſwayed by intereſt, they will tranſgreſs ſuch poſitive and acknowledged commands, as *thou ſhalt not commit adultery, thou ſhalt not ſteal, &c.* as we ſee that, in fact, they do, it will not, however, be without reluctance, and remorſe; and therefore tranſgreſſions will be leſs frequent, and leſs flagrant, and repentance and amendment may be more reaſonably expected to follow. But where no ſuch poſitive command is acknowledged to exiſt, and the voice of nature alone is to be conſulted about the proper conduct of life, moſt men will miſtake their own inclination for the voice of nature, and conſequently ſin without reluctance or remorſe. Of this it would be eaſy to give inſtances in the cleareſt of all

all cafes, but this would take up too much of our time, and fomething of this was mentioned in my laft difcourfe.

2. Still lefs would men, by the mere light of nature, have ever attained to any fatisfactory conclufion with refpect to the ultimate defign of the author of nature in the formation of man. I mean the prolongation of his exiftence beyond the grave. On this moft interefting of all queftions nature is altogether filent. Judging from appearances, as the brutes die, fo does man; and all his faculties and powers die with him. That at death any things efcapes, unaffected by this cataftrophe, is a mere arbitrary fuppofition, unfupported by any appearance, or probability of any kind.

That the belief which the ancient Greeks and Romans had of a future life, imperfect,' and of little value, as it was, was originally derived from revelation, but exceedingly corrupted by tradition, is pretty evident from this circumftance, that when they began to *fpeculate* on the fubject, subject, and examine the *reasons* they could produce for it, all serious belief in the doctrine soon vanished. With the Platonists, who made the most of this doctrine, it was only a curious speculation, of no real use in the conduct of life, such as it is with Jews and Christians. Indeed, the *reasons* which the Platonists gave for this doctrine, and which Plato puts into the mouth of Socrates, are such as could not possibly have any weight with thinking men. That on which he lays the greatest stress, is the doctrine of pre-existence, that the souls of men were originally without bodies, and afterwards confined in them as in a prison, and that death is the breaking of this prison. But where is the evidence of men having pre-existed? This doctrine of pre-existence we find most fully established in Egypt and the East, whence Plato and other Greeks derived it. With modern unbelievers it certainly has no weight.

It is well known that the first philosophers among the Greeks did not pretend to to discover any thing by their own reasoning. They only taught what they had learned of others, who had received the tenets that had been transmitted to them from early times, and that what they taught was delivered to their pupils on their sole *authority*, as what was not to be contradicted. This was the established custom of the Pythagorean school. Reasoning came into their schools afterwards, and with it the wildest theories on all subjects, as I shall shew in its proper place, and a total scepticism with respect to the doctrine of a future state of retribution, as a motive to virtue.

Supposing that it were possible by the mere light of nature to arrive at the belief of a future state, yet judging from present appearances, it could not be the future state announced in the Scriptures, a state in which virtue will find an ample recompence, and vice its just punishment, but only such a life as *this*, and in all other respects resembling the present; which is the belief of the North American Indians, and

and moſt other barbarous nations. If becauſe we diſlike any thing in the preſent ſyſtem, we entertain an idea that the inconvenience complained of will be removed in a future ſtate, where is the evidence that, under the ſame powers, or principles, of nature, whatever they are, things *will* be ordered in a better manner? Is it poſſible to infer from what we ſee (and we have nothing elſe by which to guide our conjectures) that thoſe evils which the author of nature has thought proper, for whatever reaſon, to introduce, or to permit, here, will not be continued there alſo? If we ſay that it is not agreeable to *juſtice* that good and bad men ſhould be treated as they are here, where is the evidence, from any preſent appearances, that the author of nature *intended* that they ſhould ever be treated otherwiſe? Left to the light of nature, we could only reaſon from what we know, and this would lead us to expect that, if there be any life after death, it will be ſimilar to the preſent. It is only from the expreſs aſſurance of the

author

author of nature, communicated by revelation, that we believe the future ſtate will be better than the preſent, that in it the righteous will be fully rewarded, and the wicked puniſhed. It is evident, therefore, that when we abandon revelation, we give up all *religion* properly ſo called, all that can have any ſalutary influence on the hearts and lives of men.

3. With reſpect to *men*, there is certainly a great advantage in precepts and commands, promiſes and threatenings being delivered in *words*, proceeding as from a real perſon, it being by this means that inſtructions are delivered with the greateſt diſtinctneſs. It may indeed, be ſaid, and with truth, that nature ſpeaks to men, and that nature teaches, and nature threatens, but beſides that the information is more indiſtinctly communicated, it is in a manner leſs apt to make an impreſſion, and command reſpect. It is, therefore, of great advantage that the attention of men be directed to ſomething beyond mere nature, viz. to the author and lord of

of nature, and that he be confidered not as an allegorical perfonage, but a real intelligent Being, capable of communicating his will in words, and fuch figns as men are daily accuftomed to, and apt to be impreffed by.

Befides, all men feel an unavoidable propenfity to *addrefs* themfelves to the Being on whom they depend; and without fome mode of intercourfe with him, they would foon lofe fight of him, as a child would of his father, if he never faw him, and had no accefs to him. Without an idea of God different from what we could collect from the contemplation of nature, there would be no fuch thing as *prayer*. Indeed, unbelievers in revelation ridicule the idea of prayer as unnatural and abfurd, though all nations, without exception, have had recourfe to it; which is a clear proof that it is natrual, as every thing that is univerfal muft be.

Authority is beft fupported by a mixture of *affection*, but there cannot be any thing of *this* except towards a being refembling sembling other beings which have been the object of an affection, and which have engaged our confidence. And in revelation, but by no means in nature, the Supreme Being appears to us in the familiar character of a parent, a 'person with whom we can have communication, who may be conceived to be always present with us, who encourages us to address ourselves to him, who always hears us, and sometimes answers us. By this means God easily becomes the object of real affection, and attachment. Here we find a solid foundation for *love* and *fear*, which are the chief motives for men's actions. With believers in revelation, this sometimes degenerates into an absurd enthusiasm, by which the Divine Being becomes the object of a fond and improper affection.

We may say that it is beneath the Supreme Being, and unworthy of him, to have this familiar intercourse with men; but it is of great importance to our virtue and happiness; and to a being of perfect benevolence, and who knows, the frame that

that he has given us, nothing will appear beneath him that is so well adapted to answer his benevolent purpose respecting us. Nor, indeed, would the most absolute prince, if he really wished to appear as the father and friend of his people, think any thing beneath him that tended to promote the happiness of his subjects.

It is said by modern unbelievers, that the expectaion of such a being as the great author of nature condescending to act this humble part is unreasonable, and that miracles of all kinds, the only evidence of it, are necessarily incredible. I answer that the assertion betrays a great unacquaintedness with human nature, and the history of man. For it has been the belief of all nations, and all ages, that the highest beings of whom they had any idea have acted this very part. Socrates himself expressed an earnest wish for a divine instructor. This expectation and belief is, therefore, by no means unnatural, and there must be something in human nature that leads to it.

If

If we look to the laſt, and therefore what we may ſuppoſe to be the moſt improved ſtate of heathen philoſophy, that of the later Platoniſts, or Eclectics, to which the emperor Julian (whoſe ſuperior good ſenſe is ſo much the boaſt of modern unbelievers) attached himſelf, we ſhall find them in this very reſpect the moſt ſuperſtitious, the moſt enthuſiaſtic, and the moſt credulous of men. Far from ſuppoſing that men had no intercourſe with the ſupreme being, they expected to unite themſelves to him by contemplation, and corporeal mortification. " The piety of
" Proclus, one of the moſt celebrated of
" them, is highly extolled by his biogra-
" pher. He ſpent whole days and nights
" in repeating prayers and hymns, that
" he might prepare himſelf for an imme-
" diate intercourſe with the gods. He
" obſerved with great ſolemnity the new
" moons, and all public feſtivals, and on
" theſe occaſions imagined that he con-
" verſed with ſuperior beings, and was
" able by his ſacrifices, prayers, and hymns,

to

"to expel difeafes, to command rain, "to ftop earthquakes, and to perform "other fimilar miracles." Whether, therefore, we look to the vulgar, or the philofophers among the ancients, we fhall find the idea of divine communications and of miracles, to have been natural to man. Thefe philofophers did not deny the miracles of Chrift, but maintained that he wrought them by the fame magical or theurgic powers, as they were termed, which they themfelves poffeffed. See Enfield's Hiftory of Philofophy, Vol. i. p. 83, 92.

4. They who give fo decided a preference to the light of nature, the appearances of which are uniform, to that of revelation, which fuppofes an occafional departure from the ufual courfe of nature, betray their ignorance of the nature of man, by whom all *uniform appearances* are apt to be difregarded, but who never fail to be ftruck by what is *unufual*. Does not every human being fee the regular rifing and fetting of the fun, the periodical returns

returns of summer and winter, seed time and harvest, but how few ever think of the wisdom or benevolence of these appointments? They content themselves with observing *effects*, and directing their conduct by them, without ever reflecting on the *cause*. But wherever any thing *unusual* happens, when comets are seen, or eclipses of the sun or moon take place, their attention is forcibly arrested; and after reflecting on the cause of the extraordinary appearances, they may be induced to give some attention to those that are constant. I shall illustrate this by a case which I have put on a former occasion.

Let a person unacquainted with clocks, watches, and other machines, be introduced into a room containing many of them, all in regular motion. He sees no maker of these machines, and knows nothing of their internal structure; and as he sees them all to move with perfect regularity, he may say, on the principles of the atheistical system, that they are *automata*, or self-moving machines; and so long

long as all thefe machines continue in regular motion, and he knows nothing of the making of them, or the winding of them up, this theory may appear plaufible.

But let us fuppofe that, coming into this room again and again, and, always attending to the machines, he fhall find one of them much out of order, and that at length its motion fhall intirely ceafe; but that after continuing in this ftate fome time, he fhall again find it in perfect order, moving as regularly as ever. Will he not then conclude that fome perfon, whom he has not feen, but probably the maker of the machines, had been in the room in his abfence? The reftoration of motion to the difordered machine would imprefs his mind with the idea of a *maker* of them in a much more forcible manner than his obferving the regular conftruction, and uniform motion of them. It muft convince him of the exiftence of fome perfon capable of *regulating*, and therefore probably of *making* thefe machines,

machines, whether he should ever see this person or not.

Thus do miracles prove the existence of a God in a shorter and more satisfactory manner than the observation of the uninterrupted course of nature. If there be a Being who can *controul* the course of nature, there must be one who originally *established it*, in whatever difficulty we may still be left with respect to his nature, and the manner of his existence.

Why men should be struck with unusual appearances it is not my business to explain, though it would not be difficult to do it, the fact of their *being so* is sufficient to my purpose. And therefore a person acquainted with human nature, and this property of it, would not neglect to avail himself of it when he wished to engage the attention of men, for the purpose of their instruction and improvement. Why then should we think it unnatural, or improper, in the divine Being, who, as the maker of men, best knows what they are, and in what way to apply to them?

Let

Let no one then say that occasional interpositions, or miraculous appearances, are an unnatural, or improper mode of instructing mankind, when it is in a manner necessary to draw their attention to a superior being, as a foundation for their intercourse with him.

4. No less are they mistaken who imagine that the *evidences* of revealed religion have more of difficulty in them than those of natural religion, by which we mean the arguments from nature for the being, perfections, and providence of God. On the contrary, far greater difficulties occur with respect to *these*, than with respect to the others, and all that can be said is, that great difficulties must give way to greater. Far am I from supposing that the evidence for the being of a God, is not *demonstrative*, since marks of design, with which the world abounds, necessarily imply a designing or intelligent cause. But notwithstanding this, we can never fully satisfy ourselves with respect to the objection of the atheist, that if the universe

universe require a cause, this cause must require another; and if the author of nature, or the being we call *God*, exist without a cause, so may the universe itself.

All that we can say in answer to this, is that, whatever difficulty we may labour under with respect to this subject, which will always be above our comprehension, the actual existence of a visible world, and of marks of design in it, cannot be denied, and therefore, whether we be able to proceed any farther or not, we *must* acknowledge a designing cause. Otherwise we might say that a house had no architect, or a child no father. If the eye of a man require no designing cause, neither would a telescope, which is an instrument of a similar nature, evidently adapted to answer a similar purpose. And at this supposition every mind would revolt.

More and greater difficulties occur when we proceed to the consideration of the unity, the omnipresence, the constant agency, and what is of more consequence still,

ſtill, the *benevolence* of the Supreme Being, on the principles of the light of nature. So forcibly were the minds of men in the early ages, impreſſed with a view of the *evils* which abound in the world, and ſo inconſiſtent did they conceive them to be with the deſigns of a benevolent author, that they ſuppoſed there was an original *principle of evil,* independant of that of good. And they who ſuppoſed there was a multiplicity of deities (to which they were led by the extent and variety they obſerved in the works of nature) imagined ſome of them to be of a benevolent, and others of a malevolent diſpoſition. That the author of nature is one, that he is ſimply, invariably, and infinitely good, and that all the evils we ſee and experience, are calculated to promote good, are great and ſublime truths, which we derive from revelation only, though, on a ſtrict examination, they appear not to be inconſiſtent with the appearances in nature.

On

On the other hand, the evidences of revelation are level to every capacity. That it is the author of nature who interpofes muft be evident from every interuption of the ufual courfe of it. For no other than he who eftablifhed the laws of nature can controul them; and though there may be fome difficulty in diftinguifhing fome preternatural appearances from fuch as are merely unufual, this cannot be the cafe with refpect to numberlefs others. If it was a fact that the Ifraelites walked through the Red Sea, and the river Jordan, if all the firftborn of the Egyptians, and the firft-born only, of man and beaft, died in one night, and that announced before-hand; if an articulate voice was actually heard to pronounce the ten commandments from mount Sinai, fo as to be heard by a million of people, there could be no doubt of a divine interpofition in any of the cafes. And the fame may be faid of numberlefs other facts in the fcripture hiftory. If the *facts* be afcertained, there can be no doubt concerning their *caufe*.

Now,

Now, all facts may be ascertained by sufficient testimony, or that of a competent number of credible witnesses, i. e. of persons who were in circumstances not to be imposed upon themselves, and who had no apparent motive to impose upon others. This is fully equal to the evidence of a man's own senses. Nay, there are many persons who would distrust their own eyes and ears rather than those of other persons, who they thought were better judges than themselves.

Though single persons may be imposed upon in a variety of ways, or may take it into their heads, for reasons which it is not in the power of any man to investigate, to impose upon others, this can never be said to be the case with respect to thousands who believe, or attest, things evidently contrary to their interest, and previous inclinations. That great numbers of persons, and others in succession to them, all of whom had sufficient opportunity to investigate any particular fact, which required no other evidence than that

that of the senses, and who were interested in the investigation, their fortunes or their lives depending upon it, should persist in their attestation of it, would be a greater miracle, more contrary to what we know of human nature, than any fact contained in the scripture history.

As to the evidence of a future state, what are all the arguments derived from the light of nature compared to that which is furnished by the gospel, which is therefore justly said (2 Tim. i. 10.) to *bring life and immortality to light?* There we see a person commissioned by God, teaching the doctrine with the greatest plainness and emphasis, enforcing it by miracles, among which was the raising of several persons from a state of death to life, and, what was infinitely more, submitting to die himself in the most public and indisputable manner, and rising to life again at a fixed time. Had mankind in general been asked what evidence would satisfy them, they could not have demanded more.

Whatever

Whether therefore, we confider the precepts of religion, i. e. the rules of a virtuous aud happy life, the authority requifite to enforce the obfervance of them, the motives by which they are enforced, or the evidence of their truth, revealed religion has unfpeakably the advantage of natural; and therefore fo far is the fcheme of revelation from being improbable *a priori*, that it muft appear fuch as a wife and good Being, who was acquainted with human nature, and wifhed to engage the attention of men, and imprefs their minds with fentiments of reverence of himfelf, and refpect for fuch laws as were calculated to promote their greateft happinefs, would adopt in preference to any other; being the beft adapted to gain his end. It was of the greateft importance to mankind to be made acquainted with thofe moral principles and rules of conduct on which their happinefs depended, and which they would never have difcovered of themfelves, to have their attention drawn to them in the moft

moft forcible manner, and to have the moft fatisfactory evidence of their truth; and this is what we find in revelation, and in revelation only. It is therefore as the apoftle juftly calls it (1 Cor. i. 24) *the wifdom and the power of God*, though objected to, and ridiculed, by light and fuperficial men.

DISCOURSE III.

A View of Heathen Worship.

For the wrath of God is revealed from heaven against all ungodliness and unrighteousness of men, who hold the truth in unrighteousness. Because that which may be known of God is manifest in them, for God hath shewed it unto them. For the invisible things of him, from the creation of the world, are clearly seen, being understood by the things that are made, even his eternal power and godhead, so that they are without excuse. Because that when they knew God, they glorified him not as God, neither were thankful, but became vain in their imaginations, and their foolish heart was darkened. Professing themselves to be wise, they became fools, and changed the glory of the incorruptible God, into an image made like to corruptible man, and to birds and fourfooted beasts, and creeping things. Wherefore also God gave them up to uncleanness, through the lusts of their own hearts, to dishonour their own bodies between themselves, who changed the truth of God into a lie, and worshipped and served the creature more than the Creator, who is blessed for ever. For this cause God gave them up to vile affections.
ROMANS, i. 18---26.

IN order to give you a just idea of the real value of revelation, it is necessary that I lay before you the state of things with respect to *religion* in the heathen world,

world, especially in the early ages of mankind, about the time of Moses; that when I come to give you a view of his institutions, the difference may be the more striking. Very few, I am persuaded, of the modern unbelievers have a just knowledge of this subject. If they had, it would, I hope, be impossible for them to treat the religion of the Hebrews with so much contempt. Not only the extreme ignorance, but the great depravity, of mankind in a state of heathenism, would not be credible at this day, if there did not exist a superfluity of the most authentic documents of it, so that the facts cannot be denied without the extreme of effrontery. This, however, we find in Voltaire, who says that " the religion of the " heathens consisted in nothing but *mora-* " *lity*, and festivals; morality" which he says " is common to all men, and *festivals* " which were no more than times of re- " joicing, and could not be of prejudice to " mankind." The particulars which I shall be obliged to mention, and which could not be unknown to this writer, though they are to many others, will shew how shamefully the truth is disguised in this reprefentation. The religion of the heathens had nothing to do with morality, and their public festivals were almost without exception, scenes of the greatest riot and debauchery. Believing their gods to be cruel or sensual, there is no vice how detestable and unnatural soever, that did not find a place in the most solemn acts of their worship.

It is not necessary for me to give any account of the manner in which mankind fell into this deplorable state of depravity it being sufficient to shew that such *was* their state, and that it was evident, from the experience of ages, in which men made the most of their powers of reason, that they were not able to relieve themselves. *Why* the Supreme Being permitted the rise and progress of this species of evil, may be as inscrutable to us, as the permission of any other evil, natural or moral, none of which it must be acknowledged, could have taken place without his

his knowledge and permiſſion, and all of which, and this among the reſt, we have reaſon to believe will lead to good, and hereafter appear to have done ſo. In the mean time it is well worth our while to contemplate the magnitude of the evil, and the goodneſs of God in the cure of it, in what, no doubt, was the proper time, and in the moſt proper and effectual manner.

That the great principles of religion, concerning the being and providence of God, and a future ſtate of exiſtence, were communicated by God to the firſt parents of mankind, is probable from ſeveral circumſtances. Obſcure traces of this knowledge are found in all antient nations, and the farther we go back into antiquity, the purer we find their religion to be. But in procefs of time it became more and more corrupted, till, inſtead of coming in aid of virtue, it was itſelf, a great ſource of the corruption of morals, as the progreſs is well deſcribed in my text.

The

The world ever bore sufficient marks of its being the production of an omnipotent and good Being, a lover of virtue, and a hater of vice; but men, contemplating, as we may suppose, the immense variety, and seeming contrariety, of the works of creation, could not believe that the whole was under the direction of *one being:* And being left to their own imaginations, and judging of other intelligent beings by what they observed in themselves, and others, they concluded that there must be a *multiplicity of beings*, concerned in the government of the world, and the direction of human affairs, some well and others ill disposed towards them. For it required more knowledge and comprehension of mind than they had attained, to perceive that all the evils with which the world abounds were calculated to promote good. They thought they saw in them the effects of malice, and ill will, at least of caprice, and their conduct naturally corresponded to their ideas.

The

The mind of man is never satisfied without looking for the *causes* of events, especially those that take place only occasionally, and to appearance, irregularly, and still more if they be favourable or unfavourable to themselves, because they hope by this means to be able to avoid the one, and secure the other. And not being able to discover the true causes, they must, of course, acquiesce in what they *imagine* to be the true causes. It appears from all history that, in the most early ages, mankind in general ascribed every thing that affected them to the influences of the heavenly bodies, the sun, moon, stars, and planets, and to an intelligent principle which they supposed to reside in them. For heat and cold, storms and rain, often coming unexpectedly, they naturally enough imagined that they did not come without design, and that, if these heavenly agents had been so disposed, their influences would have been always favourable. To these objects therefore, they, of course, directed all their regards, and their worship.

They

They alfo came to fuppofe that there was an intelligent principle in the earth, and in the feveral parts of it, as the air, the fea, the rivers, mountains, forefts, &c. fo that they foon became poffeffed of a great multiplicity of objects of worfhip, whofe favour they thought it of importance to gain, and whofe difpleafure they wifhed to deprecate.

Having got the idea of different fuperior intelligences, whether fubordinate to the fupreme Being or not, they foon loft fight of the fupreme Being himfelf, and gave their whole attention to thofe inferior beings, whom they fuppofed to be the immediate authors of the good and evil that befel them. This was on the fame natural principle that tenants look to the fteward, with whom they tranfact all their bufinefs, and not to the proprietor of the land, with whom they have nothing to do.

We have this farther evidence from fact, that this practice was natural. When Chriftians got the idea of Jefus Chrift,

Chrift, of faints and angels being proper objects of worfhip, they generally fell into the habit of looking no higher, neglecting the worfhip of God; and had it not been for the prayers addreffed to him in the fcriptures and in the antient liturgies, he would, I doubt not, have been as much overlooked and forgotten, as if no fuch being had exifted.

But on whatever principle this took place, the fact cannot be denied, and the number of gods kept increafing, inftead of diminifhing by time and reflection. Orpheus reckoned only as many gods as there were days in the year, but in the time of Hefiod, the Greeks had no lefs than thirty thoufand divinities. The Romans in the time of Varro had three hundred Jupiters, that is the fame God was worfhipped under fo many different titles, under which he was fuppofed to poffefs different powers, and fome have reckoned no lefs than two hundred and eighty thoufand gods.

The Egyptians, from whom the Greeks originally received their religion, imagined that particular animals were the favourites of particular deities, and communicated their powers to them. At leaſt, they conſidered their ſeveral qualities as ſymbols of divine power, and at length paid a proper worſhip to them. Plutarch expreſsly ſays, that "the greater part of the Egyptians "worſhipped the animals themſelves," which he ſaid "led ſome to the moſt ex- "travagant ſuperſtition, and precipitated "others into atheiſm." Cotta, in Cicero, ſays that "though there have been many "inſtances of temples plundered, and the "images of the gods carried away, by "the Romans, it had never been heard "that a crocodile, an ibis, or a cat, had "been ill treated by the Egyptians," ſo far did they carry their ſuperſtitious reſpect for them.

Another ſource of the multiplication of deities was an idea that particular ſuperior beings preſided over particular circumſtances

cumstances relating to men, and their affairs, so that they had gods corresponding to many abstract ideas. Thus the Romans had temples and altars dedicated to the *fever*, and ill *fortune*, and the Athenians to *contumely* and *impudence*. At length, after deifying all the parts of nature, and many of the qualities and properties of things, they deified particular *men*, and worshipped them after their death. Nay the Romans, in the time of the emperors, carried their adulation so far as to pay divine honours to some of them, and those the very worst of them, while they were alive.

The heavenly bodies being sometimes invisible, the heathens had recourse to some symbols of their power, or some visible object, to which they imagined their powers were in some way or other attached, and to which they could always have recourse. These were at first *pillars*, or only large stones, consecrated in certain positions of those heavenly bodies, which they wanted to represent. Refining upon this, they afterwards made use of the forms of men and

and animals for that purpofe. The forms of fome of their deities being altogether unknown, they made ufe of fuch figures as they conceived to be proper fymbols of their powers. The idols of the Egyptians had the heads of particular animals, as that of a dog, on the body, or part of the body of a man. At Rome the god Janus had two faces, and the idols of Indoftan have a great number of arms, &c. Hence Varro, fpeaking of thefe images fays, that " if they had life, and any perfon fhould " meet them unexpectedly, they would " pafs for monfters." He alfo cenfures the cruel and lafcivious rites that were introduced into the worfhip of feveral of their gods, efpecially of Cybele; yet he fays that " a wife man will obferve all " thefe things, not as asceptable to the " gods, but as commanded by the laws," and fpeaking of the " ignoble rabble" as he calls them " of the gods," which, he fays, " the fuperftition of ages has heaped " together," he adds, " we fo adore " them, as to remember that this worfhip "ſhip is rather matter of cuſtom, than "founded on nature and truth." So far were the heathen philoſophers, who were ſenſible of the abſurdity and pernicious tendency of this worſhip, from being diſpoſed to reform it. It was a maxim with them, as with the generality of modern unbelievers, to think with the wiſe, and act with the vulgar. But had Chriſt and his apoſtles acted on this princple, we ſhould now have been worſhipping Thor and Woden, and imbruing their altars with human blood.

The moſt horrid of all the rites of the heathen religion was that of *human ſacrifices*, which, however, were univerſal in ancient times, and eſpecially among the Canaanites, and in the countries that bordered upon Paleſtine, as, indeed, the hiſtory of the Carthaginians, who were deſcended from the Tyrians, abundantly proves.

We ſhall not much wonder at the introduction of this rite, ſhocking as it is to humanity, when we conſider the deſtruction of life, and other evils occaſionally produced

produced by natural causes, as by heat, drought, lightning, earthquakes, &c. These the heathens, of course, ascribed to the agency of their gods. They would, therefore, imagine that they were sometimes very angry, and that great sacrifices were necessary to appease them. Apprehensive, then, of greater evils, they willingly subjected themselves to those that were less.

In general, the heathens thought the sacrifice of slaves and captives would satisfy the blood thirsty appetites of their gods; but on particular occasions, fearful that this would not be deemed sufficient, they sacrificed the children of the most distinguished persons in the state, as those of their kings themselves. The Carthaginians, after some great disaster in war, sacrificed at one time three hundred young men of the first families in their commonwealth. In this the Israelites, during their apostacy from their own religion, imitated their heathen neighbours as we read, Psalm cvi. 37. *They sacrificed their sons and their daughters*

daughters to demons, and shed innocent blood, even the blood of their sons and daughters, whom they sacrificed to the idols of Canaan. Jer. vii. 31. *They built the high places of Tophet which is in the valley of the son of Hinnom, to burn their sons and their daughters in the fire. They built also the high places of Baal, to burn their sons with fire for burnt offerings unto Baal.* This place was called *Tophet*, from a Hebrew word which signifies a drum, or sistrum, instruments which made a loud noise, which the priests made use of to drown the cries of the victims, as it was the custom to burn them alive.

By Baal was meant the sun, the principal object of worship in all antient nations; and as the heat of the sun is sometimes very destructive, it is no wonder that they supposed him to be actuated by the passion of anger. Lord Herbert observes that victims of less dignity were deemed sufficient for the inferior deities, but that to their highest god, the sun, human sacrifices, as the most valuable, were to be offered.

Human

Human sacrifices appear to have been universal in antient times. They were in use among the Egyptians till the reign of Amasis. They were never so common among the Greeks or Romans; yet with them they were in use on extraordinary occasions. Porphyry says that the Greeks were wont to sacrifice men when they went to war. Clemens Alexandrinus says that both Erectheus king of Athens, and Marius the Roman general, sacrificed their own daughters. Plutarch, in his life of Themistocles, relates that three beautiful Persian women, richly habited and adorned, were, by the advice of the prophet Euphrantides, offered as sacrifices to Bacchus Omestes, as a vow for victory at the commencement of the Persian war; and though Themistocles was shocked at the inhumanity of it, the people with one voice, invoking Bacchus, and bringing the victims to the altar, compelled him to perform the sacrifice.

The same historian says that the Romans, in the beginning of a war with the Gauls,

Gauls, and in obedience to an oracle in the Sybilline books, buried alive a Gaulish man and a Gaulish woman, and alfo a Greek man and a Greek woman, in the ox market by way of facrifice. Livy fays that they repeated this facrifice at the beginning of the fecond Punic war.

Human facrifices were offered at Rome, fays Porphyry, till the reign of Adrian, who ordered them to be abolifhed in moft places. This writer, who lived in the time of Diocletian, mentions it as a thing well known, that in the city of Rome itfelf a man was wont to be facrificed at the feaft of Jupiter Latiaris. Lactantius, who wrote a little after this, fays that the fame was practifed in his time. Human facrifices were fo numerous among the Gauls and Britons, that the Romans forbad the public exercife of their religion. According to Cæfar (De Bello Gallico, lib. 6. § 15) they fometimes made images of an immenfe fize, conftructed of wicker work, which they filled with men, and then burned them alive.

In

In later times we find human sacrifices as numerous among the Mexicans and Peruvians, who, of all the inhabitants of America, had arrived at the greatest degree of civilization, as in any of the antient nations. The most authentic record says that the Mexicans sacrificed annually twenty thousand men, and at the dedication of their great temple, not less than sixty or seventy thousand. If any person will only read with attention the history of this country by Clavigero, he will be convinced that such was the rooted attachment of that people to their religion in general, and this horrid rite in particular, that nothing but such a conquest of them as that by the Spaniards, would ever have put an end to that custom. His account of the state of facts will abundantly justify the conduct of divine providence in the utter extirmination of the inhabitants of Canaan. It was for the good of mankind that such nations should be extirpated from the face of the earth.

If

If any perfons will fay that the author of nature could not give a commiffion, which they think to have been fo cruel and unjuft, let them fay whether the author of nature does not continually do things which they themfelves muft fay are more cruel and unjuft; as the promifcuous deftruction of perfons of all ages and characters by peftilence and famine, by hurricanes and earthquakes, as alfo by difeafes and death, which are univerfal. Did not the author of nature clearly forefee thefe calamities, and therefore intend that they fhould take place? And where is the difference, in a moral view, between doing any thing by laws of his appointment, or by a fpecial commiffion. The thing to be objected to is the ultimate event, not the means by which it was effected. In fact, they who make this objection, and others of a fimilar nature, firft form to themfelves an idea of the author of nature from their own imagination, and not from the obfervation of his works, which is the only method of forming a juft idea

idea of any character, and then pronounce that such and such things as they wish to have been otherwise are incompatible with his character. Besides, the firmest believer in the divine benevolence (and justice, strictly considered, is only a modification and branch of benevolence) will say that any kind or degree of evil that may, directly or indirectly, be productive of a greater good, is compatible with it, and of this ultimate tendency of things God himself, and not man, is the judge. This conduct, however, is not to be imitated by man, on account of the imperfection of our knowledge. We must not *do evil that good may come*, though this is constantly done by the Divine Being, because we cannot tell whether the evil *will* be productive of good, whereas, he always knows the end from the very beginning, and therefore cannot be mistaken with respect to the final result.

Besides the horrid custom of human sacrifices, which were thought to be necessary to appease the wrath of some of the

the heathen deities, they had other rites, which, though they did not terminate in death, were extremely painful. The priests of Baal, as we read, 1 Kings xviii. 28. *cut and flashed themselves with knives and lancets till the blood gushed out*, when they were desirous of getting a favourable answer from him. The same, according to Herodotus, was practised in the worship of Isis, an Egyptian deity, and of Bellona among the Romans. Also in the festivals of Cybele, called *the mother of the gods*, the priests, who were castrated, made hideous noises and howlings, and cut themselves till the blood gushed out. The worship of this goddess was introduced from the East to Rome. At a festival in Sparta boys were whipped with so much severity, on an altar of Diana (the priestess attending to see that it was done in a proper manner) that they often died in consequence of it. When this was the case, and the boys had borne the torture with sufficient fortitude, they had the honour of a public funeral, as having died in the service of

their

their country. This custom was instituted by Lycurgus, the great Spartan lawgiver, in exchange for the sacrifice of a man every year at the same altar, the oracle having only declared that the altar of that goddess must be sprinkled with human blood. There was also an altar of Bacchus in Arcadia, on which many young women were beaten with rods till they died.

The rites of heathen religions now or lately existing, are as cruel as those of any of the antients. In Indostan it is frequent, and deemed particularly meritorious, for widows to be burned alive with the bodies of their husbands, and their Faquirs voluntarily undergo such tortures as it is painful to read of. They will often continue so long in the most constrained postures, that their limbs are incapable of any motion; so that they remain so until they die, their wants supplied, and their prayers requested, by great numbers of persons. Sometimes, having strong iron hooks, thrust through the skin of their backs, they get themselves to be drawn up,

up, and whirled round in the air, with the greateſt violence, by means of a machine conſtructed for the purpoſe. The Mexicans, accuſtomed to the bloody ſacrifice of their priſoners, " failed not," ſays Clavigero, " to ſhed abundance of their
" own blood. It makes one ſhudder to
" read of the auſterities which on ſome
" occaſions they exerciſed on themſelves,
" either as an atonement for their ſins, or
" a preparation for their more ſolemn
" feſtivals. They mangled their fleſh as
" if they had been inſenſible to pain, and
" let out their blood in the greateſt pro-
" fuſion. This was practiſed every day
" by ſome of their prieſts. They pierced
" themſelves with the ſharp ſpines of aloes,
" and thruſt them through ſeveral parts
" of their bodies, making the holes larger
" on every repetition of the operation.
" They had alſo ſevere watchings and
" faſtings in their religious rites."

At the faſt of the Tlaſcalans, which laſted one hundred and ſixty days " the
" chief prieſt, attended by about two
" hundred

"hundred perſons aſcended a high mountain, and when they deſcended, they had a number of little knives, and a great quantity of ſmall rods delivered to them. The firſt day they bored holes through their tongues, through which they drew the rods, and notwithſtanding the exceſſive pain, and loſs of blood occaſioned by it, they were obliged to ſing aloud hymns to their gods. This cruel operation was repeated every twenty days. When eighty days of this faſt of the prieſts was elapſed, a general faſt of the people, from which the heads of the republic were not exempted, began, and was continued an equally long time."

Inconſiſtent as it may ſeem to have been with this auſterity, other rites of the antient heathen religions, and thoſe which occurred the moſt frequently, encouraged, and indeed required, the extreme of ſenſual indulgence; and ſometimes that of the moſt unnatural kind. It is not eaſy to ſay by what particular train of thinking they

they were led to conclude that such practises as these could be pleasing to the gods, but some of those deities that were to be appeased by human sacrifices were supposed to be no less pleased to see their worshippers indulge themselves in whatever could gratify their appetites; and their groves, and the temples themselves, were scenes of open prostitution.

It is well known that, in general, the heathens ascribed to their gods the passions and actions of men, and too many of the oriental princes, and those the most celebrated for their warlike and other exploits, gave into the extreme of both cruelty and lust. It is possible, however, that the indecent symbols of their worship, which might be originally designed to represent what is, no doubt, the most remarkable circumstance in the constitution of nature, viz. its *reproductive power*, or that of generation, might lead to those acts of lewdness with which the heathen worship abounded. And, incredible as it may appear to us, figures which cannot be named

named with decency, were expofed and carried about in thefe facred proceffions, hymns were fung to them, and religious worfhip paid to them. This was done by the Egyptians, and moft other antient nations, efpecially the Greeks, who borrowed the cuftom from them*.

To recite the particulars of the indecencies of the heathen worfhip would be difgufting, and the account could hardly be given in language proper for a public affembly; but as fomething of this kind is become neceffary, in order to give a juft idea of the ftate of *facts* which have been ftrongly difguifed by unbelievers, and to fhew the great fuperiority of revealed religion to that which almoft all mankind naturally fell into, I muft, be excufed if, for the fake of thofe who may have

---

* Lucian, a heathen writer, fays that, in the portico of the temple at Hierapolis, which ftood on an hill, there was a tower three hundred cubits high, built in that indecent form, to the top of which a man afcended twice a year, where he continued feven days, that he might with more advantage converfe with the gods above. In the worfhip of the people of Indoftan, figures even more fhocking to modefty than thofe of the antient weftern nations are now made ufe of.

been

been misled by such writers as Voltaire and others, (who have smoothed over the enormities of the heathan worship) recite as many particulars as may be necessary to give you an idea of the general character of the system, which they represent as perfectly innocent, and not at all unfavourable to purity of morals, their festivals, as Voltaire says, being only seasons of rejoicing, which could not be prejudicial to mankind. This would be true if their festivals had been nothing more than seasons of rejoicing. But judge for yourselves, whether they were not something more.

That lewdness was a part of the antient heathen worship, is evident from the account that Moses gives of that of Baal Peor, to which the Israelites were inticed by the Moabites and Midianites. For during that festival, Phinehas asserted the honour of his religion by killing a man and a woman in the very act of fornication; which, from the narrative, appears to have been committed without any concealment. For we read, Numb. xxv. 6. *And behold*

behold one of the children of Israel came, and brought unto his brethren a Midianitish woman, in the sight of Moses, and in the sight of all the congregation of the children of Israel, who were weeping before the door of the tabernacle of the congregation; and when Phinehas the son of Eleazar the son of Aaron the priest saw it, he arose up from among the congregation, and took a javelin in his hand, and he went after the man of Israel into the tent, and thrust both of them through, the man of Israel and the woman, through her belly. Now the name of the Israelite who was slain was Zimri the son of Salu, a prince of the chief house among the Simeonites, and the name of the Midianitish woman that was slain was Cozbi the daughter of Zur, who was head over a people, and of a chief house in Midian.

This worship of Baal-Peor, if we may credit several antient writers, consisted in such obscene practices, or postures at least, as are not fit to be mentioned; so that it is not easy to say whether they were more ridiculous, or impure. Hosea says of this worship, ch. xi. 10. *They went unto Baal-Peor,*

Peor, and separated themselves unto their shame; and *their abominations were according as they loved,* or, as the Bishop of Waterford renders it, and *became abominable as the objects of their love,* or worship.

The farther we go back into antiquity or so much nearer to the time of Moses, the more undisguised were these shameful practices. It appears from Herodotus, the oldest Greek historian, that the temples of the heathen gods had been universally places of prostitution. For he says the Egyptians were the first who forbad it in their temples. He says that all other nations, except the Greeks (who borrowed much of their religion from the Egyptians) scrupled not to perform those actions in the temples. Nor did the Greeks wholly abstain from them. For when Antiochus Epiphanes converted the temple at Jerusalem, into a temple of Jupiter Olympius, we read, 2 Mac. vi. 4. *The temple was filled with riot and revelling by the Gentiles, who dallied with harlots, and had to do with women, within the circuit of the holy places.* Julius

Julius Firmicus fays that, after the feafon of *mourning*, with which the principal feftival of the oriental nations commenced, the reft of the time was fpent with every expreffion of mirth and jollity, to which they added the moft abominable debauchery, adultery, and inceft. Thefe were conftantly practifed in their groves and temples*.

Surely, then, we may fay, with the apoftle in my text, that, as a punifhment for men's apoftacy from his worfhip, *God gave up the heathen world to vile affections*; and that there was infinite wifdom and goodnefs in the Jewifh and Chriftian difpenfations, in which we are taught a mode of worfhip worthy of a pure and holy God, a religion the great object of which is the pureft morality, and in which all the abominations of the heathen worfhip are treated with juft abhorrence. For our unfpeakable happinefs in being favour-

---

* " In what temple," fays Juvenal, a Roman heathen poet, " are not women debauched?" *Quo non proftat femina templo.*
Sat. ix. 24.

ed with thefe revelations, we cannot be too thankful. But I muſt defer the farther confideration of thefe, and other enormities of the heathen worſhip, with which the generality of chriſtians are little acquainted, but which you muſt be fenfible, it is highly ufeful for them to know, though difguſting to contemplate, to another difcourfe, with which I ſhall conclude this part of my fubject.

DISCOURSE IV.

A View of Heathen Worship.

For the wrath of God is revealed from heaven against all ungodliness and unrighteousness of men, who hold the truth in unrighteousness. Because that which may be known of God is manifest in them, for God hath shewed it unto them. For the invisible things of him, from the creation of the world, are clearly seen, being understood by the things that are made, even his eternal power and godhead, so that they are without excuse. Because that when they knew God, they glorified him not as God, neither were thankful, but became vain in their imaginations, and their foolish heart was darkened. Professing themselves to be wise, they became fools, and changed the glory of the incorruptible God, into an image made like to corruptible man, and to birds and fourfooted beasts, and creeping things. Wherefore also God gave them up to uncleanness, through the lusts of their own hearts, to dishonour their own bodies between themselves, who changed the truth of God into a lie, and worshipped and served the creature more than the Creator, who is blessed for ever. For this cause God gave them up to vile affections.

ROMANS, i. 18---26.

THE most plausible objections made to the system of revelation, and those by which persons who have no knowledge of antiquity are most liable to be impressed, are

are thofe which relate to the Jewifh religion, and the books of the Old Teftament, with which the generality of Chriftians are too little acquainted. Voltaire, and other unbelievers, are more particularly fond of reprefenting the inftitutions of Mofes as unreafonably intolerant, with refpect to the heathens who, they fay, only differed from the Hebrews in religious opinions. It therefore behoves thofe who undertake the defence of revealed religion to fhew, what it is very eafy to do, that antient heathenifm was by no means a mere fyftem of fpeculative opinions, and innocent practices; but that, befides being abfurd in the extreme, it really promoted the moft deftructive and the moft execrable vices, and that the religion of the Hebrews was free from every tendency of the kind, and infinitely fuperior to it in every other refpect.

In my laft difcourfe I gave you an idea of fome of the enormities of the heathen religion, fuch as, though well known to the learned, are not fo to the generality of Chriftians,

Chriftians, and yet without this knowledge it is impoffible that they can have a juft idea of the value of their own religion, or a right underftanding of the fcriptures, efpecially thofe of the Old Teftament, in which there are perpetual allufions to the principles and rites of the heathen worfhip. I particularly mentioned the multiplicity of the heathen deities, the vile characters of many of them, the horrid rite of human facrifices, the painful aufterities to which their religion fubjected them, and the open proftitution which was encouraged by it, and practifed in their very temples; and in fupport of my reprefentations, I recited a variety of facts, from the authority of the fcriptures, and other antient writings. Had I contented myfelf with exclaiming in general terms only againft the religion of the heathens, faying of it, as Voltaire does of the religion of the Jews, that it was an *execrable fuperftition*, without reciting any of the circumftances which fhew it to have been fuch, all that you could have inferred would have been, that I was

was defirous of impreffing your minds with an abhorrence of that religion, but then you would have had no knowledge of the reafons why it deferved that abhorrence, and therefore might have paid no regard to my unfupported reprefentation.

My laft difcourfe concluded with obferving that a moft prominent feature in the religion of the antient heathens, was the encouragement it gave to lewdnefs, and this continued with increafe, when, in the progrefs of civilization, the cruel rite of human facrifices, and their painful aufterities, became lefs frequent. For this reafon the apoftle Paul, in the chapter which contains my text, and in other parts of his epiftles, particularly dwells upon it.

On this fubject I fhall only mention one more circumftance, which is feveral times mentioned, or alluded to, in the fcriptures. It is that a confiderable revenue arofe to many of the heathen temples, as is now the cafe in Indoftan, from the proftitution that was encouraged in them, or in places provided for that abominable purpose adjoining to them. The Divine Being, alluding to this practice of the heathens, says, by Moses, Deut. xxiii. 18. *Thou shalt not bring the hire of a harlot into the house of the Lord thy God. There shall be no harlot of the daughters of Israel, nor a Sodomite of the sons of Israel.* For, incredible as it may appear to us, who have had the happiness of being educated in the principles of the purest of all religions, even unnatural pollution was allowed, and encouraged, in the religion of the antient heathens. For this we have the clear evidence of the scriptures, as well as of many antient writers. Concerning the pious king Josiah, we read, 2 Kings, xxiii. 7. that *he brake down the houses of the Sodomites that were by the house of the Lord, where the woman wove hangings for the grove,* or rather for *Asteroth,* or *Astarte,* a famous Syrian goddess*.

Besides

---

* Herodotus informs us that at Babylon, a city the most devoted to the worship of idols of all the nations of antiquity every woman was obliged once in her life to prostitute herself

In the time of Conſtantine, and no doubt from times of the moſt remote antiquity, the Egyptians had religious rites in which ſodomy was practiſed, and they imagined that the riſe of the Nile depended on the obſervance of them. Theſe this Chriſtian emperor ordered to be diſcontinued; and whereas the ſuperſtitious heathens

ſelf to ſome ſtranger in the temple of Venus. Becauſe the moſt wealthy diſdained to expoſe themſelves in public, among the reſt, they went in covered chariots to the gates of the temple, with a numerous train of ſervants attending at a diſtance But the far greater part went into the temple itſelf, and ſat down covered with garlands. The galleries in which they ſat were in a ſtraight line, and open on every ſide, that all ſtrangers might have free paſſage to chuſe ſuch as they liked beſt. The beautiful women, he ſays, were ſoon diſmiſſed; but the deformed were ſometimes obliged to wait three or four days before they could ſatisfy the law. The perſon who made choice of any of them made her a preſent, which was ſacred to the deity, and could not be refuſed, though ever ſo ſmall.

The ſame hiſtorian ſays that the women of Cyprus had a cuſtom not unlike this of the Babylonians. There was the like in the temple of Venus at Sicca in Africa, at Corinth, and at Comana in Cappadocia. In the temple of Venus at Aphaca, on mount Libanus, there was a kind of academy of lewdneſs, open to all debauched perſons, where the moſt beaſtly crimes were committed in the temple, as a privileged place, exempt from all law and government. The *ludi Florales* at Rome were celebrated by a company of proſtitutes, who

thens had imagined that the confequence of this fuppreffion would be that the river would not rife as ufual, the Chriftians faid it rofe higher than before.

Sodomy, fays Julius Firmicus, who wrote in the time of the fons of Conftantine, was then practifed in the temple of Juno. He adds that they were fo far from being afhamed of it, that they gloried in it. And it appears from various writers, that the gains of this abominable kind of proftitution were a fource of revenue to the heathen temples, as well as thofe of the women who belonged to them. And yet of this religion Voltaire fays that " it

who ran up and down naked, ufing the moft lafcivious poftures. The temple of Venus at Corinth maintained above a thoufand proftitutes, facred to her fervice, and what they got was given to the goddefs. The fame is the cafe at this day with refpect to many of the temples in Indoftan. Tavernier fays there is a Pagod near Cambaye, where women proftitute themfelves, and Marco Polo fays that the like cuftom prevailed at Camul; and that when it was forbidden by the Mahometan prince Mongou Khan, and the order had been obeyed three years, the people fent deputies to get it repealed, as they faid that their fields had not been fo fruitful as they had been before.

" could

" could not be of any prejudice to man-
" kind."*

Besides the rites which were performed in public, and at which all persons were permitted, and often required, to be present, there were in the antient heathen religions, rites of a private nature, to which none were admitted but under an oath of secrecy, the violation of which was deemed to be the greatest act of impiety. Some have supposed that the design of these *mysteries*, as those rites were called,

---

* How the rites of the goddess Cybele operated as an incentive to lewdness may be seen in Juvenal, Sat. vi. 313. &c.

That these practices thus sanctioned by religion, had a fatal influence on the public opinion and the public morals, is evident from the writings of the heathens, especially those of the poets, which abound with the most disgusting obscenities. One of the most admired eclogues of Virgil, who is esteemed the chastest of the Roman poets, celebrates the love of a man to a boy, and the only remaining, and much admired poem, of the Greek poetess Sappho, describes that of a woman to a woman, which is an abundant confirmation of what to us appears most incredible in the apostle Paul's representation of the depravity of the Gentile world. And with the disbelief of revelation we find in fact, that the just abhorrence which all the Christian world entertain for these unnatural vices disappears; a proof of which might be given in some well authenticated anecdotes of the late king of Prussia, but not to be related in this place.

was

was to shew the abfurdity of the popular worfhip; but this is in the higheft degree improbable. Indeed, nothing which fhould have been fufpected to have that tendency would have been borne with, and they who made the greateft account of thefe myfteries were the moft devoted to the popular fuperftitions. The moft probable opinion is, that whatever was the original intention of thefe private myfteries, they became a fcene of fuch exhibitions and practices, as were worfe than any that were tranfacted in public.

Socrates, the moft moral of all the heathen philofophers, and the leaft attached to the vulgar fuperftition, would never be initiated into thefe myfteries. In the time of Cicero the very term *myfteries* was almoft fynonymous to *abominations*, and we may well fuppofe what the nature of them muft have been when it is known that they were celebrated in the night, in honour of Bacchus, Venus, or Cupid, and that indecent images were carried in proceffion in them, fo that they could not fail

fail to countenance that impurity, and diffoluteneſs of manners, which was ſo general in the Pagan world. To theſe myſteries it is moſt probable that Paul refers, when he ſays, Epheſ. v. 12. *It is a ſhame even to ſpeak of thoſe things which are done by them in ſecret.* Clemens Alexandrinus called theſe myſteries, " the myſteries of atheiſtical men," adding, " I may rightly call them
" atheiſts, who are deſtitute of the know-
" ledge of him who is truly God, and who
" moſt impudently worſhip a boy torn in
" pieces by the Titans, women lamenting,
" and the parts which modeſty forbids
" to name." A Roman conſul diſcovered that " the Bacchanalian myſteries
" conſiſted of ſuch things as the moſt un-
" bounded proſtitution could exhibit in
" private and nocturnal aſſemblies, that no
" perſon could be initiated into them
" without renouncing his modeſty, while
" the prieſts who preſided over them pre-
" ſcribed in public, to thoſe who were to
" be admitted to them, a ten days
" abſtinence." Conſtantine, who forbad the

the practice of sodomy in the religious rites of the Egyptians, forbad all secret rites of initiation in all the Roman empire.

But there is no occasion to pry into the secret mysteries of the heathen religion for scenes sufficiently shocking to decency. Public games and plays, in which the flagitious actions of the heathen gods were represented, were always considered as acts of religion, and celebrated in their honour, though some of the wiser of the antients were ashamed of these exhibitions. Cicero, speaking of the adulteries of Jupiter, his ravishing the boy Ganymede, and carrying him off to be his cup-bearer, says, " Homer feigned these things, and ascrib- " ed human actions and qualities to the " gods. I had rather that he had raised " man to the imitation of what is divine." It is not, however, true that Homer invented those stories. He only introduced into his poems what was generally believed in his time. " The same gods," says Austin, " that were ridiculed on the thea- " tre, were adored in the temples." And what

what is particularly remarkable, is that worfe things were afcribed to gods of the greateft dignity, as Jupiter, than to any of an inferior rank. Such was the religion which Voltaire reprefents as perfectly innocent, with refpect to its moral tendency.

Some of the rites of the antient heathen religions, which were not remarkable for their cruelty or lewdnefs, confifted of fuch inftances of favage ferocity and extravagance, as are not eafily accounted for. But whatever was the *caufe* that led to fuch rites, the *facts* that I fhall mention are unqueftionable, and perhaps fuch perfons as Voltaire would not have been fhocked, but only amufed, with them.

When the fun entered Aries, at the time of the vernal equinox, the Egyptians celebrated a feftival in honour of the fun, when perfons of both fexes counterfeited madnefs, ran about the ftreets, and alfo up hills, and through deferts, pulling in pieces the carcafes of the animals they facrificed, breaking their bones, and eating

ing the flesh raw with the blood running out of their mouths, and committing every sort of extravagance. From Egypt this rite passed into Greece. At Chios, and also at Tenedos, they sacrificed a man, whom they tore in pieces in this manner. Plutarch, speaking of these things, says " These festivals and direful sacrifices, " which are celebrated with eating raw " flesh, torn with men's nails, as others " in which men fast, and beat their breasts, " were not, I think, performed on the " account of any of the gods, but rather " to mollify and appease the fury of some " evil demon. For it is not probable that " there ever was a god, who required " men to be sacrificed to him, as has " been antiently done, or received such " sacrifices with approbation." But Plutarch, from his own better reason, thought too favourably of the religion of his ancestors.

In the *Omophagia*, which was a festival of the Greeks in honour of Bacchus, the priests tore with their teeth, and devoured, the

the entrails of the goats which they sacrificed, raw and reeking, in imitation of their god. And the *Lupercalia,* one of the moſt antient of the Roman feſtivals, in honour of the god Pan, was celebrated by the prieſts running about the ſtreets, naked, all but the middle, and ſtriking all they met, and eſpecially women, with thongs made of the ſkins of the goats, which they ſacrificed. And the women, thinking there was great virtue in thoſe laſhings, rather threw themſelves in their way than avoided them.

What a ſtriking contraſt with reſpect to all the things I have enumerated do we ſee between the religious rites of the heathens, and thoſe preſcribed to the Hebrews, in none of which is there any thing that favours of cruelty, immorality, or indecency; and yet Voltaire is ever loading the religion of the Jews with every term of reproach, and apologizing for that of the heathens.

The proper parent of all ſuperſtition, and falſe religion, is, as I have obſerved

ignorance

ignorance of nature, and the true causes of events; and men being naturally anxious about the good or evil that may befal them, not knowing their true causes, but ascribing every thing to some cause or other, were led, from circumstances which it is impossible at this distance of time to trace, to fix upon causes entirely foreign to the purpose. But though their opinions, and some of the practises derived from them, cannot now be mentioned without exciting a smile of contempt, they were serious things in times of antiquity; and to have laughed at them then would have cost a man dear.

When the sun, and his emblem fire, were the principal objects of worship, it was imagined that no child would live or thrive, that was not made to pass through the fire, and therefore the drawing them over lighted straw, or any kind of flame that would not materially injure them, was deemed a necessary rite of religion. This we find practised by the Israelites, in imitation of their neighbours, during their defection from their own religion. Thus we we read concerning Manaſſey Chr. xxxiii. 10, that *he cauſed his children to paſs through the fire, in the valley of the ſon of Hinnom, as alſo that he obſerved times, uſed inchantments, and dealt with a familiar ſpirit, and wizards,* all which practices were of heathen origin, and deſerve to be particularly noticed.

The *obſerving times*, or diſtinguiſhing days into the lucky and unlucky, when they cannot have any real influence on the buſineſs tranſacted in them, was a very antient heathen ſuperſtition, and even continues to this day, though one of the remains of heatheniſm, in moſt Chriſtian countries.

Lucian, a heathen philoſopher, ſpeaking of unlucky days, ſays " on them neither " do the magiſtrates meet to conſult about " public affairs, neither are law ſuits de-" cided in the hall, nor ſacrifices offered, " nor in fine any ſort of buſineſs under-" taken, in which a man would wiſh " himſelf fortunate." He ſays that Lycurgus the great Lacedemonian lawgiver made a fundamental inſtitution of government

ment, never to enter upon any warlike expedition, but when the moon was at the full; being of opinion that all things were under the influence of the moon, and that neither would their forces abroad act with sufficient vigour and success, nor would their affairs at home be so well conducted, in the increase, as in the decrease, of that planet. The emperor Augustus was so much a slave to this superstition, that he never went abroad on the day after the *nundinæ*, on which the public markets were held, nor did he begin any serious undertaking on the *nones* of any month. Ambrose says that the first converts from heathenism were much addicted to these observances.

What is called *witchcraft*, which is another of the superstitious practices to which Manasseh was addicted, was very common among the heathens. It consisted in the invocation of demons, in order to produce by incantation, charms, medicated compositions of herbs, &c. the most surprizing effects. This art Maimonides says

says was much practifed by the Zabii, and the Chaldeans; and it was very common among the Egyptians, and Cannanites.

None of thefe magical operations could be performed without a regard to the ftars. For they held that every plant had its governing ftar. With the heathens, therefore, thefe magical practices were acts of religion. By this means they believed that the demons were fubject to them. In the antient heathen religions the moft extraordinary effects, efpecially of the mifchevious kind, were afcribed to charms, and talifmans, but it was fuppofed that they might be counteracted by more potent charms, though alike infignificant. A fuperftitious perfon, fays Theophraftus, if he fees a weafel crofs his path, goes no farther, till fome other perfon goes before him, or till he has thrown three ftones acrofs the way. Many of thefe things, though abfurd in the extreme, made fo deep an impreffion on the minds of the heathens, that it was with great difficulty that they were brought to to difregard them when they embraced chriftianity.

It might be imagined that thefe idle notions and cuftoms were peculiar to the vulgar among the heathens, but they were regularly practifed by the graveft magiftrates of the wifeft ftates in antiquity. For in fact when thofe ftates were conftituted, the legiflators themfelves were not, in thefe refpects, more knowing than the reft of the people. When any great public calamity was to be averted at Rome, the firft magiftrate went in folemn proceffion, and drove a nail of brafs into the temple of Jupiter Capitolinus. This was deemed to be the moft effectual method of appeafing the anger of the gods.

The greateft ftrefs was laid by the antients on folemn *imprecations*, as we fee in the cafe of Balak, king of Moab, who at a great expence, fent for the prophet Balaam to curfe Ifrael. For the curfes of prophets and priefts, were thought to be the moft efficacious. Hence it was cuftomary for men condemned for any notorious crime
to

to be publicly curfed by the priefts. It was alfo often done from particular enmity and faction. Thus when Craffus the Roman triumvir undertook his famous expedition againft the Parthians, his opponent Ateius Capito, the tribune, running to the gate of the city through which he paffed, placed there veffels full of burning coals, on which he offered odours and oblations, and then he pronounced the moft direful curfes againft him as he went along.

Prying into futurity was always a great object in the religion of the heathens; and from their ignorance of nature, they imagined that the gods, who were the rulers of the fates of men, gave indications of future events by various figns, which it was the bufinefs of the priefts to ftudy. This was the act of divination,

Divination was moft commonly made by facrifices, and efpecially by the obfervation of the entrails, and more particularly the livers, of the victims. This among the Romans was a fcience of itfelf, and a diftinct order of priefts, called *Harufpices ruspices*, were appointed to the study and practice of it. Another solemn divination was by the observation of the flight of birds, and this was the business of another order of priests, called *Augurs*; and unless their reports were favourable, no public business could be transacted. A peculiarly solemn rite of this kind called *taking the auspices*, was by observing the manner in which a coop of poultry, which was kept for the purpose, ate their food. If they did it heartily, the omen was thought to be favourable, if otherwise, unfavourable; and so much were the minds of the Roman soldiers impressed by this circumstance, that no prudent general would risk an engagement with the enemy, till the augurs made a favourable report.

Nebuchadnezzar, king of Babylon, did not undertake his expedition against Jerusalem without first consulting the gods, according to the rites of divination practised in his time, though we know but little of them at present. Thus we read, Ez. xxi. 21. *The king of Babylon stood at the parting*

parting of the way, at the head of the two ways, to ufe divination. He made his arrows bright, he confulted with images, he looked in the liver. At his right hand was the divination for Jerufalem, to appoint captains, to open the mouth in the flaughter, to lift up the voice with fhouting, to appoint battering rams againft the gates, to caft a mount, and to build a fort.

It were endlefs to enumerate all the various modes of divination practifed by the antient heathens, as by lots, by ominous words and things, &c. with allufions to which the Greek and Roman writers abound, fo that they are well known to every fchool-boy. But one of the moft extraordinary and direful of thefe modes of divination, that by having recourfe to the dead, I muft briefly mention. This was the ferious art of *necromancy*, to which Manaffeh was faid to have been addicted; and to this king Saul had recourfe in his diftreffes. Thus alfo Ulyffes is reprefented by Homer as facrificing a black fheep in a ditch, and after pouring libations, inviting the ghoft of Tirefias and others to drink of the blood, in order to their anfwering the queftions that would be put to them.

Similar to this was the *having to do with familiar fpirits*, and *wizards*, with which Manaffeh is likewife charged; for the anfwers received by this means are reprefented as feeming to come from under the ground, the place of the dead; as we read If. viii. 19. *Seek unto them that have familiar fpirits, and unto wizards, that peep and that mutter*, and If. xxix. 4. *Thou fhalt be brought down, and fhalt fpeak out of the ground, and thy fpeech fhall whifper out of the duft.* Sometimes the perfons who pretended to this art feemed to fpeak out of their own bellies. Of this kind Maimonides fays is the oracle of Pytho. " He is one," he fays, " who after a kind of fumigation, " flourifhes a myrtle rod in his hand, and " pronounces certain fet words of in- " chantment. Then he feems to confult one " who is talking with him, and anfwers " his queftions, as it were from under the " ground, with fo low a voice, that he " cannot

"cannot diftinctly hear it, but muft col-
"lect the meaning by his imagination."

Thus have I endeavoured to give you a general idea of the nature of the heathen religion, as it was practifed in the earlieft ages, and indeed as it continued, with little or no improvement, till the promulgation of chriftianity. It was not, you fee, a merely contemptible fuperftition, founded on the groffeft ignorance of the laws of nature, but fuch as in the higheft degree muft have debafed the minds, and have corrupted the morals, of men. How juftly is the ftate of the heathen world defcribed by the apoftle Paul in my text, and other facred writers; and how remote from truth, and the appearance of truth, is the account that Voltaire, and other unbelievers, out of a defire to difcredit revelation, have given of it. Surely then the rectifying thefe fundamental errors, into which all the world had fallen, with refpect to religion, and the putting an end to practices fo debafing to the human character, and fo deftructive of human happinefs, happiness, was an object not unworthy of the great parent and friend of mankind.

That there was no prospect of men, by any use they could make of their own reason, recovering from this deplorable ignorance and corruption, was evident by the experience of three thousand years, in which, though many parts of the world became enlightened in other respects, they grew, if possible, more confirmed in their attachment to their religions received from their ancestors; continuing to believe, notwithstanding the strongest appearances to the contrary, that the prosperity of their several states, and even the fertility of the ground, depended upon the observance of their particular rites. And therefore as soon as the heathen magistrates saw the rapid spread of christianity, and the danger to which their antient religions were exposed in consequence of it, they employed all their power to suppress it, persecuting the professors of the new religion in every form, though happily in vain. Truth, supported by clear evidence,

evidence, could not be overcome by power.

That nothing lefs than repeated interpofitions of the deity could have preferved any part of the human race from this fhocking idolatry, fo deftructive of virtue and of happinefs, is particularly evident from the hiftory of all the nations defcended from Abraham, whofe founders were, no doubt, inftructed by him in the knowledge and worfhip of the one true God, and who, notwithftanding this, all became idolaters. This was the cafe with the Arabs, defcended from Ifhmael, and other fons of that great patriarch, though in the time of Job, who was probably prior to Mofes, fome of them were not fo. This was alfo the cafe with the Edomites, though defcended from Ifaac, and of the Moabites and Ammonites, defcended from Lot, the friend and companion of Abraham. There muft, therefore, have been fome thing exceedingly fafcinating and plaufible in the fyftems of heathen worfhip, though to us, who have been enlightened by revelation, nothing appears more abfurd and fhocking.

But

But *when the world by its own wisdom knew not God, it pleased God,* as the apostle says, 1 Cor. i. 21, *by the foolishness of preaching,* i. e. by the gospel (which at its first publication was ridiculed as foolish by those who were reputed wise) to effect a reformation. And to this day there has not been any reformation of the most absurd of the heathen religions, but by means of the gospel. All that Mahometanism has done in this respect was by means of the principles derived from the Jewish and Christian religions, the truth of which it supposes. Thus was verified the declaration of our Saviour, John xiv. 6. *No man cometh to the father* (or attains to the knowledge and worship of the one true God) *but by me;* a most extraordinary prediction, but abundantly verified by facts.

Can we then be too thankful to God, for the promulgation of the gospel which has not only *brought life and immortality to light,* by the clear revelation of a future state; but has freed mankind from the grossest ignorance, and superstitious addictedness to innumerable practices of the most
hor-

rid and abominable nature; such as furnished incentives and opportunity for every vice, the most debasing of the characters of men, and the cause of infinite mischiefs to them, both as individuals, and as members of society. The gospel, whatever else may be said of it, has been, if there be any truth in history, the only, but it has been an effectual, remedy of these great evils; while all the evils that have been charged upon *it*, are clearly owing to a departure from its genuine principles, as they are now to be seen in the New Testament, the rise and progress of them being investigated with the greatest ease and certainty. And as the reformation advances they are now every where abated, and may therefore be expected soon to disappear, when the gospel will again appear in its purity, the greatest of blessings to all the human race.

DISCOURSE V.

The excellence of the Mosaic Institutions.

Behold I have taught you statutes and judgments, even as the Lord my God commanded me, that ye should do so in the land whither ye go to possess it. Keep therefore and do them. For this is your wisdom and understanding, in the sight of the nations which shall hear all these statutes, and say, Surely this great nation is a wise and understanding people. For what nation is there so great, who hath God so near unto them as the Lord your God is, in all things that ye call upon him for; and what nation is there so great that hath statutes and judgments so righteous, as all this law which I set before you this day.

DEUT. iv. 5---8.

HAVING, in the two preceding discourses, given you a view of the religions of the antient heathen nations, I shall now, by way of contrast, give you a similar view of that of the Hebrews; and this it will be the easier to do, as the original records of it are extant in the writings of Moses, which were composed at the time of its institution; so that there cannot be
any

any difficulty in diftinguifhing the genuine principles of this religion from the corruptions and abufes of it. No other nation can give fuch an account of the origin of their religion. For it is not pretended that any other has writings coeval with their inftitutions. All the accounts of them are traditional, and their traditions are derived from the moft remote antiquity; fo that much is necefsarily left to conjecture with refpect to them.

The fuperior excellence of the fyftem of Hebrew religion and policy, for they had the fame fource, and the moft intimate connection, is ftrongly afserted by Mofes in my text. On the other hand, Voltaire, followed by the generality of unbelievers, fays, that " the Jews were " an ignorant and barbarous people, who " have for a long time joined the bafeft " avarice to the moft deteftable fuperfti- " tion. They have done much hurt," he fays, " to themfelves, and to the hu- " man race." This writer had, no doubt, read the books of Mofes, and the other books

books of the Old Testament, for he frequently quotes them; but many persons, without ever reading these books themselves, take for granted that what he says of them is true. But, my brethren, be persuaded to make use of your own eyes, and judge for yourselves. To assist you in this, I shall, as briefly as possible, lay before you the most important particulars of which the institutions of Moses consist, and occasionally compare them with particulars of a similar nature in the systems of the heathens, which were cotemporary with them.

In order to throw the greater odium on the Hebrew nation, Voltaire says, "they were ignorant and barbarous, that "they were never famous for any art, "they never were natural philosophers, "geometricians, or astronomers." Admitting this to be the case, if there be any wisdom, or superior excellence, in their religious or political institutions, it will be the more probable that they had some other source than any knowledge of their own.

own. But I do not defire to take any advantage of this circumftance.

It is not true that, in ancient times, the Hebrews were much, if at all, inferior to other nations with refpect to the arts. In the art of war, which, even in the age of Mofes comprized many other arts, it will hardly be denied that the Hebrews, if there was nothing miraculous in their hiftory, muft have excelled. For to fay nothing of their emancipating themfelves from the yoke of the Egyptians, then the moft warlike people in the world, when they were wholly unprovided for the conteft, they completely expelled the inhabitants of Canaan, ten times more numerous than themfelves, who had horfes and chariots of iron, and whofe cities are faid to have been *fenced up to heaven*, when they only fought on foot. The whole land of Canaan was of no great extent, and yet David conquered, and held in fubjection, all the neighbouring nations; and it is probable that they continued tributary to the Ifraelites all the reign of Solomon.

Solomon. There are few nations in all antiquity that can boaſt of two ſuch princes as David and Solomon with all their faults.

The conſtruction of the tabernacle in the time of Moſes, and of the temple in the time of Solomon, ſhows that there were ingenious artiſts among them, as well as in other countries, and the knowledge that any people in theſe early ages had of real *ſcience*, that is, of the laws of nature, and the application of that knowledge to any uſeful purpoſe, was very inconſiderable. Knowledge of this kind would have prevented that miſerable ſuperſtition, in which, as I have ſhewn, the antient heathen religion conſiſted.

As to what is properly called *literature*, or the art of writing, and compoſing books, no antient nation can pretend to vie with the Hebrews. We have no account of any books ſo old as thoſe of Moſes, and though there is not in them the leaſt appearance of *art*, or ſtudied compoſition, they are written with that engaging ſimplicity, which has not yet been exceeded by by any writings whatever. The pathos in the addrefs of Mofes to his nation in the book of Deuteronomy, written juft before his death, is inimitable. It is not poffible to read it, if I may judge of the feelings of other perfons by my own, without the ftrongeft emotions.. The incidents in the hiftory of Jofeph were not the invention of Mofes, but they have loft nothing in going through his hands. There is not, in all antiquity, fo affecting a narrative.

With refpect to the knowledge of human nature and human life, the proverbs of Solomon difcover as much of it as the fayings of the feven wife men of Greece, in a much later period; and for fublimity of fentiment, and energy of expreffion, the pfalms of David, and the writings of Ifaiah, and other Hebrew prophets, though in a language but imperfectly known, and though they have fuffered more than any writings whatever by frequent copying, are infinitely fuperior to any poetical compofitions of the Greeks or Romans in any age;

age; especially if they be read in profe translations, which is all that we can do with respect to the poetry of the Hebrews, the measure of which is now lost. Both are extant. Let them be compared by the principles of just criticism; but not by so prejudiced a person as Voltaire.

The Egyptians had the art of writing, but they had no books of which we have any certain account. The same was the case with the Chaldeans. And as to the Greeks, they were, in a period long after the time of Moses, as barbarous and ignorant as the North American Indians at this day. If we may judge of the antient Hebrews by the Jews, who are descended from them, we must say that, with respect to natural ingenuity, or industry, they are far from being inferior to the rest of mankind. They are perhaps rather superior, not by nature (for in that respect probably all mankind are nearly equal) but in consequence of the greater exercise of their faculties, owing in a great measure to the treatment they have met with from other nations,

tions, and the manner in which they are compelled to provide for their maintenance among them. In Europe at leaft, a very filly, or a very idle, Jew could hardly fubfift.

But without any regard to the *people*, let us confider their *inftitutions*; and in doing this we muft endeavour to forget, or overlook, principles that are familiar to us Chriftians, and which we derived from the fcriptures, and attend fimply to the ftate of the world in the time of Mofes, and the principles and cuftoms which were then moft prevalent, and which the Ifraelites themfelves had in a great meafure adopted while they were in Egypt. Admitting that Mofes, in confequence of his having been educated at the court of Pharoah, was acquainted with all the learning of the Egyptians, he had no opportunity of acquiring *more*, or indeed any knowledge of a different kind; and he was not likely to improve his knowledge of any kind by living afterwards forty years among the Arabs, where he married, and was

was fettled; having probably given up all thoughts of ever returning to Egypt, his life being in danger if he did.

Notwithftanding this, at the age of eighty, he did return, and though Egypt was then in a ftate of its greateft power, and his countrymen in a ftate of the moft abject fervitude, deftitute of arms or friends, he effected their complete emancipation, in a very few months without the lofs of a fingle life, while the Egyptians were fo weakened, or overawed, that, though the Ifraelites continued many years in their neighbourhood, and without any connection with other nations, their old mafters never attempted to get them back again: and yet on account of the fervice they had derived from them, they had been moft unwilling to part with them. This, however, is a circumftance, which, though highly favourable to the fuppofition of there being fomething miraculous in their deliverance, I only mention by the way, before I recite the particulars of thofe inftitutions, which, in their ftate of emancipation

emancipation from their bondage in Egypt, and before they had got any other settlement, Moses delivered to them.

In considering these institutions, let us pay no regard to what Moses says of their having been delivered to him by God, but only what they are in themselves, that we may judge, from the circumstances of the times, whether it be more probable that they were devised by himself, or that they were communicated to him in the manner that he relates. In this view of the Mosaic institutions I shall not, however, strictly confine myself to what may be drawn from the writings of Moses, but take advantage of the farther lights that are thrown upon them in other books of the Old Testament, the authors of which had no other sources of information. They are all written on the same principles, and in the same spirit.

1. You have seen the monstrous polytheism of all the nations of antiquity. In direct opposition to this, the first, and most fundamental, principle in the religion of the Hebrews,

Hebrews, was that of the *unity of God*. The firft of the ten commandments, delivered from mount Sinai is (Exodus. xx. 2.) *Thou fhalt have no other Gods befides me.* This precept is repeated with the greateft emphafis through all the writings of Mofes, and thofe of the fubfequent prophets. Deut. vi. 4. *Hear, O Ifrael, the Lord our God is one Lord; and thou fhalt love the Lord thy God with all thine heart, with all thy foul, and with all thy mind,* that is, with an undivided affection, there being no other legitimate object of worfhip befides him.

That this principle is a juft one, will not now be queftioned; but, compared with the principles and practices which then prevailed in the world, it muft be pronounced to be not only juft, but alfo great, and fublime; being entirely remote from the apprehenfions of the moft enlightened of mankind in that age. That fuch an immenfe, and infinitely various, ftructure as that of the world, or rather what was called the univerfe, confifting of all the

the visible objects in nature, the system of the sun, moon, and stars, as well as the earth and sea, should have had any proper author, and much more only *one* author, that one mind should perfectly comprehend, and direct, the whole, was utterly incomprehensible by mankind; and therefore they had recourse to a multiplicity of superior beings, each presiding in his separate province; and hence the idea of the different characters and dispositions, of the heathen gods, and the varieties in their modes of worshipping them. It is in vain that we look for such an idea as Moses gives of the Deity, even among the learned Greeks, two thousand years after his time, when they had long been possessed of leisure, and every other advantage, for speculations concerning the origin of the universe, which was indeed the great object of their philosophy.

2. You have seen in what strange *forms* the heathens represented their divinities, and under what symbols, as the figures of animals, and others, they worshipped

shipped them, a practice that must have suggested low and degrading ideas of their gods. And it actually led to the worship of the animals, and the images themselves, divine powers being supposed to reside in them. This was universal among the nations that bordered on Judea. The Persians, indeed, who worshipped the sun, had no images of their god besides fire: but all the nations that the Hebrews in the time of Moses, were acquainted with, were properly *idolaters*, worshipping their gods by means of images in various shapes, and the Egyptians the animals themselves.

This source of corruption and abuse was effectually cut off in the institutions of Moses. The second commandment expressly says, Exod. xx. 4. *Thou shalt not make to thee any graven image, or the likeness of any thing that is in heaven above, or that is in the earth beneath, or that is in the waters under the earth. Thou shalt not bow down to them nor serve them.* Also when Moses, a short time before his death, reminds the Israelites of what they had seen and heard,
and

and of their obligation to respect his laws, he says, Deut. iv. 14. *When the Lord spake to you out of the midst of the fire, ye heard the voice of the words, but ye saw no similitude, only ye heard a voice. Take ye therefore good heed to yourselves, for ye saw no manner of similitude on the day that the Lord spake to you in Horeb out of the midst of the fire, lest ye corrupt yourselves, and make you a graven image, the similitude of any figure, the likeness of male or female, the likeness of any beast that is on the earth, the likeness of any winged fowl that flies in the air, the likeness of any thing that creepeth upon the ground, the likeness of any fish that is in the waters under the earth; and lest thou lift up thine eyes unto heaven, and when thou seest the sun, and the moon, and the stars, even all the host of heaven, which the Lord thy God hath divided unto all nations under the whole heavens, should be drawn to worship and serve them.*

The very idea of an intelligent Being, immense and omnipotent, and without any definite form, never occurred to any of the heathens. It is in vain that we look among their philosophers for any thing
so

so great and sublime. The least degree of attention will convince us of the greatness and sublimity of it, and yet it was familiar to this *ignorant and barbarous people* as Voltaire represents the Hebrews to have been.

These great and splendid objects, the sources of light and heat, and, as was supposed, of other beneficial influences, which were the primary objects of worship to other nations, Moses always described as having been created by the one supreme God, as well as the earth, which was another great object of worship to the heathen world. According to the just and sublime description of the writers of the Old Testament, all things are subject to the controul of this one great Being, Dan. iv. 35. *He doth whatever he pleases in the armies of heaven above, as well as among the inhabitants of the earth beneath.* Heaven is the throne, and the earth the footstool of God.

According to the principles of the wisest of the heathen nations, *matter*, if not the world itself, with all the visible system

system of things was eternal, and the gods who were the objects of the popular worship, arose out of it, and of course after it. For the idea they had received by tradition of *one God* having created all things, was soon lost and forgotten, so that he was no object of their worship at all.

The supremacy of this one God, as the author, and lord, of universal nature, is declared in the most emphatical terms on a variety of occasions in the Hebrew scriptures. On a solemn fast, after the return from the Babylonish captivity, we find an address made to God, in which they say, Neh. ix. 5. *Blessed be thy glorious name, which is exalted above all blessing and praise. Thou, even thou, art Lord alone. Thou hast made the heaven, and the heaven of heavens, with all their hosts, the earth, and all things that are therein, the sea, and all that is therein, and thou preservest them all, and all the host of heaven worship thee.* Do such sentiments as these, and such language as this, bespeak the Hebrews to have been that ignorant, barbarous, and superstitious,

superstitious nation, that Voltaire describes them as having always been?

3. Let us now see what are said to have been the *attributes* of this one God, the sole object of worship to the Hebrew nation, according to their own writings. The objects of the worship of the heathen nations, we have seen, were according to themselves, all limited in their knowledge and powers, and indeed by one another, one of them being occupied in this province, and another in that. But the God of the Hebrews is always represented as omnipotent, omnipresent, and omniscient.

According to the sublime language of the prophet Isaiah (xl. 12.) *It is he who has measured the waters in the hollow of his hand, who has meted out the heavens with a span, and comprehended the dust of the earth in a measure, hath weighed the mountains in scales, and the hills in a balance. Who*, says he, *has directed the spirit of the Lord, or being his counsellor has taught him? With whom took he counsel, and who instructed him, and taught him knowledge, and*

and shewed him the way of understanding? Behold, the nations are as the drop of a bucket, and are counted as the small dust of the balance. Behold, he taketh up the isles as a very little thing. All nations before him are as nothing, and they are counted to him as less than nothing, and vanity. To whom then will ye liken God, or what likeness will ye compare unto him? Have ye not known, have ye not heard, has it not been told you from the beginning? It is he that sitteth upon the circle of the heavens, and the inhabitants of the earth are as grashoppers, who stretcheth out the heavens as a curtain, and spreadeth them out as a tent to dwell in. Hast thou not known, hast thou not heard, that the everlasting God, the Lord, the creator of the ends of the earth, fainteth not neither is weary? There is no searching of his understanding.

What a sublime idea doth Solomon give of the attributes of God, on occasion of the dedication of the temple. 1 Kings viii. 27. *But will God indeed dwell on earth? Behold the heaven, and the heaven of heavens, cannot contain thee. How much less this house which I have built?* In the prophet Jeremiah,

miah, the divine Being is reprefented as faying, *Am I a God at hand, and not a God afar off? Can any perfon hide himfelf in fecret places that I cannot find him? faith the Lord. Do I not fill heaven and earth? faith the Lord.* The fecrets of the hearts of men are reprefented as known to God. Jer. xvii. 9. *I the Lord fearch the heart, I try the reins, even to give to every man according to his ways, and according to the fruit of his doings.*

Where fhall we find in any of the Greek or Latin poets fuch an idea of any of the heathen gods as David gives us of the God of the Hebrews in the cxxxix. Pfalm? *O Lord thou haft fearched me, and known me. Thou knoweft my down fitting, and my uprifing. Thou underftandeft my thoughts afar off. Thou compaffeft my path, and my lying down, and art acquainted with all my ways. For there is not a word in my tongue but lo, O Lord, thou knoweft it altogether. Thou haft befet me behind and before, and haft laid thine hand upon me. Such knowledge is too wonderful for me. It is high, I cannot attain unto it. Whither fhall I go from thy fpirit,*

or

or whither shall I flee from thy presence? If I ascend up into heaven, thou art there. If I make my bed in the grave, behold thou art there. If I take the wings of the morning, or dwell in the uttermost parts of the sea, even there shalt thy hand lead me, and thy right hand shall hold me. If I say, surely the darkness shall cover me, even the night shall be light about me. Yea, the darkness hideth not from thee, but the night shineth as the day. The darkness and the day are both alike to thee.

 The absurdity of the heathen worship, and the vain pretensions of the heathen gods, are finely ridiculed by the Hebrew prophets. Isaiah, foretelling the destruction of Babylon, a city peculiarly devoted to the worship of idols, says, chap. xlvi. 1. " Bel boweth down, Nebo stoopeth. " Their idols were upon the beasts, and " upon the cattle, your carriages were " heavy laden, they are a burden to the " weary beast. They stoop, they bow " down together, they could not deliver " the burden, but themselves are gone " into captivity." Jeremiah expresses equal

equal contempt of them, when he says chap. viii. 1. " Thus saith the Lord, Learn
' not the ways of the heathen, and be
' not dismayed at the signs of heaven,
' for the heathen are dismayed at them.
' For the customs of the people are vain.
' For one cutteth a tree out of the forest
' (the work of the hand of the workman,)
' with the ax. They deck it with silver
' and with gold, they fasten it with nails
· and with hammers, that it move not.
' They are upright as the palm-tree, but
' speak not. They must needs be borne,
' because they cannot go. Be not afraid
' of them, for they cannot do evil, nei-
' ther is it in them to do good. For as-
' much as there is none like unto thee, O
' Lord. Thou art great, and thy name
' is great in might. Who would not fear
' thee, O King of nations, for to thee doth
' it appertain.

4. Considering the shockingly cruel and abominable customs of the heathens, we do not wonder that such worship as theirs was most strictly forbidden to the Israelites.

ites. Indeed, to preserve in the world the knowledge and worship of the one true God, was the great object of the institutions of Moses; and a greater and more worthy object cannot be conceived. In the directions that Moses gives his countrymen, how they should conduct themselves in the land of Canaan, he says, Deut. xii. 2. ' And ye shall utterly de-
' stroy all the places wherein the nations
' that ye shall possess served their gods,
' upon high mountains, and upon hills, and
' under green trees. And ye shall over-
' throw their altars, and break their pillars,
' and burn their groves with fire. And
' ye shall hew down the graven images of
' their gods, and destroy the names of
' them out of their places.' No idolater was permitted to live in the country of the Hebrews, which was appropriated to the worship of the one true God; and every Jew conforming to the heathen worship was to be put to death without mercy. It is to be observed, however, that the Israelites were not directed to propagate

gate their religion by the sword, and compel other nations to conform to their worship. Their conquests, and the extirpation of idolatrous worship were confined to the boundary of the land of Canaan, the country promised by God to Abraham. Accordingly when David, who had more zeal for his religion than any of the kings of Israel, conquered all the neighbouring nations, he did not compel any of them to change their religion for his.

5. The characters of the principal of the heathen gods we have seen to have been stained with vices of the grossest kind, and the most abominable rites were practised in their groves, and the temples themselves, as peculiarly proper for their worship. The reverse of every thing of this kind is always represented by Moses, and the prophets, as the disposition of the God of the Hebrews. Nothing of impurity, or indecency, was admitted into his worship. Nay the great object of the whole system of the Hebrew religion was to form men to the perfection of mo-

ral

ral character; and all the rites and ceremonies of it are constantly said to be wholly insignificant without this. *Be ye holy*, says Moses, Lev. xix. 2. *for the Lord your God is holy.*

When the Psalmist describes the character of the man who was acceptable to God, and fit to be admitted to his presence, he says, (Psalm xv. 1.) *Lord, who shall abide in thy tabernacle, who shall dwell in thy holy hill? He that walketh uprightly, and worketh righteousness, and speaketh the truth in his heart.* On the other hand, vice and wickedness is always represented as the great, and indeed the sole, object of his displeasure. *There is no peace, says God, to the wicked*, Is. vi. 22.

The insignificance of all merely ritual observances, in which the whole of the heathen religion consisted, compared with moral virtue, is expressed in the most emphatical manner by several of the sacred writers as Is. i. 11. ' To what purpose is
' the multitude of your sacrifices to me,
' saith the Lord? I am full of the burnt-
' offerings

'offerings of rams, and the fat of fed
'beasts, and I delight not in the blood of
'bullocks, or of lambs, or of he goats.
'When ye come to appear before me,
'who hath required this at your hand, to
'tread my courts. Bring no more vain
'oblations. Incense is an abomination unto
'me. The new moons, and sabbaths,
'the calling of assemblies, I cannot away
'with. It is iniquity, even the solemn
'meeting. Your new moons, and your
'appointed feasts, my soul hateth. They
'are a trouble unto me, I am weary to
'hear them. And when ye spread forth
'your hands, I will hide mine eyes from
'you, yea when ye make many prayers
'I will not hear. Your hands are full of
'blood. Wash ye, make you clean, put
'away the evil of your doings from be-
'fore mine eyes, cease to do evil, learn
'to do well, seek judgment, relieve the
'oppressed, judge the fatherless, plead for
'the widow. Come now and let us rea-
'son together saith the Lord, though your
'sins be as scarlet, they shall be as white

'as

'as snow, though they be red like crim-
'son, they shall be as wool.

'Wherewith,' saith Micah, ch. vi. 6.
'shall I come before the Lord, and bow
'myself before the high God. Shall I come
'before him with burnt offerings, with
'calves of a year old? will the Lord be
'pleased with thousands of rams, or ten
'thousands of rivers of oil? Shall I give my
'first born for my transgression, the fruit of
'my body for the sin of my soul? He hath
'shewed thee, O man, what is good, and
'what doth the Lord require of thee, but
'to do justly, to love mercy, and to walk
'humbly with thy God." Passages equally excellent, and as purely moral as these, abound in the scriptures of the Old Testament.

6. The public festivals of the heathen gods were seasons of rioting and lewdness, but those of the Israelites were scenes of innocent rejoicing, joined with acts of devotion, which are by no means incompatible with it; and every thing relating to the service of the tabernacle and the tem-

P 2   ple,

ple, was conducted with the greatest regard to decency; while the utmost abhorrence is expressed for the horrid customs of the heathens. 'Thou shalt not, says Moses, Deut. xii. 29. ' inquire after their ' gods, saying how did those nations serve ' their gods, even so will I do likewise. ' Thou shalt not do so unto the Lord ' thy God. For every abomination to the ' Lord, that he hateth, have they done ' unto their gods. For even their sons and ' their daughters have they burned in the ' fire to their gods.' And yet this very thing, which is here mentioned as the greatest enormity in the worship of the heathens, viz. human sacrifices, Voltaire says was practised in that of the Jews. Is it possible for effrontery to go farther than this? (except indeed his maintaining that the Jews were canibals, and fed on human flesh) while without any evidence, but his own, and contrary to every representation of the facts by heathen writers themselves, he speaks of the heathen festivals as mere seasons of perfectly innocent festivity. But, justly juftly or unjuftly, every thing not Jewifh muft be harmlefs, and their religion muft be, as he calls it, a *deteftable fuperftition*.

7. While the religion of the Hebrews was free from every ftain of impurity, it contained nothing of unneceffary aufterity. It had no painful rite, except that of circumcifion, which, being performed on children of eight days old, who can have no apprehenfion of the thing before hand, and whofe wounds foon heal, is a very trifling inconvenience. The Hebrews had only one faft, and that of no more than a fingle day in the year, but three feftivals of fome continuance.

In the principal of the heathen feftivals there was firft a folemn mourning, all the people performing whatever was cuftomary at funerals, or in feafons of great calamity. They tore their hair, fhaved their heads, and mangled their flefh. But the Ifraelites were exprefsly forbidden to do any of thofe things, Deut. xiv. 1. ' Ye ' are the children of the Lord your God. ' Ye fhall not cut yourfelves, nor make any
' baldnfs

'baldnefs between your eyes for the dead, '(that is for idolatrous ufes) for ye are an 'holy people to the Lord your God.' Thefe directions had no view to private mournings, for on thofe occafions they always did thefe very things, but to the worfhip of God.

It was the cuftom of the heathens to imprint on their fkin various indelible marks, being figures and characters expreffive of their devotednefs to their gods, which muft have been a painful operation. But this was alfo forbidden to the Hebrews, Lev. xix. 27. 'Ye fhall not make 'any cuttings in your flefh for the dead, 'nor print any marks upon you, I am the 'Lord.'

8. If the extreme of aufterity was with fo much care avoided in the Hebrew inftitutions, that of fenfual indulgence was avoided with more. Every incentive to lewdnefs, which was encouraged, and openly practifed, in the heathen temples, was far removed from the worfhip of Jehovah. The heathens were fond of worfhipping

shipping on the tops of mountains, and in groves, in which every species of abomination was committed; and for this reason both were forbidden in the Hebrew worship, Deut. xvi. 21. ' Thou shalt not plant ' thee a grove near to the altar of the ' Lord thy God, which thou shalt make ' unto him.'

In the rites of some of the heathen deities men were habited like women, and women like men. This was more especially the case in the worship of Venus. This manner of worship was also common among the Syrians, and Africans, and thence it passed into Europe, the Phœnicians having brought it to Cyprus. In a religious rite of the Argives, Plutarch says the women were clothed like men, and men like women. But in the laws of Moses it is said, Deut. xxii. 5. ' The wo- ' man shall not wear that which appertain- ' eth unto man, neither shall a man put on ' a woman's garment. For all that do so ' are an abomination to the Lord thy God.'

You

You have seen that the heathens had places adjoining to their temples, in which both men and women proſtituted themſelves in honour of their deities, and to augment the revenues of the place. With a view, no doubt, to this abominable cuſtom, the Hebrews were commanded to avoid theſe practices. Lev. xix. 9. 'Do not 'proſtitute thy daughter, to cauſe her to 'be a whore, leſt the land fall into whore-'dom, and the land become full of wick-'edneſs. Ye ſhall keep my ſabbaths, and 'reverence my ſanctuary, I am the Lord 'your God.

9. A ſuperſtitious reſpect for the heathen temples and altars made them aſylums for all kinds of criminals, and it was deemed the greateſt act of impiety to take any perſon from thence, whatever his guilt had been, and however clear the proof of it. But this was not the caſe in the religion of the Hebrews, which Voltaire repreſents as the extreme of the moſt deteſtable ſuperſtition. Ex. xxi. 12. 'He that 'ſmiteth a man ſo that he die, ſhall ſurely 'be

'be put to death. If a man lie not in wait,
'but God deliver him into his hand, then
'will I appoint thee a place whither he
'shall flee. But if a man come presump-
'tuously upon his neighbour, and slay him
'with guile, thou shalt take him from
'mine altar, that he may die." Where
then do we find the proper characters of
superstition, and where are those of good
policy and good sense?

DISCOURSE VI.

The excellence of the Mosaic Institutions.

Behold I have taught you statutes and judgments, even as the Lord my God commanded me, that ye should do so in the land whither ye go to possess it. Keep therefore and do them. For this is your wisdom and understanding, in the sight of the nations which shall hear all these statutes, and say, Surely this great nation is a wise and understanding people. For what nation is there so great, who hath God so near unto them as the Lord your God is, in all things that ye call upon him for; and what nation is there so great that hath statutes and judgments so righteous, as all this law which I set before you this day.

DEUT. iv. 5---8.

IN my last Discourse I began to give you a general view of the religious institutions of Moses, corresponding to that which, in two preceding Discourses, I gave you of the religion of the heathens, to which they were opposed: in order to enable you to judge whether it was probable that the former were devised by men,

men, or were of divine origin. You have seen that, in a variety of important respects, the religion of the Hebrews, said by unbelievers to be a barbarous and superstitious people, had doctrines and rites infinitely superior to those of the heathens. I particularly mentioned the great doctrine of the Scriptures concerning the unity of God, in opposition to the multiplicity of heathen deities, his being represented as having no definite form, so as to be worshipped under any image, his attributes of creating and governing the world, his omniprefence, omniscience, and infinite wisdom, the perfection of his moral character, and his making the strictest virtue the great end of his worship. I mentioned the decency of all the religious festivals of the Hebrews, as the reverse of the licentiousness encouraged in those of the heathens, and at the same time their freedom from any unnecessary or painful austerity, and the peculiar abhorrence in which human sacrifices, and other rites of the heathen worship were held by the Hebrews.

I also

I also observed that the Hebrew altars afforded no asylum for criminals, which those of the heathens constantly did.

10. I now proceed to observe that, whereas much of the attention of the heathen nations was taken up with the superstitious practice of *divination*, in a great variety of forms, with witchcraft and necromancy; these being essential parts of their religion, and more studied than any other (so that at Rome to despise the established *auguries* would have been reckoned the extreme of profaneness) the Hebrews of all the antient nations, were entirely exempt from this wretched superstition, the offspring of the most extreme ignorance, though they knew no more of philosophy, or the true causes of events, than other people. Every branch of this superstition was strictly forbidden to the Israelites, as well as things of greater enormity. Lev. xix. 26. ' Neither shall ye use enchantments, nor ' observe times,' Deut. xviii. 10. ' There ' shall not be found among you any one ' that maketh his son or his daughter to

pass

'pass through the fire, or that useth divi-
'nation, or an observer of times, or an
'enchanter, or a witch, or a charmer, or
'a consulter with familiar spirits, or a wi-
'zard, or a necromancer. For all that
'do these things are an abomination unto
'the Lord, and because of these abomi-
'nations the Lord thy God doth drive them
'out from before thee. Thou shalt be
'perfect with the Lord thy God. For
'these nations which thou shalt possess
'hearkened unto observers of times, and
'unto diviners; but as for thee, the Lord
'thy God hath not suffered thee so to do.'
Is this any mark of the detestable superstition, with which Voltaire charges the
religion of the Jews? On the contrary,
it is such good sense, as we in vain look
for in the religions of other nations, that
this writer represents as in all respects
their superior.

Considering the very strong hold that
these opinions and practices still have on
the minds of men (for to this day many
christians, and even many unbelievers in
christianity,

christianity, have great faith in charms, and other things of a similar nature, relating to good or bad fortune, as insignificant as the sailors whistling for a wind) there is not a clearer and more unequivocal mark of superior, of divine wisdom, than the contempt that is so strongly expressed for every thing of this kind in the books of Moses, especially considering the times in which they were written.

11. The heathens had many superstitious rules with respect to *sacrifices.* Thus hogs were sacrificed to Ceres, an owl to Minerva, a hawk to Apollo, a dog to Hecate, an eagle to Jupiter, a horse to the sun, a cock to Æsculapius, a goose to Isis, and a goat to Bacchus: The Zabians sacrificed to the sun seven bats, seven mice, and seven other reptiles. The Egyptians were so far from sacrificing horned cattle, that they worshipped them, as also the ram. The Hebrews alone kept to the natural and rational idea of sacrifices, which was to confine them to things most proper for the food of man, in order to express

express their gratitude to God, as the giver of it, and, as it were, to be the guests at his table.

That sacrifices, though not required of Christians, was a natural mode of worship cannot be denied, because they were universal, and are used by all heathen nations to this day. No philosopher, in the most enlightened period of the heathen world, ever objected to them.

The heathens were used to reserve some of the flesh of the animals they sacrificed for superstitious uses, as the christians, when superstition crept in among them, did of the consecrated bread in the the eucharist. For the christians derived all their superstitious practices from the heathens. When the Mahometans sacrifice a sheep, as they always do on their pilgrimage to Mecca, they dry a great part of the flesh, which by this means may be kept two years, and make presents of it to their friends at their return. This was probably an antient idolatrous custom, which Mahomet kept up. But to prevent every

every superstitious use of sacrifices, the Hebrews were directed to keep nothing of theirs till the next day; and no flesh of the paschal lamb was to be carried out of the house in which it was eaten. They were also strictly forbidden to eat any part of it raw, Exod. xii. 9. which has been observed to have been a superstitious and indecent custom with the Egyptians, and others.

12. Some part of the first fruits of their harvests were reserved by the heathens for magical purposes. On the contrary, the Israelites were directed, when they presented their first fruits, to recount the goodness of God to them in the following pious form. Deut. xxvi. in the presence of the priest. ' I profess this ' day unto the Lord thy God, that I am ' come unto the country which the Lord ' sware unto our fathers for to give us." When the priest had taken the basket out of his hand, and presented it, he was to say farther. ' A Syrian ready to perish ' was my father, and he went down into
' Egypt,

'Egypt, and sojourned there, with a few, and there became a great nation, mighty and populous, and the Egyptians evil intreated us, and afflicted us, and laid upon us hard bondage, and when we cried unto the Lord God of our fathers the Lord heard our voice, and looked on our affliction, and our labour, and our oppression. And the Lord brought us forth out of Egypt with a mighty hand, and an outstretched arm, and with great terribleness, and with signs, and wonders; and he hath brought us into this place, and hath given us this land, even a land that floweth with milk and honey; and now behold I have brought the first fruits of the land which thou, O Lord, hast given me.'

When some of the antient idolaters had gathered all their fruits, they took a kid and boiled it in its mother's milk, and with magical rites sprinkled with it their fields, gardens, and orchards, thinking that by this means they would become fruitful. This practice was expresly for-

bidden to the Hebrews, no doubt, as superstitious and idolatrous. 'Thou shalt 'not seethe a kid in its mother's milk." (Exod. xxiii. 19. Deut. xiv. 21.) To this custom it is not improbable that Isaiah, alludes, when speaking of idolaters, he says (Chap. lxv. 4.) 'Who eat swine's 'flesh, and broth of abominable things is 'in their vessels.' For they might put other things into the pot along with the flesh of the kid. And on this account, when they had distributed their tythes, they were directed to say, (Deut. xxvi. 13.) 'I have brought away the hallowed 'things out of mine house, and also have 'given them to the Levite, and unto 'the stranger, to the fatherless, and to 'the widow, according to all thy com-
'mandments, which thou hast commanded
'me. I have not transgressed thy com-
'mandments, neither have I forgotten
'them. I have not eaten thereof in my
'mourning (alluding to the solemn mourning in the festival of Isis) neither have I
'taken away ought thereof for any un-
'clean

'clean ufe, nor given ought thereof for the dead,' (that is for idolatrous purpofes) 'but I have hearkened to the voice of the Lord my God, and have done according to all that thou haft commanded me. Look down from thy holy habitation, from heaven, and blefs thy people Ifrael, and the land which thou haft given us, as thou fwareft unto our fathers, a land that floweth with milk and honey." Here certainly is piety and good fenfe, and nothing of that *deteftable fuperftition,* which Voltaire afcribes to this antient people.

13. The rules laid down in the books of Mofes for the *diet* of the Ifraelites, permitting the ufe of fome kinds of food, and prohibiting others, will, no doubt, be deemed fuperftition by fome perfons. But if the particulars be confidered, it will be found that the Ifraelites were confined to that food which was the moft wholefome, and beft fuited to the climate they were deftined to inhabit. On the contrary, there was real and mere fuperftition in the reftrictions that many of the heathens laid themfelves

themselves under in this respect, and in all antient nations religion was concerned in the choice of food. Thus the Egyptians would not eat the flesh of a cow. It was commonly said of them, they would as soon eat that of a man. Their priests, and the Pythagoreans, who followed them in it, abstained from beans. The priests in Syria ate no fish, the Phœnicians no pigeons, and the antient Arabians abstained from eating a variety of things, because they thought them particularly consecrated to some of the heavenly bodies, which were the objects of their worship, and because they made use of them in their divinations. Moses, therefore, or rather God by him, in order to counteract and prevent this superstition, (for it cannot be called any thing else, as the things refrained from cannot be denied to be wholesome food,) established a distinction of meats on a quite different, and perfectly rational, principle.

The article that will perhaps be most objected to is the prohibition to eat *swines flesh*, which we find not to be unwholesome. But the

the Egyptians, Arabians, and all the eastern nations, from Ethiopia to India, detest swines flesh, and so do the Mahometans universally. As to *blood*, I believe it is generally allowed to be gross and unwholesome food; but probably the principal reason why it was forbidden to the Hebrews, was the use that was made of it in some of the sacrifices of the heathen nations, who drank of the blood, by way of communicating with the infernal deities. For this reason too, it might be that, in the Hebrew sacrifices, the blood was directed to be sprinkled on the altar, or poured out at the foot of it. The blood was also considered as, in a peculiar manner, the seat of animal life; and by giving it back, as it were, to God, they acknowledged that it came from him.

14. There is, indeed, hardly any species of superstition that was practised by the antient idolaters that is not either directly noticed, or alluded to, and particularly guarded against, in the religion of the Israelites. The Zabians, it is said, constructed

ed certain images, according to the conſtellations, which they called *taliſmans*, by means of which they expected to perform the greateſt wonders, and eſpecially to foretel future events. Theſe were probably the *teraphim* of which mention is made in the Hebrew ſcriptures; and it is well known that the uſe of them was condemned by Moſes; and the Iſraelites were directed to other means of becoming acquainted with ſuch future events, as it was proper for them to be informed of. But this I ſhall make the ſubject of a ſeparate difcourſe.

There are ſeveral things in the Hebrew ritual for which we are not at preſent able to give any ſatisfactory reaſon. But this is probably owing to our not being ſufficiently acquainted with remote antiquity, and eſpecially the worſhip of the moſt antient idolaters, which it was the great object of the Moſaic inſtitutions to oppoſe. For this reaſon, and perhaps, in ſome caſes, for no other, the cuſtoms of the Iſraelites were ordered to be the very reverſe

verſe of thoſe of other nations. When the heathens worſhipped their ſuperior divinities, who were ſuppoſed to have their reſidence above the clouds, they did it not only on mountains, and in high places, but on high altars, thinking that by that means they had a nearer acceſs to the objects of their worſhip. For this reaſon the Hebrews were directed not to build ſuch altars, or to worſhip in ſuch places. The heathens uſed *leaven* and *honey*, in the cakes which they offered to their gods, whereas in thoſe of the Iſraelites they were both forbidden, but they were always to uſe *ſalt*. The heathens bowed towards the Eaſt, as an act of homage to the riſing ſun; and therefore their temples were made to front the Weſt, that when they entered them, which they always did bowing, it might be towards the Eaſt. For this reaſon the tabernacle and temple of the Iſraelites were made to look to the Eaſt, that on entering them, the worſhippers might bow towards the Weſt, turning their backs on the place of ſun riſing.

The

The antient idolaters held *heifers* in peculiar veneration, and for this reason perhaps, it was ordered, (Deut. xxi. 3.) that if any person was found murdered, and the murderer could not be discovered, a heifer which had not been used to the yoke should be slain in his place. It was not sacrificed, but its head was to be struck off. The Egyptians held in peculiar abhorrence animals that had *red hair*, which they supposed to have been that of Typhon. In opposition, perhaps, to this, the Israelites were commanded to prepare their water of purification with the ashes of a red heifer, without spot, or perfectly red. Numb. xix.

15. Many unbelievers think that wherever there are *priests*, there must be *priestcraft*, and of course the interest of the people sacrificed to their emolument; it being always, as they think, in the power of that order of men to impose upon the rest. But there were several circumstances in the situation of the Hebrew priests, which shew that they could have had no such power.

In

In the first place, the Hebrew priests had no *secrets*. Every thing that they knew or that they did, was as well known to the whole nation as to themselves. It was all detailed in the books of the law, which were not confined to themselves, as the sacred books of the Hindoos are to the Bramins, but directed to be read in the hearing of all the people. To these books they always had access, and the Levites were dispersed all over the country, that they might with the more advantage instruct the people in them.

So far was Moses from wishing that the priests should have any advantage over the people by their superior knowledge, that his exhortations to all the people to make themselves accurately acquainted with the law are peculiarly emphatical, (Deut. vi. 6.) *These words, which I command thee this day, shall be in thine heart. And thou shalt teach them diligently unto thy children, and shalt talk of them when thou sittest in thy house, and when thou walkest by the way, and when thou liest down, and when thou risest up. And*

And thou shalt bind them for a sign upon thine hand, and they shall be as frontlets between thine eyes. And thou shalt write them upon the posts of thy house, and on thy gates. Had the Israelites observed this excellent precept, they could never have revolted, as they did, from their own religion to that of the neighbouring nations. It were to be wished that Christians would observe this excellent rule, or adopt the spirit of it. There would not then be so many unbelievers as there now are in Christian countries.

There was indeed, a part of the tabernacle, and of the temple, into which only the priests entered, and another into which the high priest only entered. But there was nothing deposited in those places, or done in them, but what was perfectly well known to the whole nation, and they did not, and could not, pretend to derive any extraordinary powers from their having access to those particular places. Whereas, in all the antient heathen religions, there were *mysteries* or *secrets*, with which only

the

the initiated were acquainted, and which were communicated to them under the moſt ſolemn oath of ſecrecy. Which of theſe inſtitutions then, bears moſt of the marks of prieſtcraft?

In the next place, though the Hebrew prieſts were of a particular family, and conſidered as the moſt reſpectable order of perſons in the nation, as being more immediately employed in the ſervice of God, they could have no landed property, and without this they could never attain any great degree of civil power; and in fact their judges, who were occaſionally appointed to direct the civil power, and the kings, who held it permanently, were never of the order of prieſts, till the time of the Maccabees, which was a long time after the Babyloniſh captivity, when they had departed very far from their original plan of government.

However, the prieſts of Iſrael were not ſo far a ſeparate order of men, but they were capable of civil offices. They were alſo married, and ſo much mixed with the reſt

reſt of the people, that they could have no intereſt ſeparate from theirs. Their chief dependance was upon the tythes which they received from the people, who by this means had them completely in their power. By this means, however, it was wiſely provided that it ſhould be their intereſt to inſtruct the people in the law, and keep them to the obſervance of it. But when the prieſts and Levites did their duty in this reſpect, and received all the advantages they could from it, it does not appear that the tribe of Levi, which comprehended the family of the prieſts, the deſcendants of Aaron, was upon the whole ſo well provided for as any of the other tribes. The Levites in general muſt have been poor; for when mention is made of charity, the caſe of the Levite is generally recommended together with that of the ſtranger, the fatherleſs, and the widow. Indeed ſome part of the tythes, as you have ſeen, were given to all theſe without diſtinction. Jacob, who foretold the future condition of all his ſons, ſpeaks of of the Levites as well as the Simeonites, as under a kind of curfe. For he fays of them, Gen. xlix. 7. *Curfed be their anger for it was fierce, and their wrath for it was cruel. I will divide them in Jacob, and feparate them in Ifrael.* This was a punifhment for their treachery, and cruelty with refpect to the inhabitants of Sichem.

Whatever advantage the Hebrew priefts were poffeffed of, it muft have depended upon their keeping the people to the ftrict obfervance of their religion. But in this they notoriously failed (which is an abundant proof that their influence was not great) through the ftrong predilection of the Ifraelites in favour of the religions of the neighbouring nations; and many times, but more efpecially during the reign of Ahab, the priefts of Baal had far more influence than the priefts or prophets, of Jehovah. Elijah was then the only prophet who made his appearance, while the priefts of Baal including thofe of the groves, or rather of Aftaroth or Aftarte, were eight hundred and fifty (fee 1 Kings, xviii. 19.)

19.) and there were not more than seven thousand persons in all the country who were not worshippers of Baal (1 Kings xix. 18.) At the same time the influence of the court, and of the nobles, was in favour of that foreign religion. As to the priests of Jehovah, there is no mention made of them in any transactions of those times, so that they could not have been at all conspicuous. Whatever, therefore, of priestcraft there was at that time in the country, it must have been in the hands of the priests of Baal, and not of those of Jehovah.

16. In all antient states, religion and political institutions had a very near connection. With the Hebrews, there was a peculiar reason for its being so. They were a nation separated from all others, for the sole purpose of preserving in the world the knowledge and worship of the one true God, in a time of universal defection from it, and they were made to depend upon the providence of God, more immediately than other nations, God, according

cording to their original conſtitution, being their proper King, or ſupreme civil magiſtrate. He was *their God*, and they were *his people* in a peculiar ſenſe. In his addreſs to them, when they had left Egypt, he ſays, Exod. xix. 4. *Ye have ſeen what I did to the Egyptians, and how I bare you on eagles wings, and brought you unto myſelf. Now therefore if ye will obey my voice indeed, and keep my covenant, then ye ſhall be a peculiar treaſure unto me. For all the earth is mine. And ye ſhall be to me a kingdom of prieſts, and a holy nation.* He alſo ſays, Exod. xxv. 8. *Let them make me a ſanctuary, that I may dwell among them.* Agreeably to this, when, in imitation of the neighbouring nations, they wiſhed to have a king, it was conſidered as a rejection of the government of God, to which they had been ſubject, and therefore God ſays to Samuel on the occaſion, 1 Sam. viii. 7. *They have not rejected thee, but they have rejected me, that I ſhould not reign over them.* Under the immediate government of God, that of the Hebrews was an equal republic, while all the neighbouring

bouring nations were governed by kings, and in the moſt arbitrary manner. What could have led Moſes to think of ſuch an excellent mode of government as this? He could not have ſeen, or heard, of any thing reſembling it. For at that time no ſuch thing exiſted in any part of the world.

The religion and civil government of the Hebrews having this intimate connection, I ſhall mention ſome particulars of the latter, that we may ſee whether it was ſo very barbarous and abſurd a ſyſtem as Voltaire and other unbelievers repreſent it to have been, and whether the civil inſtitutions of other antient nations bear greater marks of wiſdom and liberality. But on this ſubject I mean to be very brief.

The great object of the inſtitutions of ſeveral of the antient nations was *offenſive war*, and *conqueſt*. That of the Hebrews was ſimply *agriculture*, which is certainly the moſt natural and rational object, leading to the happieſt ſtate of human ſociety. Foreign commerce was not encouraged, on account of the danger that was to be

appehended

apprehended with respect to their religion, from an intercourse with foreign and idolatrous nations. And as a purely agricultural, and not a commercial nation, they were forbidden to take any interest for money lent to one another.

In order to attach them to the lands of their inheritance, the Hebrews had in their laws an excellent provision unknown in any other, viz. their reverting to the family of the original proprietors at the year of Jubilee, which was every half century, at which time also any contract which a Hebrew might make to bind himself to servitude was dissolved. By this means it was not in the power of the most improvident spendthrift intirely to ruin his family. He could only mortgage his possession for a limited time, nor could there be any instance of a permanently excessive landed property. What an excellent institution was this for preserving a reasonable equality among this people, the only security for liberty, and also for creating an attachment to the soil, and of course the

R love

love of their country, in which all hiſtory ſhews that no nation ever exceeded, or equalled, the Jews.

Beyond the boundary of the land of Canaan, which was promiſed by God to their anceſtors, and of which they got poſſeſſion not by any power of their own, but by the immediate hand of Gód, they were not to attempt any conqueſt. All their wars were to be defenſive, and when they took arms to repel an invaſion, they were ordered in the firſt place to propoſe terms of peace. In caſe of ſucceſs in war, and when, in conſequence of it, they marched into the country of the enemy, they were required to do no unneceſſary injury to it; and eſpecially not to cut down the fruit trees, and to ſpare all who did not bear arms.

Every Iſraelite of an age capable of bearing arms was, as in all antient nations, obliged to join the army; but at the head of it a proclamation was directed to be made, excuſing every perſon who had either lately married a wife, built a houſe,

or

or planted a vineyard, which would naturally make him more attached to life. Even if any man felt himſelf on any other account fearful and faint hearted, he might return home. It is in vain that we look for maxims of ſuch moderation, and good ſenſe, in any other antient nation.

The great ſtrength of any country conſiſts in its population, and ſuch were the principles of the Iſraelites, that with them beyond all other nations, celibacy was deemed to be a misfortune, barrenneſs a reproach, and a multitude of children the greateſt bleſſing. But in heathen nations many perſons devoted themſelves to a ſingle life as an act of religion; as the Veſtal Virgins among the Romans. They were heathen principles and practices that led to the ſyſtem of monks and nuns among Chriſtians.

The Hebrew inſtitutions allowed of ſervitude, but enjoined more humanity to ſlaves than thoſe of any other nation. If a maſter, in beating his ſlave, ſtruck out an eye, or even a tooth, he was obliged to to set him free. Exod. xxi. 16. If a slave committed a capital offence, the judge, and not his master, was to pronounce the sentence. If the master wilfully murdered his slave, he was to suffer death. The Israelites were not permitted to use the captive women, who were of course slaves, at their pleasure. The law is so express on this subject, that I shall recite it. Deut. xxi. 10. *When thou goest forth to war against thine enemies, and the Lord thy God hath delivered them into thine hands, and thou hast taken them captive, and seest among the captives a beautiful woman, and hast a desire unto her, that thou wouldest have her to thy wife, thou shalt then bring her home to thy house, and she shall shave her head, and pare her nails,* (as it is in our translation; but the meaning is that she should make them beautiful by colouring them, which is at this time done in the East, and considered as a great article of beauty,) *and she shall put the raiment of her captivity from off her, and shall remain in thine house, and bewail her father and her mother a full month; and after that thou shall go in unto*

unto her, and she shall be thy wife. And it shall be if thou have no delight in her, then thou shalt let her go whither she will, but thou shalt not sell her at all for money, thou shalt not make merchandise of her, because thou hast humbled her. We shall find no law approaching to the humanity of this among the Greeks or Romans, a thousand years after this time, and still less among nations of greater antiquity. How little will the treatment of slaves by Europeans bear to be compared with this?

Voltaire charges the Jews with a violent hatred of all other nations; but let us attend to their original laws and institutions on this subject, Deut. xxii. 8. *If a stranger sojourn with you in your land, ye shall not vex him, but the stranger shall dwell with you. He shall be unto you as one born among you, and thou shalt love him as thyself. For ye were strangers in the land of Egypt. I am the Lord your God. The Lord loveth the stranger.* Exod. xxii. 22. Many antient nations made great difficulties about the naturalization of foreigners; but among the Hebrews

'any

any perfon, being circumcifed, and conforming to the laws of the land, became one of themfelves in all refpects. Only, for particular reafons, perfons of certain nations could not be completely naturalized till after the expiration of a certain number of generations.

In all antient nations, and many modern ones, *torture* was made ufe of both in the punifhment of crimes, and for procuring evidence. But no ufe whatever was made of it among the Hebrews. Punifhment by fcourging was limited to forty ftripes, murder and fome other atrocious crimes were punifhed with death, but executions were performed by ftoning or hanging, and the body buried before funfet. Where, then, are thofe " cruel and tor-
" turous executions, and that unrelenting
" vindictivenefs" which Mr. Paine fays contribute to make him confider the Bible as " the word of a demon rather than the
" word of God," and which makes him
" deteft it," as he fays " he detefts every
" thing that is cruel." They have no exiftence

exiftence whatever, but in his own imagination. How eafy is it to calumniate what a man does not underftand, and what he is ftrongly predifpofed to diflike and mifreprefent. In cafes of mere manflaughter, a city of refuge was provided, in which the innocent author of the death of another, was fafe from the purfuit of the relations of the deceafed. Theft was punifhed by reftitution, by fine, or flavery, but not with death.

Such, my brethren, is the general outline, and fome of the principal features, of that fyftem of religion, and civil policy, which Voltaire treats as moft execrable; but judge for yourfelves with what juftice. On the contrary, I have no doubt but that, if all the circumftances of the Hebrew nation, and of other antient and neighbouring nations, could be known, we fhould be fatisfied that it was, in all refpects, the beft fyftem poffible, as much fuperior to any of thofe of human invention, as the works of nature are fuperior to thofe of art.

DISCOURSE VII.

The Principles of the Heathen Philosophy compared with those of Revelation.

The world by wisdom knew not God.
1. Cor. i. 21.

IN my two last discourses I shewed you how greatly superior were the religious institutions of Moses, though so much decried by modern unbelievers, to those of the heathens, the shocking enormities, and gross abominations, of which are so much disguised and smoothed over by them. But because it will be said that what I then exhibited was only the system of *superstition*, adopted by the *vulgar*, and that the more intelligent persons among the heathens (though for political reasons, they did not chuse to oppose, and even countenanced it) held a more rational system, I shall now

now show you what that more rational system was.

For this purpose I shall lay before you and in as intelligible a manner as I can, (for I will not undertake to make the two discourses which, it will be necessary for me to give on this subject, perfectly intelligible to *all*) what it was that the philosophers among the antients really thought concerning the system of nature, and the government of the world, and also concerning the nature of man, and his future destination, with some of their ideas concerning the principles of morals, that you may compare them with those that are advanced in the scriptures. And if it appear that those are more consonant to reason, it will afford a considerable presumption that they were of divine origin. For how can it be supposed that the authors of the books of scripture, who had no advantage of literature, and whom unbelievers treat with the greatest contempt, for their ignorance and barbarity, should have adopted a more rational system on these great subjects

jects than those who have been the most celebrated for their wisdom in the most polished and civilized nations in the world. It will be very easy to make this comparison, as there is sufficient evidence what the tenets of the antient philosophers were, many of their own writings being now extant, as well as the scriptures of the Old and New Testament.

1. It was a fundamental maxim with all the philosophers of antiquity, that *creation from nothing* was absolutely impossible; and many of those who admitted a principle of intelligence in the universe, maintained that *matter* in some confused chaotic mass was another principle, coeternal with it, and independent of it, and therefore could only be modified, but not destroyed by it. Moses on the contrary, asserts a proper *creation* of every thing that exists, antecedent to the *chaotic state* which he describes. Gen. i. 1. *In the beginning God created the heavens and the earth, and the earth was without form and void, and darkness was upon the face of the deep.* And since the

properties

properties of bodies are all that we know of them, the appointment and changing of *thefe*, which the philofophers admitted to be within the province of the intelligent principle, implies a power of proper *creation*, and proper *deftruction*. For if we take away all the properties of any thing, nothing will be left. The fyftem of Mofes therefore, is more rational than theirs. This, however, continued to be the doctrine of the Greek philofophers to the lateft period of their hiftory. Plato held that matter exifted coeternally with God. Alfo, according to Zeno, the founder of the ftoical philofophy, " there exifted from " all eternity a dark and confufed chaos, in " which were contained the principles of " all future beings."

2. Another fet of philofophers, and perhaps of greater antiquity than the other, equally maintaining that creation from nothing was impoffible, maintained that every thing, was originally emitted from the fubftance of the felf-exiftent and fupreme Being. And not only did they fuppofe

suppose that *intelligent* beings of all orders proceeded from him, by this mode of *emenation*, as rays of light from the sun; but that other substances of an inferior nature proceeding in the same manner from *them*, at last *matter* itself, the most remote from the divine essence, came into existence, and therefore that this substance, of which they speak with the greatest contempt, had its origin from the divine essence. This was the system of the Oriental philosophy, which is still found in Indostan, and other parts of the East, and from them was derived the doctrine of the *Gnostics*, by which Christianity was corrupted in the time of the apostles. I need not say how far this notion of the derivation of every thing from the substance of the divine Being, deviates from reason. There is certainly nothing so wild and absurd as this in the writings of Moses, who always supposes God to have created all things, but not by the projection of them from his own essence.

The

The same class of philosophers who held that every thing had been produced from the substance of the Supreme Being, also supposed that, after a certain period, they would be absorbed into it again; and as originally nothing had existed besides this self-existent being, he would again exist alone; but that after another period, other beings would be again produced from him, and that these successive revolutions would go on forever. This ever has been, and still is, the established doctrine in the East, and it was adopted by some of the Grecian philosophers, especially the Stoicks, who said that " the world, including the whole
" compass of nature, both God and mat-
" ter, had subsisted from all eternity, and
" would for ever subsist; but that the
" present regular frame of nature had a
" beginning, and would have an end,
" from the alternate prevalence of *moisture*
" and *dryness*; that when the former pre-
" vails, all things are destroyed by an *in-*
" *undation*, and when the latter prevails,
" by a *conflagration;* that, however, from
" both

"both of these cataſtrophe's every thing
"will again emerge, by the energy of
"an efficient principle, when all the forms
"of regular nature will be renewed, but
"to be again diſſolved, and again renewed,
"in an endleſs ſucceſſion."

This ſcheme excludes all idea of *melioration*. For according to it, every thing has been, and in all future revolutions ever will be, juſt what it now is. Accordingly Seneca ſays, that "many perſons "would reject this reſtoration of being, "were it not this reſtoration will be ac-"companied with a total oblivion of paſt "events." How far leſs rational, as well as leſs pleaſing, is this ſyſtem, than that of the ſcriptures, which ſuppoſes a conſtant tendency to a better ſtate of things, every rational being retaining his ſeparate conſciouſneſs, always diſtinct from the ſupreme Being, but making nearer approaches to him in perfection and happineſs to all eternity. As to any proof, or evidence, of the truth of this philoſophical ſyſtem, of every thing having been produced

by

by way of emanation from the divine effence, and being abforbed into it again, it is only this; that there cannot be *two* eternal principles, and therefore every thing that exifts, muft have been derived, immediately or mediately, from *one*, and this one muft have been the fpiritual and intelligent principle. But will any modern philofopher admit the validity of fuch an argument as this, and adopt the conclufion? It is univerfally rejected with contempt.

As to the *effence*, or *fubftance*, of the Supreme Being, from which they fay that all things were derived, it is a queftion of no moment; fince all that we have to do with are his *attributes*, as thofe of power, wifdom, and benevolence, in whatever it be that they may be faid to refide. But according to our apprehenfions, there is fomething degrading in the idea of his being of the fame nature with all other beings, as he muft be, if every thing was produced by mere protrufion from his fubftance. Zeno, however, fuppofed that both " the active and paffive principles

"ples in nature," that is, both *God*, and *matter*, "were alike corporeal, only that "the former was a pure ether, or fire, "occupying the external furface of the "heavens, that is, a more attenuated kind "of matter." And Epicurus, conceiving the human form to be the moft perfect, faid that, "though the gods were of an "ethereal fubftance, they were fhaped "like men."

3. Both the claffes of philofophers, whofe opinions I have now defcribed, admitted a principle of *intelligence* in the univerfe, and a real diftinction between *God* and *matter*. But in later times this was by many denied, and fome philofophers even proceeded fo far as not to admit the exiftence of any fuch being as *God*, in any fenfe of the word. Sanchoniatho, explaining the philofophical fyftem of the Phœnicians, fays, that "the uni-"verfe arofe from the neceffary energy "of an eternal principle, active but with-"out intelligence, upon the eternal paffive "chaotic mafs." This is fuppofed to have

have been advanced in oppofition to the principles of Mofes; but certainly thefe will not fuffer any thing by the comparrifon. If there be no marks of *intelligence*, that is, of *defign*, in the univerfe, where fhall we find them? not furely in the works of men. How much more juft and noble are the fentiments and language of the Pfalmift, Pfalm civ. 24. *O Lord how manifold are thy works, in wifdom haft thou made them all.*

Ariftotle did not in words deny the being of a God, but he fuppofed the univerfe to have exifted from all eternity, independent of any wifdom or contrivance, of his. He only confidered him as the ' main fpring
' of the whole machine, and therefore
' properly a part of it, employed, in fome
' inexplicable manner, in communicating
' motion to it.' Strato of Lampfacus, a difciple of Ariftotle, held that ' the world
' was neither formed by the agency of the
' deity, diftinct from matter, nor by any
' intelligent animating principle, but that
' it arofe from a force innate in matter,

originally

'originally excited by accident, and since
'continuing to act according to the pecu-
'liar qualities of natural bodies. He neither
'denied nor asserted the existence of a di-
'vine nature, but, in excluding all idea
'of a deity from the formation of the
'world, he indirectly excluded him from
'his system.'

These atheistical doctrines were not confined to a single philosopher, or his disciples, many of them, and those of the greatest eminence, entertained the same, or similar, sentiments. Democrates held that ' the first principles of all things were
' *atoms* and a *vacuum*, in which, by a natural
' necessity, or fate, they perpetually move,
' and that from their combinations arise
' all the forms of things.' Pythagoras, also
' had held that ' motion is the effect of a
' power essential to matter.' Protagoras in one of his books, said concerning the gods;
' I am unable to determine whether they
' have any existence, or not. For the
' weakness of the human understanding, and
' the shortness of human life, with many
' other

' other causes, prevent us from attaining
' this knowledge.' But Diagoras openly
denied the existence of a deity. Heraclitus
' made use of the term *God*, but not to
' denote a distinct being of a peculiar na-
' ture, but merely a *natural force* in that
' primary *fire*, from which he supposed
' all things to have proceeded, and by means
' of which he supposed that its particles
' had been in eternal motion, and at length
' to have united, to form the present
' system of nature. To this *force*, con-
' sidered as distinct from *matter* on which
' it acts, he applied the term god.'

Epicurus admitted a deity into his system, but it was chiefly to avoid popular
odium. For he maintained that " the
" universe always existed, and will always
" continue to exist; for that there is no-
" thing by which it can be changed.
" There is nothing, he said, in nature, nor
" can there be conceived to be any thing,
" besides *body* and *space*; that the atoms,
" from which all things were composed,
" are not only all the materials of which

bodies

" bodies are made, but that the *energy*, or
" *principle of motion*, which eſſentially be-
" longs to them, is the ſole agent in the
" operations of nature."

As the Oriental philoſophers ſuppoſed that all things would be reſolved into the divine eſſence, from which they originally ſprung, Epicurus ſuppoſed that they would be reſolved into their original atoms. " The world," he ſaid, " is preſerved by
" the ſame mechanical cauſes by which it
" was framed, and from the ſame cauſes
" it will at laſt be diſſolved. The inceſſant
" motion of the atoms which produced
" the world is continually operating to-
" wards its diſſolution. For nothing is
" ſolid and indiſſoluble beſides atoms;
" whence it may be concluded, that the
" time will come when nothing will re-
" main but the original atoms, and infinite
" ſpace."

Epicurus abſolutely denied all *wiſdom* in the conſtruction of the univerſe, even in the moſt obvious inſtances. " The
" parts of animals," he ſaid " were not
" originally

"originally framed for the ufes to which they are now applied; but having been accidentally produced, they were afterwards accidentally employed. The eye, for example, was not made for feeing, nor the ear for hearing; but the foul being formed within the body, at the fame time with the organs, and connected with them, could not avoid making ufe of them, in their refpective functions."

Can we attend to thefe things, and not be ftruck with the truth of the apoftle's obfervation in my text, *the world by wifdom knew not God.* It was not even able to retain that knowledge of God which had been originally communicated to man. And how juftly is their cafe defcribed by the fame apoftle, in another paffage, where he fays, Rom. i. 21. *They became vain in their imaginations, and their foolifh heart was darkened.* But are not their minds equally, or more, darkened, who can prefer the abfurd conceits of thefe philofophers, to the rational doctrines of revelation?

tion? We shall, however, see more of the wanderings of the human imagination when left to itself, in what I have farther to observe.

4. The existence of *evil* always created the greatest difficulty to those who speculated concerning the origin and construction of the universe, and the causes of events. Indeed, so difficult is the question, that nothing but revelation could have solved it. In the scriptures we learn that *evil*, as well as *good*, is the appointment of the same great Being, but always for the most benevolent purposes. *Shall we receive good at the hand of God,* says Job, chap. ii. 10, *and shall we not receive evil?* ch. i. 21. *The Lord gave, and the Lord hath taken away, Blessed be the name of the Lord.* In Isaiah, xlv. 6, 7, *I am the Lord, and there is none else. I form the light, and create darkness; I make peace, and create evil; I the Lord do all these things.* All these evils, in the administration of this greatest and best of Beings, are subservient to good, as the Psalmist says, Ps. xcvii. 1, *The Lord reigneth*

let

let the earth rejoice, let the multitude of the isles be glad thereof. Clouds and darkness are round about him, righteousness and judgment are the habitation of his throne. But through these clouds and this darkness, the heathens, by the help of their greatest wisdom could not see. Some of the antients, as the Persians, thought that there were *two independent principles* in nature, one the author of good, and the other of evil. The good principle they called *Oromazes*, and the evil *Arimanius*. The Egyptians also worshipped an evil principle under the name of *Typhon*.

The Greek philosophers in general considered *matter* as the cause of all evil. In their antient cosmogonies it is ascribed to *chaos*. Plato held that 'there is in matter
' a necessary but blind and refractory force,
' from which arises a propensity to disorder
' and deformity,' which he said, ' was the
' cause of all the imperfection which is
' found in the works of God;' so that he appears to have thought that matter, from its nature, resists the will of the supreme artificer,

artificer, so that, on this account, he cannot perfectly execute his designs. Plato was also influenced by the argument from *contraries*. 'It cannot be,' he said, 'that evil 'should be destroyed; for there must al-'ways be something contrary to good.'

The Stoics said that 'evil was the ne-'cessary consequence of eternal *necessity*, to 'which the great whole, comprehending 'both God and matter, was subject.' When Chrysippus was asked whether diseases were to be ascribed to divine providence, he replied, that 'it was not the in-'tention of nature that these things should 'happen, nor were they conformable to 'the will of the author of nature, and the 'parent of all good; but that, in framing 'the world, some inconvenience had ad-'hered by necessary consequence to his wise 'and useful plan.'

How different is this from the sublime doctrine of the scriptures on this subject, as when we read, Psalm cxxxv. 23. *I know that the Lord is great, and that our Lord is above all gods. Whatever the Lord pleased that*

that did he in heaven and in earth, in the seas, and all deep places.

5. It is in vain that we look for the rational and sublime doctrine of an *universal providence* among the philosophers of antiquity. But according to the scriptures, there is no event, great or small, but what comes to pass according to the will of God. Dan. ii. 20. *Blessed be the name of God for ever and ever; for wisdom and might are his. He changeth the times and seasons, he removeth kings and setteth up kings.* The proud king of Assyria, in the midst of his conquests, is represented, If. x. 5. as the *staff* in the hand of God. At the same time we are assured by our Saviour, Mat. x. 33. that *a sparrow falleth not to the ground without his will, and that the very hairs of our heads are numbered.* And this is true philosophy, for so connected are all the parts of the system, that the smallest things are as necessary as the greatest, and in many cases we cannot but see that the greatest things depend upon the smallest. Voltaire justly observes that had a particular stone been thrown

thrown with a little more force, it would have given a different turn to the whole history of the East. It was a stone by which Mahomet was knocked down, as he was engaged in battle, but not killed.

There is most of the appearance of the doctrine of a providence among the Stoics. But according to Zeno and Chrysippus, 'there is in nature a *fate*, or an eternal 'and immutable series of causes and ef-'fects, within which all events are includ-'ed, and to which the Deity himself is 'subject,' though the later Stoics, who wrote after the promulgation of christianity, changed this *fate* into the *providence of the gods*.

Other philosophers did not pretend that God, or the gods, had, in any sense, or in any respect, the government of the world. According to Aristotle; the Deity, if it can be said that he believed in any proper deity, ' is eternally employed in the ' the contemplation of his own nature. ' He observes nothing (this philosopher ' says) he cares for nothing beyond himself. ' Residing in the first sphere, he possesses
' neither

'neither immensity nor omnipresence.
'Removed from the inferior parts of
'the universe, he is not even a spectator
'of what is passing among its inhabitants,
'and therefore cannot be a proper object
'of worship.'

Epicurus, I have observed, said that there were gods, only to avoid popular odium. According to his own account of them, they were of no manner of use in creating or governing the world. "There "are," he said, "in the universe divine "natures, but that it is inconsistent with "our natural notions of the gods, as hap- "py and immortal beings, to suppose that "they encumber themselves with the ma- "nagement of the world, or that they "are subject to the cares and passions "which must necessarily attend so great "a charge. We are not, therefore, to "conceive that the gods have any inter- "course with mankind, or any concern "in the affairs of the world." But, according to the scriptures, every thing is conducted by the Supreme Being, without trouble.

trouble. With respect to creation itself, it is said, *He spake and it was done, he commanded and it stood fast.* He said *Let there be light, and there was light;* and the government of the world, is no doubt, as easy to him as the creation of it. It is, in fact, a continuation of the same exertion, whatever that be. But no idea so sublime as this was ever entertained by any heathen philosopher.

It was the consideration of the immensity of the universe, and the idea men had of the multiplicity of cares that was necessary to the government of it, that led those of the philosophers who supposed that the world was in any sense, governed by superior Beings, to think it necessary to provide a great number of them, each to superintend his particular province. They had no conception of the sublime, but truly rational doctrine of the scriptures, according to which one intelligence, one mind, perfectly comprehends, and directs, the whole. And yet the uniformity we observe in the works of nature might have

suggested

suggested the idea of one mind having arranged and directed the whole, immense as that whole is. But the amazing variety, and seeming discordancy, of many parts of the system prevented their perceiving their uniformity, nor could Moses, or any of the Hebrews, have been able to discover it of themselves.

6. Mention is made in the scriptures of *angels*, as created beings, superior to man; but they are never supposed to interfere in the affairs of men, except on particular occasions, and by the express appointment of the Supreme Being, never by their own voluntary agency. They are employed merely as *messengers* (for so their name in the Hebrew signifies) to convey the orders of the Almighty. But according to the system of all the philosophers, as well as that of the vulgar, among the heathens, there are beings inferior to the Supreme, who *at their own pleasure*, interfere in the affairs of men, and act according to their peculiar humours and passions.

Among

Among the Egyptians the idea of one supreme God was, from the earliest times, connected with the belief of inferior divinities, residing in the various parts of nature, whence arose the worship of those parts of nature. According to the mythology of the Greeks, those inferior deities sprung from chaos. Pythagoras supposed the region of the air to be peopled with these beings. whom he calls *gods, demons,* and *heroes,* according to their rank, these last approaching the nearest to the nature of man, ' These,' he said, ' at their pleasure,
' by means of dreams and other instru-
' ments of divination, communicate to men
' the knowledge of future events, and the
' good demons are to be invoked by pray-
' er.' Socrates admitted the existence of beings ' possessed of a middle nature be-
' tween the Supreme Being and man; and
' to their agency he ascribed the ordinary
' phenomena of nature, and the particular
' conduct of human affairs; and he encou-
' raged the practice of divination, under
' the notion that the gods sometimes dis-
' cover future events to good men.'

Plato supposed that there were " sub-
' ordinate divinities appointed by the su-
' preme Being, both to form the bodies
' of animals, and to superintend the affairs
' of the visible world.' Xenocrates, a
disciple of Plato, taught that ' the heavens
' are divine, and the stars celestial gods,
' and that besides these divinities, there
' are terrestrial demons, of a middle na-
' ture between God and man, and par-
' taking both of mind and body, like
' human beings, capable of passion, and
' liable to a diversity of character.'

Aristotle, who believed in no particular providence, yet supposed that there
were ' intelligent natures inferior to the
' first mover, who presided over the lower
' celestial spheres.'

Though Democritus rejected the doctrine of a Supreme Deity, he admitted
the popular belief of divinities inhabiting
the aerial regions, saying that ' they made
' themselves visible to favoured mortals,
' and enabled them to foretel future events.'
He said, ' they were in form like men, but
of

'of a larger size, and a superior nature; being composed of the most subtle atoms, and less liable to dissolution than human beings, but nevertheless mortal.' According to the Stoics, 'portions of the ethereal soul of the world, being distributed through all the parts of the universe, and animating all bodies, there are inferior gods and demons, with which all nature is peopled. They conceived them, however, to be limited in their duration, returning at length to their original, and losing their separate existence.'

DISCOURSE VIII.

The Principles of the Heathen Philosophy compared with those of Revelation.

PART II.

The world by wisdom knew not God.
1 COR. i. 21.

HAVING given you a comparative view of the religion of the Hebrews, and that of the antient idolatrous nations, I began, in my last discourse, to give you a similar view of the principles of the *heathen philosophy*, that it might not be said that I took an unfair advantage, in relating nothing more than the opinions and practices of the vulgar among the heathens, instead of the real sentiments of the wisest among them. These, however, I shewed you were, in several respects, far less rational than those of the scriptures. I mentioned their univerfal opinion of the impoffibility of creation out of nothing, of the eternity and indeftructibility, of matter; its neceffary evil tendency; the doctrines of many of them, of the production of all inferior beings by emanation, or protrufion, from the fubftance of the deity, and their abforption into it again; the abfolute denial of the being of a God by many, and thofe fome of the moft eminent, of the Greek philofophers; their various and unfatisfactory opinions concerning the origin of evil; their denial of a divine providence, their belief of the exiftence of intelligent beings, inferior to the fupreme, who at their pleafure, and contrary to the will of the Supreme Being, interfered in the direction of human affairs. I now proceed to obferve,

7. If the heathen philofophers became fo *vain in their imaginations*, when they fpeculated concerning the nature of God, and the origin and government of the univerfe, and were not able to retain the great truths which mankind had received by tradition relating to them, much more did they wander

wander in uncertainty and error, with respect to the doctrine of a *future state*, concerning which, as I have observed, the light of nature gives us no information at all. On this subject, so important that without it the doctrine concerning God and providence is merely a curious speculation, of no practical use, the principles of those philosophers who admitted a future state are totally discordant with those of the scriptures, which alone are agreeable to reason, though not discoverable by it. On this subject, I must be excused if I advance some things which will not be approved by the generality of Christians, who, in my opinion, have not intirely got rid of doctrines introduced into Christianity from a heathen source, from which have been derived almost all its corruptions.

According to the scriptures, the future state of man depends intirely upon a *resurrection*, to take place at a distant period, called the *last day*, and nothing is said concerning the rewards of the righteous, or the punishment of the wicked, antecedent to that time. Our Saviour recommending acts of charity, says, (Luke xiv. 14) *Thou shalt be recompensed at the resurrection of the just,* and on no occasion did he refer his hearers to any state of things prior to this. When he speaks of being *cast into hell,* it is with hands and eyes, which are members of the body; and the rich man in the parable is represented as with a tongue, tormented with burning thirst, though for the sake of some circumstances in the parable the future state is represented as taking place before the proper time.

The Apostle Paul, comforting the Thessalonians on the death of some of their friends, refers them only to the resurrection, and gives no hint of their enjoying any degree of happiness at the time that he was writing, which would have been unavoidable if, in his opinion, they *had* been happy then, 1. Thess. iv. 13. *I would not have you be ignorant, brethren, concerning them that are asleep, that ye sorrow not as those who have no hope. For if we believe that Jesus died and rose again, even so also them that sleep*

sleep in Jesus will God bring with him, and the dead in Christ shall rise first, that is, before any change take place on those who will be then alive. Why, indeed, did he use the term *sleep,* if, in his idea, the dead were not in a state of *insensibility,* and not to be awaked to life and action, but at the resurrection?

Again, when the same apostle exhorts Christians to live sober, righteous, and godly lives, Tit. ii. 13. he directs them *to look for that blessed hope, even the glorious appearing of the great God, and our Saviour Jesus Christ,* when he shall come again to raise the dead and judge the world. When our Saviour says that he will receive the apostles to himself, he refers them to the same time, and nothing prior to it, John xiv. 3. *I will come again, and take you to myself, that where I am there ye may be also.* When, therefore, the apostle Paul speaks of being *absent from the body and present with the Lord,* he must have meant the same great period, overlooking all that passed between the time of his death and his resurrection, which indeed

indeed will only appear as a moment: as in the cafe of a man awaking from a profound fleep.

When Mofes defcribes the formation of man, he reprefents him as made wholly, and not in part only, of the *duſt of the ground*, and fays after this, God put breath and life into him, thereby giving motion to the curious machine, which was before a lifelefs mafs. It is to this doctrine of Mofes, that our Saviour refers, when he fays that God is able *to deſtroy both body and foul*, or the power of life, *in hell*. For the word that is here rendered *foul*, is elfewhere rendered life, meaning that men, by killing the body, which God has been pleafed to put in their power, cannot prevent its returning to life, this being in the power of God only. There is not, in reality, any more reafon to fuppofe *life* to be a real fubftance, than *death*, which we neverthelefs perfonify, when we fay that *death comes*, and *furprifes men*, and *takes* them. In the fcriptures, both *death*, and *fin*, are perfonified.

The

The Gnostics, who were the first of the philosophers who embraced Christianity, could not divest themselves of their prejudices with respect to *matter*, as the source of all evil; and thinking it the happiest state of the soul, to be entirely detached from it, they explained away the doctrine of the *resurrection*, as to be understood of something that took place during life. To them the apostle Paul alludes, when he says, 2 Tim. ii. 18. that *they erred concerning the faith; saying that the resurrection was past already, and overturned the faith of some.* Justin Martyr, the first Christian writer after the apostolic age, whose works are come down to us, enumerating the particular tenets of the Gnostics, who were deemed to be *heretics*, and not allowed to be properly Christians; says of them, Dial. p. 2. 'They also say that there is no re-
'surrection of the dead, but that immedi-
'ately after death, souls are received into
'heaven. Do not take these to be Chris-
'tians.'

This

This language of this antient and venerable writer, is not a little remarkable. Think not, however, that I approve of his harſh cenſure of the Gnoſtics. Others will ſay that they who reject the doctrine of a ſoul, are not Chriſtians. Both are equally reprehenſible. The Gnoſtics as well as Juſtin, believed the divine miſſion of Jeſus, and a life of retribution after death, and many of them were martyrs as well as himſelf. The doctrine of a future life, is the moſt important article of Chriſtian faith. The time, the place, or the manner, in which it will be effected, are all comparatively of little moment.

Though after this Chriſtians in general adopted the doctrine of a ſoul diſtinct from the body, they thought that, after death, it remained in a place under ground, called *Hades*, where it waited for the reſurrection of the body, when, and not before, it would be admitted to the immediate preſence of God and of Chriſt, in heaven. This continued to be the faith of the Chriſtian world, for about a thouſand years. They
pretty

pretty foon, however, made an exception in favour of the fouls of the martyrs, which they thought went directly to heaven.

There are thought to be fome traces of the doctrine of a refurrection in the heathen world, as among the Chaldeans and Zabians. But if this was the cafe, the doctrine was foon obliterated, and fpeculative perfons, thinking a proper *refurrection* to be abfolutely impoffible, and yet unwilling to give up all hope of fome *future ftate*, imagined that there was fome fpiritual, or ethereal, principle in man, which having exifted long before his birth, would fubfift after his death. For with the heathens thefe two doctrines always went together; and Origen, one of the moft learned of the early Chriftians, believed both the pre-exiftence of the foul, and its feparate exiftence after death. Afterwards Chriftians in general abandoned the former, but retained the latter, though originally they were both derived from the fame fource.

But what evidence is there, from any appearances in nature, which is all that
the

the heathens had to look to, on which their belief either of the pre-exiftence, or the feparate exiftence of the foul is founded. The former will be allowed to have been wholly chimerical. But with refpect to the latter, is it not evident that the power of thinking depends upon the brain; and if thought is fufpended in the ftate of found *fleep*, and during a *fwoon*, muft it not be more effectually fufpended in a ftate of *death?*

It will be faid that we cannot conceive of any connection between the properties of perception or thought, and the idea of matter. But we know nothing at all of the connection of any properties with thofe of any fubftance whatever. Who can explain the connection between the magnet and the property of attracting iron, or the caufe of the gravitation of all material fubftances towards each other? And what clearer ideas have we of the connection between the power of perception and thought with an *immaterial* fubftance any more than with a *material* one. Let us us then no longer cover our ignorance, or our fancied knowledge, with the repetition of mere words, to which we have no ideas, but confine ourselves to known *facts*, such as the strict connection between the powers of thought and the organization of the brain. When that is destroyed, sensation and thought cease; so that there cannot be any rational ground to expect the restoration of the one without the restoration of the other. And certainly the great Being who made man of the dust of the ground, can make him again, though reduced to the same dust. As to the *manner* in which this is to be effected, we know as much of the one as of the other; which is just nothing at all. But as the one has been effected by the same Being who has promised the other, we have no reason to entertain any doubt of its accomplishment at the time appointed.

The only rational hope of a future life must, therefore, be founded on the scripture doctrine of a *resurrection*, when the whole man, with all his powers, will be be revived. That this doctrine of a resurrection is inconsistent with that of a soul, which survives the body, and retains all its faculties, not only unimpaired, but improved, (for such is the original and proper doctrine on the subject) is obvious to the slightest consideration. For if such be the condition of the soul, when freed from the clog and obstruction of the body, a resurrection would not only be unnecessary, but even undesirable. The two systems are, therefore, repugnant to each other, and cannot be rationally held together.

The doctrine of a soul, and consequently that of an intermediate state between death and the resurrection, has been the foundation of the worship of dead men and women, called saints, of the doctrine of purgatory, and many other doctrines of popery. These, and almost every other corruption of genuine christianity, came from the same heathen source, as I have shewn at large in my *History of the Corruptions of Christianity*.

The

The imagination of man being let loose in speculations on the origin and nature of souls, and their existence after death, we do not wonder at the wildest and most extravagant hypotheses on so obscure a subject. The general opinion of the philosophers was, that all souls, having been portions of the divine essence, or of the great soul of the world, and having contracted various impurities in their state of separation from their source, must pass through a course of purgation, by going through various animal bodies, before they could be reunited to the fountain from which they sprung, and to which they always tend.

The Egyptians, according to Herodotus, believed that when the body was decayed, the soul passed into that of some other animal, which was just then born, and that after it had made the circuit of beasts, birds, and fishes, through a period of three thousand years, it again became an inhabitant of a human body. They, therefore, endeavoured to delay this transmigration,

migration, by embalming the body, and thereby preferving it uncorrupted, and in a ftate fit for the refidence of the foul, as long as poffible.

Pythagoras, who borrowed his doctrines from the Eaft, carried this of tranfmigration into Greece. He alfo held that of the final return of all fouls into the eternal fource from which they fprung. It does not, however, appear that the doctrine of tranfmigration, though ftill held in the Eaft, remained long in Greece; but the doctrine of *pre-exiftence*, ever accompanied that of a *foul*, and on this principle, the Grecian philofophers believed its natural independence on the body, and its continued exiftence after its feparation from it by death. Socrates held this doctrine, but either with fome degree of doubt, or having no high opinion of the happinefs of a future ftate*. Plato reprefents him as

---

* The heathens in general, at leaft the Greeks, do not appear to have had any high idea of the happinefs of the beft of men after death. For Homer makes Achilles fay to Ulyffes,

as faying to his friends, who attended him at his trial, ' whether it is better to ' live or die, was known only to the gods."

Plato, though a difciple of Socrates, combined his doctrines with thofe of other philofophers, and had fome peculiar ideas on this fubject. Thefe, on account of his great celebrity, I muft not omit to mention, if it were only to fhew what very abfurd and extravagant notions the greateft of men have adopted when deftitute of the light of revelation. He fuppofed that ' there exifts fomething between *God*, and ' the *matter* of which the world was form' ed, which he calls *ideas*, exifting in the ' divine mind; and as external objects are ' perceived by the *fenfes*, thefe can only be ' perceived by the *intellect*.' Senfible things, he faid, ' being in a ftate of continual ' fluctuation, cannot be the object of ' *fcience*, but thefe *ideas*, being permanent, ' *may*, and by the contemplation of them,

---

Ulyffes, when he found him in the Elyfian fields, ' I had ' rather be a poor man, and ferve another poor man, who ' had himfelf a bare fuficiency of food, on earth, than rule ' over all the dead.'

' he

'he supposed that men might attain to a
'kind of union with God, in whose mind
'those ideas exist. He also supposed that
'there is a *third substance*, composed of
'spirit and matter, diffused through the
'universe, and the animating soul of
'the world; that the souls of men are
'not derived immediately from God, but
'from this soul of the world, which from
'its origin was debased by a mixture of
'material principle. He said that when
'God formed the universe, he separated
'from the soul of the world, a number of
'inferior souls, equal in number to the
'stars, and assigned to each its proper ce-
'lestial abode; but that these souls (from
'what reason does not appear) were sent
'down to the earth, as into a sepulchre,
'or prison, and that it is only by disen-
'gaging itself from animal passions, and
'rising above sensible objects, to the con-
'templation of the world of intelligence,'
(the *ideas* above mentioned) 'that the
'soul of man can be prepared to return
'to its destined habitation.'

He

He moreover held that 'the soul con-
'sists of three parts, the first the seat of
'intelligence, the second of the passions,
and the third of appetite, and he assigned
to each its proper place in the human body.

The Stoics thought very differently
from each other concerning the duration
of souls. 'Some of them were of opinion
'that they would all remain till the general
'conflagration; some that only those of
'the wise and good would continue so
'long; some thought that all souls, on be-
'ing released from their bodies, would be
'immediately absorbed in the soul of the
'world; some that souls being of the na-
'ture of *fire*, would be extinguished at
'death; others that the soul was so con-
'fined in the gross body, that it could not
'find a passage out even at death, but
'must remain till it was intirely destroyed.
'Some of the Stoics thought that, in the
'universal restoration of nature, each in-
'dividual would return to its former body,
'but others thought that then only similar
'souls would be placed in similar bodies.

Uncertainty

Uncertainty cannot be more strongly indicated than in this diversity of opinion.

It does not appear whether Aristotle thought the human soul to be mortal or immortal; but the former is the more probable, from his opinion concerning the nature and origin of it. For he says ' it ' is an intellectual power, externally trans- ' mitted into the human body, from the ' common source of rationality to human ' beings.' He does not say what he conceived this universal principle to be; but there is no proof that he supposed this principle continued with any individual after death.

If we may collect the sentiments of Aristotle from those of his followers, we may certainly conclude that he did not expect that men would in any sense, survive death. Dicæarchus, an Aristotelian, held that ' there was no such thing as *mind*, ' or *soul*, in man or beast, that the principle ' by which animals perceive is equally dif- ' fused through the body, and inseparable ' from it.' Alexander Aphrodisœus, another

other follower of Ariftotle, faid that 'the 'foul was not a diftinct fubftance itfelf, but 'the form of an organized body,' meaning probably, that it was a property that was the refult of organization. Theophraftus, an Ariftotelian, at the clofe of life, expreffed great regret at the fhortnefs of it, and complained that 'nature 'had given long life to ftags and crows, 'to whom it is of little value, and had 'denied it to man, who, in a longer du-'ration, might have been able to attain 'the fummit of fcience, but now, as foon 'as he arrives within fight of it, he is ta-'ken away.' His laft advice to his difciples was that, 'fince it is the lot of man 'to die, as foon as he begins to live, they 'fhould take more pains to enjoy life, than 'to acquire pofthumous fame.' Indeed the natural inference from this doctrine is, as the Apoftle expreffes it, *Let us eat and drink, for to morrow we die.*

The great father of modern unbelievers among Mahometans and Chriftians, was Averroes, a Saracen, devoted to the philofophy losophy of Aristotle, whose writings made all the unbelievers in the age of Petrarch, and that of Pope Leo X. He held ʻ the ʻ eternity of the world, and the existence ʻ of one universal intellect, the source of ʻ all human intelligence, into which every ʻ separate intelligence will finally be re- ʻ solved, and consequently he denied the ʻ distinct existence, and proper immortality ʻ of the human soul.' I need not say how irrational this notion, so long prevalent with those who ridiculed the scriptures, is. Modern unbelievers will smile at the extreme absurdity of it, as much as any Christians, and so they will at all the systems of their predecessors, the heathen philosophers; though in a general way, with a view to disparage the writers of the scriptures, they, but with little real knowledge of them, occasionally cry them up.

I hardly need to mention any more of these vague opinions, altogether destitute of proof, or probability. But I shall observe that Democritus said that ʻ men were first
ʻ produced

'produced from water and earth, and
'that the foul, or the principle of animal
'life and motion, is the refult of a com-
'bination of round and fiery particles, and
'is mortal, and perifhes with the body.'
And Epicurus faid, 'the foul is a fubtle
'corporeal fubftance, compofed of the
'fineft atoms.'

The principles of found reafoning and true philofophy, have fufficiently exploded all thefe crude fyftems, the beft of which never produced fuch a perfuafion concerning a future ftate as men could act upon, and fuffer and die for; whereas the faith of Jews, and Chriftians, has unqueftionably produced, and does ftill produce, thefe fubftantial fruits. And if the great end of *theory*, as it undoubtedly is, be *practice*, a doctrine which is both rational in itfelf, and fupported by fufficient authority, muft be infinitely preferable to fuch wild and incoherent fyftems as thofe of the antient philofophers, the knowledge of which, moreover, never extended beyond their own difciples, and which does not

not appear to have had any real influence even upon them.

But the great queſtion before us at preſent is this; if Moſes, and the other writers of the Old and New Teſtament, are to be claſſed with *philoſophers* or *legiſlators*, how came they to frame a ſyſtem ſo fundamentally different from any that other philoſophers and legiſlators of the ſame age had conceived? And if they were *not*, but are to be conſidered as perſons who had no advantage of learning or education, and therefore to be claſſed among the *vulgar*, and the vulgar of a rude and barbarous nation, as the Jews are generally conſidered, how came they to diſcover ſo much true knowledge, and adopt a ſyſtem of religion, laws, and morals, which cannot be denied to be free from the crude conceptions, and groſs abſurdities, with which the ſyſtems of the boaſted philoſophers of the heathen world are chargeable? The only anſwer is, that what they wrote was from a ſource of wiſdom *not their own*, or any that they could

could have borrowed from the neighbouring nations, but one much superior; and as they profess, *from God*. But what are we to think of those, who with the facts that I have recited before them, whether they will attend to them or not, are continually exclaiming against the religion of the Bible, without sparing any term of reproach, and praising the superior attainments, and philosophy, of the Greeks and Romans. Happily, however, there are facts enow before us, and abundantly ascertained, by which impartial persons may easily form a true judgment concerning both; and I hope there is yet in the world common sense, and candour too, sufficient to make a just comparison between them.

8. In a former discourse I shewed you to what horrid and abominable practices the popular religions among the heathens led. But these, it may be said, were peculiar to the *vulgar*, and that the *philosophers* would not fail to condemn those practices. This, however, was far from being the case. Many of the philosophers, no doubt, knew

knew better, and among themſelves deſpiſed and ridiculed the popular ſuperſtitions, at leaſt ſome of them; but they had not the juſt courage in the cauſe of truth and virtue, to run any riſque in oppoſing ſo deſtructive a torrent. They themſelves conformed to all the ſuperſtitious practices of thoſe times, and recommended the ſame to others. Xenophon began his account of his beloved maſter Socrates, with ſaying, that ' he wondered how he came to
' be charged with not believing in the gods
' of his country, when he not only joined
' in the public ſacrifices, but frequently
' ſacrificed in private, and openly practiſed
' divination, which was always deemed a
' part of religion.' Socrates himſelf ſaid,
' that it is the duty of every perſon, to
' follow the cuſtoms of his country, in all
' its religious rites.' In ſuch veneration did ſeveral of the philoſophers hold the laws of their country, that they maintained there was no other rule of right and wrong. This doctrine was avowed by Democritus and Ariſtippus. I need not obſerve how abſurd

abfurd this maxim was. Were the laws themfelves framed by no rules of natural right or wrong? and how are we, on this principle, to make an eftimate of the comparative excellence of different fyftems of law?

So far were the antient philofophers from entertaining the liberal fentiments which it is now the fafhion to afcribe to them, that, in a period of three hundred years, during which the Chriftians were perfecuted, as oppofers of the vulgar fuperftition, there is no example of any philofopher pleading for the toleration of them. On the contrary, they were often the foremoft to promote the perfecution. The celebrated emperor Marcus Aurelius, who was himfelf an eminent philofopher, was one of the moft unrelenting perfecutors of Chriftians.

9. As feveral of the philofophers were aware that fome of their tenets would have given offence to the vulgar, either from the nature of them, or from their being liable to be mifunderftood, they had *doctrines*, which

which they communicated only to a few, and this under a strict injunction of secrecy. This practice was adopted by Pythagoras from the Egyptian priests. He moreover enjoined upon his pupils a silence of two, and sometimes of five, years. In this state of probation they were not permitted even to see their master, or to hear him, except from behind a curtain, and when they were admitted to his presence, and favoured with his secret doctrines, they bound themselves by an oath not to divulge them. Something of this nature was adopted by Plato. He said, ' it is a difficult thing to
' discover the nature of the creator of the
' universe, and being discovered, it is im-
' possible, and would be impious, to expose
' the discovery to vulgar understandings.
' He therefore threw a veil of obscurity
' over his public instructions, which was
' only removed for the benefit of those
' who were thought worthy to be admit-
' ted to his more private and confidential
' lectures.'

But

But how much more noble was the conduct of Moses, and of our Saviour, who made no secret of any thing that they taught? How much dignity was there in the charge that Jesus gave to his apostles, to publish every thing that they knew of his doctrines, Mat. x. 27. *What I tell you in darkness, that speak ye in the light, and what ye hear in the ear, that preach ye upon the house tops.*

10. In general, no doubt, the heathen philosophers had just ideas concerning moral virtues, and in their writings they express themselves with truth and energy on the subject; but in several respects their peculiar tenets misled them, and were unfavourable to a right disposition of mind, and a proper conduct in life. This could not but be the case with the Stoics, the most rigidly moral of all the antient sects. Their opinion that all souls are portions of the divinity, from which they inferred that they were sufficient for their own happiness, inspired them with a great degree of pride. For they said, ' it was
' not

'not in the power of the gods to make a 'good man unhappy.' They maintained that pain was no evil, and that a wife man may be happy even in the midst of torture. They also held that he ought to be free from every emotion of affection or passion. Nature would never suffer any man to reduce this absurd system to practice; but the attempt to do it must have had an unfavourable influence on a man's temper and conduct. Whether consistently with their principles, or not, many of the more eminent of the Stoics put an end to their own lives. This was done by Zeno himself, the founder of the sect, when, in a very advanced age, he was in much pain from breaking his finger.

11. It is common with unbelievers to decry both Christianity and Judaism, as species of *superstition*. But no misconceptions or abuse, of the Jewish or Christian religions, led to more absurd superstitions than the doctrines of the heathen philosophers, concerning the defiling nature of matter, their consequent contempt for the body

body, and their ideas of the purification of the foul by the mortification of it, It was, in fact, from the heathen philofophers that the Chriftians of the fecond and following centuries derived their opinions and practices on the fubject. It was from them alfo that the monkifh ideas of the fuperior merit of a *contemplative* to an *active* life, and of the value of feclufion from the world, were originally derived.

Pythagoras faid that ' contemplative
' wifdom cannot be completely attained
' without a total abftraction from the or-
' dinary affairs of life, and a perfect tran-
' quility and freedom of mind.' But the later Platonifts, among whom we might expect the moft advanced and improved ftate of philofophy, carried thefe ideas ftill farther. ' They practifed the moft
' rigorous abftinence, as by this means
' they expected to purify themfelves from
' moral defilement, and they paffed whole
' days and nights in contemplation, and
' what they called devotion. Plotinus
' had fuch a contempt for the body, that
 ' he

'he never could be prevailed upon to
'make ufe of any means to cure the dif-
'eafes to which his conftitution was fub-
'ject, or to alleviate his pain. His rigo-
'rous abftinence, and determined neglect
'of his health, at laft brought him into a
'ftate of difeafe and infirmity, which ren-
'dered the latter part of his life extremely
'painful.' In Chriftians this would be
laughed at, but in this deep philofopher, it
may perhaps be admired.

To this fuperftition thefe philofophers
joined the moft extravagant enthufiafm.
They fuppofed, that 'the foul of man,
'prepared by previous difcipline, might
'rife to a capacity of holding immediate
'intercourfe with good demons, and even
'to enjoy in ecftafy an intuitive vifion of
'God himfelf,' a degree of perfection and
felicity which fome of the more eminent
among them, fuch as Plotinus, Porphyry,
Jamblicus, and Proclus, were fuppofed
actually to have attained. Plotinus is faid
'to have afcended through all the Platonic
'fteps of contemplation, to the actual vi-
'fion

'sion of the Supreme Being himself, and
'to have been admitted to such inter-
'course with him as no other philosopher
'ever enjoyed." Porphyry says that he
'himself, in the sixty-eighth year of his
'age, was in a sacred ecstasy, when he
'saw the supreme intellignece, the god,'
he says, 'who is superior to all gods, with-
'out an image.'

According to Jamblicus, 'the human
'soul has an innate knowledge of God,
'prior to all reasoning, in consequence of
'its having originally derived its essence
'from, and having subsisted in, the divine
'nature; that by the intervention of de-
'mons, it enjoys communication with
'the superior divinities, and with God
'himself. Gods, demons, and heroes,'
he says, 'appear to men under various
'forms, in dreams, or waking visions, to
'render them bodily or spiritual services,
'and to enable them to predict future
'events. But these communications with
'the divine nature are not to be obtained
'without the observance of certain sacred
                                rites,

' rites. The signs of divine communica-
' tions,' he says, ' are a temporary suspen-
' sion of the senses and faculties, the inter-
' ruption of the ordinary functions of
' life, and a capacity of speaking and do-
' ing wonders, so that in this state the per-
' son does not live an animal, or human,
' but a divine life.'

Jews and Christians are reproached for their credulity, for their faith in miracles, however well attested; but can they say that these Platonists were less credulous? ' With a view to destroy the credit which
' the Christian religion derived from mira-
' cles, or at least to advance their philoso-
' phy to a level with it, they pretended to
' a power of performing supernatural ope-
' rations, by the aid of invisible beings,
' and said that the miracles of Christ,' which they did not deny, ' were wrought
' by the same magical, or as they termed
' them, *theurgic* powers, which they them-
' selves possessed. The emperor Julian,
' made great use of magical arts in exe-
' cuting his political purposes. While he
' reported

'was at Vienna, he reported that in the
'middle of the night, he was visited by
'a celestial form, which, speaking in heroic
'verse, had promised him the possession
'of the imperial dignity.

With these facts before us, and many more of the same kind might have been adduced, surely Christianity will no longer be exclusively taxed with superstition, enthusiasm, or credulity. But no countenance is given to these idle notions, or absurd practices, in the scriptures. Christ and the apostles were not monks, nor had they any monkish ideas. Their piety was perfectly rational, and their love of God evidenced by benevolence to man. And they inculcated no austerity, or mortification, besides that temperance, which is opposed to vicious excess, and contributes to the true enjoyment of life.

On the whole, we may surely say that, had modern unbelievers found in the scriptures any of the doctrines which I have shewn to have been professed by the philosophers of antiquity, had they found there the doctrine of two coeternal principles, that of the emanation of all fouls from the substance of the supreme Being, the absorption of them into it again, with their repeated emissions and retractions to all eternity; had they found there the doctrine of the formation of all things by the fortuitous concourse of atoms, that the air is filled with demons of different characters, directing the affairs of the world at their pleasure, and giving intimations of future events by omens and divination; had they found in the scriptures the doctrine of the pre-existence of all human souls, their lapse into gross bodies, where they are confined, and also contaminated by their connection with so debasing a companion, the purification of these embodied souls by austerity and mortification, their transmigration through the bodies of animals, by way of preparation for their ascent to the empyreal regions; had they there found the doctrine of one common principle of intelligence, or soul of the universe, in all men and animals, without giving

giving to each a permanent exiftence, had all or any of thefe doctrines been found in the fcriptures, would they not have exclaimed againft fuch crude notions, and wild conceptions, and have rejected the fyftem without farther examination? It was, in fact, the finding no fuch opinions as thefe in the fcriptures, that firft led Chriftian philofophers, (after having adopted feveral of them from a heathen fource, and having long endeavoured to hold them in conjunction with their chriftian principles) that led them to fufpect their truth; and farther reflection on the fubject led many to explode them altogether. Thus is the world indebted to Chriftianity for the detection of errors which were the difgrace of human reafon, though patronized by the moft eminent philofophers of the heathen world; yet modern unbelievers, though lying, with the reft of the world, under fo great obligations to chriftianity, are now bufily affaulting it with every weapon of reafon or ridicule. Its friends, however, are under no apprehenfions

henfions about it. This very ftate of things was forefeen, and foretold, by its founder. Revealed religion is fo far from fhrinking from, that it invites, the ftricteft examination. Its friends being thofe of reafon and truth, engage in its vindication only as fupported by reafon and truth, and as favourable to the beft interefts of mankind.

DISCOURSE IX.

The evidence of the Mosaic and Christian Religions.

PART I.

God, who, at sundry times, and in divers manners, spake in time past unto the fathers, by the prophets, hath, in these last days, spoken unto us by his son.
HEB. i. 1--2.

IN the preceding Discourses I have endeavoured to prepare the way for the proper evidence of revealed religion, by explaining the nature, and shewing the importance, of the subject, and by exhibiting a comparative view of the heathen religions, and that of the Hebrews, which is that branch of revealed religion which is most objected to by unbelievers. The systems of the heathen religions, especially those

those of remote ages, coeval with the Mosaic institutions, you have seen to have been not only a confused mass of miserable superstition, arising from a total ignorance of the laws of nature, but to have consisted in rites shocking to humanity, good morals, and common decency, and that they were, in a great measure, the cause of the horrid depravity of manners which prevailed in the Gentile world. On the contrary, the tenets of the religion of the Hebrews, which has been so much decried by Voltaire and others, were, in the highest degree, rational, worthy of the Supreme Being, leading to the greatest purity of heart and life, and peculiarly calculated to counteract the effects of the absurd and mischievous religions of the neighbouring nations. Being, therefore, so much superior to, and reverse of, all the forms of religions, with which Moses or any of his countrymen, could have been acquainted, and even superior, as I have shewn, to the principles advanced by the most celebrated of the heathen philosophers,

phers, there is the greateſt antecedent probability that it came from God, the fountain of wiſdom; who thought proper to make choice of one nation, in which to preferve the true knowledge and worſhip of himſelf, amidſt the general defection from it, and by that means to diffuſe, in due time, the moſt falutary light to all his offspring of mankind. And it has already, in a great meaſure, effected this benevolent purpoſe, in the gradual unfolding of the plan, in the Chriſtian revelation, which has a conſtant reference to that of Moſes; fo that they are to be confidered as parts of the fame ſcheme; the proper evidence of which I ſhall now proceed to lay before you. In order to do this as briefly as poſſible, I ſhall not confider the evidence of each feparately, but jointly; eſpecially as I have done the former, and more in detail, in another ſet of difcourſes, which are already before the Public.

I ſhall begin with obſerving that the only proper evidence of the interpoſition

of

of God, as the author of nature, is an exhibition of something which he alone is capable of performing, that is, a proper *miracle*, or a controlling of the order of nature, which it must be allowed that no other than he who established it, and who constantly maintains it, can do. The medium of divine communications may be *men*, and where the instruction and reformation of men is the object, it is most naturally and properly so; but the power by which it is effected, must appear to be of God. Otherwise, there would be no reason to suppose that there was any thing superhuman in the scheme.

It has, indeed, been the opinion of some, that proper miracles may be wrought by beings superior to man, though inferior to the Supreme God, and even for purposes opposite to any that could be *his*, tending to mislead and injure mankind. But this is an opinion which I am persuaded will not be seriously maintained by any person at this day. It cannot, with any appearance of reason, be supposed, that the Supreme Being would put it in the power of any malevolent demon (supposing such beings to exist) thus to deceive his creatures, and without reserving to himself the power of undeceiving them. For if such beings as these were permitted to work real miracles, or perform such works as men were unable to distinguish from real miracles, it was all that himself could do; so that the mischief would be without remedy.

We must, therefore, take it for granted, and I doubt not, it will be universally allowed, that if there be a real departure from the order or laws of nature (which in the greater instances there is no danger of mistaking) it must be by the interposition of a power properly *divine*, and for a purpose worthy of divinity, of the great and good parent of the human race; for instance, to give them seasonable assistance in the discovery of interesting truth, and removing the causes of error, vice, and misery, which must otherwise have remained without remedy.

Miracles,

Miracles, then, being allowed to be the only, but a sufficient, evidence of divine interposition, it will be asked, what is the evidence of their having been wrought, to those who are not themselves witnesses of them? For it is not pretended that miracles are exhibited before all persons, but only occasionally. I answer, the testimony of those who *were* properly witnesses of them, but testimony so circumstanced, that the supposition of its being false would be more improbable on the whole than that of its being true; so that its being false shall, by a fair estimate, appear to be a greater miracle, or a greater deviation from the usual course of nature, than what is related as such. And certainly such cases may be supposed.

If, for instance, a great number of persons, universally allowed to have the use of their senses and understanding, seriously declare that they actually saw, or heard, any thing whatever, though *a priori* ever so improbable, and their *veracity* be not

not queftioned, their fenfes muft have been under a miraculous illufion, if the thing be not as they reprefent it. It will alfo be allowed, from the opinion generally entertained of human nature, that circumftances may be fuppofed, in which a great number of perfons agreeing to tell a falfehood, when they could not have any motive to do it, would be deemed nothing lefs than miraculous.

It is readily acknowledged, that miracles not being events of daily or frequent occurrence, require more definite evidence than ordinary facts, and this in proportion to their antecedent improbability, arifing from their want of analogy to events that are common. But there is no fact that is poffible in itfelf, but the evidence *may* be fuch as to make it credible. The circumftances which tend to give credit to human teftimony with refpect to miracles, are the following. The witneffes muft be in fufficient number. They muft be in circumftances in which they cannot be deceived themfelves, and they muft have no apparent

rent motive to deceive others. In order to this, the miracles muſt be in ſufficient number, and exhibited ſo long, as to afford opportunity for examining them. They muſt alſo be upon a large ſcale, or of ſuch a nature as to exclude all idea of trick or impoſition. They muſt be exhibited before perſons who had no previous diſpoſition to expect or to receive them. A ſufficient degree of attention muſt be excited to them at the time, and a number of perſons muſt be intereſted in aſcertaining their reality. The hiſtory of them muſt be coeval with the events, and the belief of them muſt produce a laſting effect.

If all theſe circumſtances ſhould be found to concur in the miracles recorded in the ſcriptures, it muſt be allowed that they have all the credibility that facts ſo extraordinary, and of ſo great antiquity *can* have, and nothing more can be required in the caſe. The moſt ſceptical of men cannot demand more ſatisfactory evidence. I ſhall therefore now proceed to conſider confider how far thefe circumftances apply to the miracles of which an account is contained in the Old and New Teftament. For it is the truth of the fyftem of religion propofed to us in thefe books that is to be proved by them.

I muft, however, remind you, that though I would by no means crave your indulgence in being fatisfied with a fmall degree of evidence, or lefs than fuch as I have defcribed, the thing to be proved is far from being improbable *a priori*, fo as to make fuch extraordinary evidence neceffary. If men, who are the offspring of God, were involved in error, vice, and mifery, from which it was not in their power to refcue themfelves, it might even have been *expected* that their benevolent parent would provide fome effectual means for their relief. And the fcheme of revelation, which gives men the fulleft information concerning the being, the perfections and the providence of God, concerning man's duty here, and a future ftate of retribution hereafter, the knowledge of which

which we have seen the wifeſt of men never attained of themſelves, is excellently adapted to anſwer this end, and therefore it is not only deſirable, but far from being improbable. On the contrary, I have ſhewn at large that the plan of revelation is, in a variety of reſpects, the moſt natural and the moſt effectual, and conſequently the moſt eligible, mode of communicating religious inſtruction to men.

In this, however, I ſpeak to the feelings of the virtuous, the worthy, and the thinking part of mankind, thoſe whoſe characters and conduct are ſuch as will naturally lead them to wiſh for, and rejoice in, the diſcovery of ſuch momentous truths, and not the profligate and thoughtleſs, who are governed by mere appetite and paſſion, like the brutes, who, looking no farther than to mere animal enjoyments, never think of a God, of a providence, or a future ſtate at all; and who, if it depended upon them, would not chuſe that there ſhould be any ſuch thing.

In

It is well known that there are ſtates of mind in which no attention will be given to any thing that is offenſive to it. A philoſopher of great eminence, having advanced an opinion concerning ſomething that might be determined by a microſcopical obſervation, refuſed to look through a microſcope that was brought to him, with the object ready prepared, when he was told that the inſpection would refute his hypotheſis. And certainly vicious propenſities lay a ſtronger bias on the mind than any ſpeculative opinions whatever.

In minds exceedingly debaſed, there muſt be an almoſt invincible bias againſt the doctrines of revelation; and probably the evidence even of their own ſenſes would not be ſufficient to convince them. To ſuch perſons as theſe, I do not addreſs myſelf at all, becauſe it would be altogether in vain. Indeed I can hardly ſuppoſe that any motive, even that of curioſity, would bring any perſon of this character to hear me on the ſubject, and therefore

therefore I will not suppose any such to be present.

1. To those persons whose minds are not absolutely shut against conviction, I would observe, in the first place, that the miracles recorded in the scriptures, and on which the truth of the Mosaic and Christian institutions rests, are sufficiently *numerous*. Passing over all that preceded the age of Moses himself, the miracles which effected the emancipation of the Israelites from their bondage in Egypt, and their settlement in the land of Canaan, will certainly be allowed not to have been deficient with respect to *number*, whatever else be objected to them. They began with the miraculous appearance of fire, in a bush which was not consumed by it, the withering and restoring of Moses' arm, and the changing his rod into a serpent, and that serpent into a rod as at first. Then follow the ten great plagues of Egypt, beginning with the changing of the waters of the river into blood, and ending

ending with the death of all the firft born of the Egyptians in one night, according to the prediction of Mofes. We then proceed to the paffage of the red fea, while the waters rofe on each fide to admit of it; the fweetning of the waters of Mara, the delivery of the ten commandments in an articulate voice from mount Sinai, the fupplying of the whole nation with manna, and the conducting of them with the appearance of a pillar of cloud by day, and of fire by night during forty years, the drawing water from a rock, enough to fupply the whole nation, at two different times, the death of Korah, Dathan, and Abiram by the opening of the earth at the word of Mofes, the death of Nadab and Alihu, the two fons of Aaron, by fire from heaven, the paffage of the river Jordan, by the dividing of its waters, the fall of the walls of Jericho, and fome others of lefs confequence, all in the compafs of one generation.

In the fubfequent hiftory of the Ifraelites, miracles were not fo numerous, but it it is probable that no long period of it was intirely without them, till they were difcontinued after the Babylonifh captivity. But in this interval the Hebrew prophets foretold in the plaineft language many future events which came to pafs in their own times, or very near to them, and among thefe the fate of all the neighbouring nations, as well as of their own, to the lateft period of time. Jeremiah foretold not only the Babylonifh captivity, but the exact duration of it. In the time of Daniel we have the deliverance of Shadrach, Mefhach and Abednego from the fiery furnace, of Daniel himfelf in the den of lions, and his foretelling the infanity (for fuch it muft have been) of Nebuchadnezar, and his reftoration after feven years, as well as his prophecies concerning the rife and fall of the four great monarchies, which have been wonderfully verified, though part of them yet remain to be fulfilled.

After this we have an interval of about four hundred years, in which we find no pretenfions to miracles, or prophecy. But during the public miniftry of Jefus, miracles

cles were more numerous than they had ever been before. His divine miſſion was announced three times by articulate voices from heaven, he cured the diſeaſes, however obſtinate, of all who applied to him, and ſome when he was at a diſtance, and he raiſed at leaſt three perſons from a ſtate of death. He twice fed ſeveral thouſand perſons with a ſmall quantity of proviſions, he alſo changed a large quantity of water into wine. He ſtilled a tempeſt at a word, he walked on the ſea, and cauſed a fig-tree to wither by only ſpeaking, he foretold the deſtruction of Jeruſalem, and the temple, and the deſolation of the country, to come to paſs, in that generation; he roſe from the dead after being publicly crucified, and viſibly aſcended to heaven.

Miracles not leſs conſiderable than theſe diſtinguiſhed the miniſtry of the apoſtles, who ſucceeded Jeſus. They not only expreſſed themſelves in languages which they had never learned, but imparted this power to all the converts; they healed many ſick perſons, they even raiſed the dead, and foretold several future events, which came to pass in their own time. If any person will say that these miracles (and many are omitted in this general view) are not sufficiently numerous for the purpose for which they were wrought, he would say that no *number* whatever would be sufficient, and therefore his objection would not be to the *number*, as such, but must be of some different kind, which will be considered under some of the following heads.

2. Many of the miracles recorded in the scriptures, were on so large a scale, or on other accounts of such a nature, that there could be no suspicion of trick or deception, with respect to them. If the *appearances* only existed (and with respect to them, the senses of men could not be deceived) the *cause* was indisputable. And such were almost all the miracles exhibited in Egypt, as the changing of all the water of such a river as the Nile, as large as any in this country, into blood, or any thing like blood, so that no use could be made of

of it; and this not momentarily, but for a confiderable time, and yet an evil of this magnitude was removed at the prayer of Mofes. Perfons fkilled in tricks of flight of hand, which was, no doubt, the cafe of the magicians of Egypt, might impofe upon a company, even of intelligent and quick fighted perfons, not ufed to them, and on Mofes himfelf, with a fmall quantity of water, contained in a bafon, or they might dexteroufly fubftitute a ferpent in the place of a rod, or a rod in the place of a ferpent; but the miracles exhibited by Mofes, convinced even the magicians themfelves, that what he did was by the *finger* of *God*, as they expreffed themfelves.

The plague of frogs, that of the lice, (as our tranflation renders the word,) of the murrain among the cattle, of the boils, of the hail, of the locufts, and of the darknefs, might each of them feparately, have been produced by natural caufes. But that they fhould all be announced before hand, that none of them fhould affect the diftrict occupied by the Ifraelites, which adjoined to the

the rest of Egypt, and that they should all be removed at the prayer of Moses, are undeniable evidences that the hand of God was in them. Still more was this evident in the death of the first-born, and of the first-born only, of man and of beast, through all the country, while not one of the Israelites died. By this display of divine power, Pharaoh and all the Egyptians were so terrified and subdued, that, unwilling as they before had been, to part with such useful servants, they *were* now desirous of getting rid of them, at any rate.

Upon a greater scale still, was the passage of the whole nation of Israelites, though not fewer than two millions of people, marching at their leisure, with all their cattle and baggage, through an arm of the red sea, while the water rose on each side of them, and all the Egyptians who had ventured to follow them were drowned. There could be no imposition on the senses in such a scene as this, or in the similar miracle of the passage of the river Jordan, in the same manner. The same may be said of other miraculous

miraculous appearances in the time of Moſes, eſpecially that of the delivery of the ten commandments in an articulate voice, heard by all the Iſraelites, then, as I obſerved, more than two millions of people, from mount Sinai, in a river, (for it could not be leſs) iſſuing from a rock, at the word of Moſes; for the blow of his ſtaff could not have had any ſuch effect, and the deſcent of the manna every morning, with the remarkable and conſtant exception of one particular day in the ſeven, on which no manna fell, for the ſpace of forty years, and the pillar of a cloud by day and of fire by night, which alſo attended them the ſame time, and directed all their marches. He muſt have been a bold impoſtor, indeed, who ſhould have attempted any thing of this kind, and not ſo reluctant and ſo timid a leader as Moſes evidently was.

Among the miracles which were on ſo large a ſcale as to exclude all idea of deception, I may mention the falling down of the walls of Jericho, on the ark being carried

carried round the place feven times, the falling down of the idol Dagon, in the prefence of the ark, the calamities which befel the cities of the Philiftines, to which it was fent, and the circumftances of its conveyance back into the land of Canaan, viz. in a carriage drawn by cows whofe calves were kept at home.

Of the miracles that come under this clafs, was the ftrength imparted to Sampfon, by which he was able to take down the gates of a city, and carry them to the top of a hill, and after lofing his ftrength, his recovering it again, fo as to pull down the building in which were aflembled all the lords of the Philiftines, when they were all killed. Such alfo was the burning of the facrifice of Elijah, on mount Carmel, while the priefts of Baal attempted the fame in vain, he being alone, and they four hundred men, favoured by an idolatrous king, who was himfelf prefent, and the people in general alfo favouring them. I might add, under this head, feveral other miracles recorded in the Old Teftament, and

and muſt not omit to mention in this view alſo, the caſe of Shadrach, Meſhach, and Abednego, who were preſerved unhurt in the fiery furnace at Babylon, and alſo the delivery of Daniel from the lions, in the ſame city.

The miracles recorded in the New Teſtament are not, in general, on ſo large a ſcale as many of thoſe recited in the Old, but they are ſufficiently ſo to be out of the reach of any charge of trick and impoſition. Such were the cures performed by Jeſus, of ſuch diſeaſes as, though ſometimes curable by medical treatment, always require a long time; whereas his cures were always inſtantaneous, and yet complete. Such were his cures of blindneſs, eſpecially of the man who was born blind, of fevers, which are never cured but by coming to a certain criſis, of leproſy, of the dropſy; and eſpecially of inſanity, called the caſting out of demons, the ſuppoſed cauſe of that diſorder. Of this claſs, more eſpecially, was his raiſing to life, the daughter of Jairus, at Capernaum, the widow's ſon at Nain,

Nain, and of Lazarus at Bethany. Of miracles of this clafs, were his feeding firſt five thouſand, and afterwards four thouſand perſons, with a few loaves and fiſhes, his ſtilling a tempeſt, his walking on the ſea, and a ſtormy ſea, and laſtly his reſurrection and aſcenſion.

In the hiſtory of the apoſtles, the miracles of this clafs are thoſe called *the gift of tongues*, by which thouſands of perſons were enabled to expreſs themſelves in languages which they had not learned, the cure of the beggar who was known to have been lame from his birth, at the gate of the temple, the deliverance of Peter and John, and afterwards of Peter only, out of priſon, when every precaution had been taken to ſecure them, and alſo the cure of many diſeaſes by Peter and others, ſimilar to the cures performed by Jeſus. Several other miracles might be mentioned under this head, but theſe are abundantly ſufficient for the purpoſe, that is, they were appearances with reſpect to which there could not have been

been any deception. Perfons who were prefent, could never have been under any miftake with refpect to the *facts*, and the facts were of fuch a nature, that they muft necessarily have been miraculous, how ignorant foever we may be of the powers, or laws, of nature in other refpects.

3. Many of the miracles recorded in the fcriptures, and almoft all thofe that are mentioned under the preceding head, were performed in the prefence of a great number of perfons. At the miracles performed by Mofes, all the inhabitants of Egypt, and the whole nation of Ifraelites, were prefent. All the latter muft have feen every thing that paffed in the wildernefs. The whole nation paffed through the river Jordan, and faw the falling of the walls of Jericho. The whole nation of the Philiftines could not but know of the triumph of the ark of God over their idol Dagon, and the manner in which it was conveyed back to the land of Canaan. Ahab and his court, and no doubt thoufands of the
common

common people, were present at Elijah's sacrifice. Nebuchadnezzar, and all the people of Babylon, must have known of the deliverance of Shadrach, Meshach, and Abednego, and so must Darius, and all people in his time, the deliverance of Daniel from the lions.

With respect to the miracles of Jesus, it is evident from the nature of them, and from his manner of life, that they could not but have been known to the whole nation of the Jews. Peter, speaking of them to a promiscuous multitude who were assembled in Jerusalem on the report of the wonderful gift of tongues, expressed himself in the following remarkable manner, Acts ii. 22, *Ye men of Israel, hear my words, Jesus of Nazareth, a man approved of God among you, by miracles and wonders and signs, which God did by him, in the midst of you, as ye yourselves also know.* Again, addressing himself to Cornelius, a Roman centurion, and his friends, he says, concerning Jesus, and the gospel, Acts, x. 36. *The word which God sent unto the children of Israel, that*

that word ye know, which was publifhed throughout all Judea. He evidently did not think it neceffary to produce witneffes of particular facts. He took it for granted that they were known to every body, *how God anointed Jefus of Nazareth with the holy fpirit, and with power, who went about doing good, and healing all that were oppreffed of the devil, for God was with him; and we are witneffes of all things which he did, both in the land of the Jews, and in Jerufalem.*

Alfo, when Paul was addreffing king Agrippa, in the prefence of Feftus, and the court, he fays, Acts xxvi. 20, *None of thefe things are hidden from him; for this thing was not done in a corner.* To the refurrection and the afcenfion of Jefus, all the country, but for the beft reafons, were not witneffes. But certainly five hundred who faw him at one time, were abundantly fufficient to afcertain the fact, as far as any number could do it.

The miracle of the gift of tongues, conferred on the apoftles, and all the primitive Chriftians, could not but be known

known to all the country, and in every place in which it was conferred. The cure of the lame beggar at the gate of the temple, was, from the circumſtances of it, as public as any thing of the kind could well be, and the deliverance of Peter and John from priſon, when the court and all the people knew of their commitment, and were in expectation of their being produced, muſt have engaged univerſal attention. Paul was a perſon ſo well known to the chief prieſts, and ſo active in the perſecution of the Chriſtians, that the circomſtances of his converſion were, no doubt, the ſubject of much converſation, and the miracles that he performed in ſtriking Elymas with blindneſs in the preſence of the governor of Cyprus, the cure of the lame man at Lyſtra, for which the people would have ſacrificed to him as to a god, his cure of the inſane woman at Theſſalonica, and of the demoniacs at Epheſus, were of the moſt conſpicuous nature.

4. The

4. The miracles recorded in the scriptures, especially the great ones which attended the promulgation of the law of Moses, and of Christianity, were all performed in the presence of enemies, at least of persons not at all predisposed to believe them, or to be convinced by them. It appears that Moses himself, who had resided forty years in Arabia, and was married, and had settled there, was exceedingly averse to undertake any thing in favour of his countrymen, and that they, seeing no remedy, had acquiesced in their state of servitude; but that his reluctance was overcome by miracles, and the positive command of God.

In his expostulation with God on the subject, he expressed the unwillingness of his countrymen to believe his mission. On the sight of the miracles which he was impowered to work in their presence, they were satisfied with respect to it, but their deliverance not being effected immediately, and their servitude being rendered more galling, they conceived great indignation

dignation againſt Moſes and Aaron, for attempting it. We read Exod. v. 20. *And they met Moſes and Aaron, who ſtood in the way, as they came forth from Pharoah, and they ſaid unto them, the Lord look upon you, and judge, becauſe you have made our favour to be abhorred in the eyes of Pharoah, and in the eyes of his ſervants, to put a ſword into their hands to ſlay us.* Moſes himſelf at this time repented of his undertaking. For we read, v. 22. *And Moſes returned unto the Lord, and ſaid, wherefore haſt thou ſo evil intreated this people? Why is it that thou haſt ſent me, for ſince I came to Pharoah to ſpeak in thy name, he hath done evil to this people, neither haſt thou delivered thy people at all.* On this Moſes received farther encouragement, but when he ſpake to his countrymen again, chap. ix. *they hearkened not unto him, for anguiſh of ſpirit, and for cruel bondage.*

When, in conſequence of a ſeries of miracles, of the moſt aſtoniſhing kind, the deliverance of the Iſraelites was actually effected, and they had marched out of the country, on perceiving that they were

were purfued, they were exceedingly alarmed, and faid unto Mofes, Exod. xiv. 11. *Becaufe there were no graves in Egypt, haft thou taken us away to die in the wildernefs. Wherefore haft thou dealt thus with us, to carry us forth out of Egypt? Is not this the word that we did tell thee in Egypt? faying, Let us alone that we may ferve the Egyptians. For it had been better for us to ferve the Egyptians, than that we fhould die in the wildernefs.* It was almoft with as much reluctance that the Ifraelites were induced to leave Egypt as the Egyptians expreffed to let them go. On every adverfe event, or hardfhip, we find them making the fame complaints, and regretting that they had left Egypt.

Thus, when they wanted water, we read, Exod. xvii. 3. *The people murmured againft Mofes, and faid, wherefore is it that thou haft brought us out of Egypt, to kill us and our children, and our cattle with thirft. And Mofes cried unto the Lord faying, what fhall I do unto this people, they be almoft ready to ftone me.* Finding no flefh meat in the wildernefs, they again repented that they had

had left Egypt, Num. xi. 4. *They wept saying, Who shall give us flesh to eat. We remember the fish that we did eat freely in Egypt, the cucumbers and the melons, the leeks, the onions, and the garlic; but now is our soul dried away. There is nothing at all but this manna before our eyes.*

On the unfavourable report of the spies, who had been sent to explore the land of Canaan, we read, Num. xiv. 2. *All the children of Israel murmured against Moses and against Aaron, and the whole congregation said unto them, Would God that we had died in the land of Egypt, or would God that we had died in the wilderness; and wherefore hath the Lord brought us unto this land to fall by the sword, that our wives and our children should be a prey. Were it not better for us to return to Egypt.* Again, when they wanted water, after passing forty years in the wilderness, and been maintained by miracle all that time, we read, chap. xx. 2. *they gathered themselves together against Moses, and against Aaron, and the people chode with Moses, and the people said, Would God we had died when*

our

our brethren died before the Lord, and why have ye brought up the congregation of the Lord into this wilderness, that we and our cattle should die there; and wherefore have ye made us come up out of Egypt, to bring us to this evil place? It is not a place of seed, or of figs, or vines, or pomegranates, neither is there any water to drink. Lastly, When Arad the Canaanite fell upon them, and took some prisoners, we read, Numb. xxi. 4. *the souls of the people were much discouraged, because of the way, and the people spake against God and against Moses, Wherefore have ye brought us up out of Egypt, to die in the wilderness; for there is no bread, neither is there any water, and our soul loatheth this light bread.*

As to the religion which Moses prescribed to this people, there is the most abundant and indisputable evidence of their having been very far indeed from having had any predilection for it. On the contrary, they from the first discovered a dislike for it, and took every opportunity of deserting it, and revolting to the more alluring

luring rites of the neighbouring nations; and such as, no doubt, they had been accustomed to, and been fond of, in Egypt. But as this is a subject of the greatest importance, I shall defer enlarging upon it to the next opportunity.

DISCOURSE X.

The evidence of the Mosaic and Christian Religions.

PART II.

God, who, at sundry times, and in divers manners, spake in time past unto the fathers, by the prophets, hath, in these last days, spoken unto us by his son.

HEB. i. 1--2.

IN my last Discourse, I observed that the only proper evidence of divine revelation, is the exhibition of something to which divine power alone is equal, or proper *miracles*, and that these, not being analogous to common events, are, on that account, improbable, *a priori*, and therefore require more definite evidence, though there is nothing that is possible in itself, but may be proved to have taken place by human

human testimony. And I farther observed, that all that the most sceptical persons could require in the case, were the following circumstances, viz. that the miracles must be in sufficient number, and also exhibited so long, as to afford sufficient opportunity to consider and examine them. They must be on so large a scale, or otherwise of such a nature, as to exclude all suspicion of trick and imposition; they must be exhibited before persons who had no previous disposition to expect or believe them; a great degree of attention must be excited to them at the time, and a sufficient number of persons must be interested to ascertain their reality, while the events were recent; the history of them must be coeval with the events, and the belief of them must have produced a lasting effect.

Three of the first mentioned of these circumstances I have already shewn are found in the miracles recorded in the scriptures, and with respect to the next, I have shewn that the Hebrew nation was
sufficiently

sufficiently indisposed to believe the divine mission of Moses in general, and I shall proceed to show that they were more particularly indisposed to receive the *religion* which he presented to them, and which it was the great object of all the miracles to establish. So far, I have observed, were they from being predisposed to receive and embrace it, that from the very first they discovered a dislike of it, and took every opportunity of deserting it, and revolting to the more alluring rites of the neighbouring nations, and this disposition continued more than a thousand years.

Upon Moses's staying in the mount longer than the people expected, and thinking they should hear no more of him (for he had been absent forty days, and where he could not find any sustenance) we read Ex. xxxii. 1. *the people gathered themselves together unto Aaron, and said unto him, Up make us gods that shall go before us. For as for this Moses, the man that brought us up out of the land of Egypt, we wot not what is become of him.* After this, they made a golden calf, built
an

an altar before it, offered burnt offerings, and peace offerings, when the *people sat down to eat and drink, and rose up to play,* no doubt in the licentious manner in which the religious festivals of the Egyptians were conducted.

A severe judgment, and the return of Moses, brought them back to the new religion. But after they had passed forty years in the wilderness, in which they had no opportunity of shewing their disposition, on coming into the neighbourhood of the Moabites and Medianites, we read Numb. xxv. 1. *the people began to commit whoredom with the daughters of Moab, and they called the people to the sacrifices of their gods, and the people did eat, and bowed down to their gods, and Israel joined himself unto Baal Peor.* Another heavy judgment recovered them from this defection, but it is not probable that any reasoning, or expostulation, would have done it.

The miraculous passage of the river Jordan, the falling down of the walls of Jericho, and their conquering the warlike inhabitants of Canaan, devoted to the worship

ship of idols, satisfied the Israelites that their God was superior to the gods of that country, and therefore we read Josh. xxiv. 31. that *Israel served the Lord all the days of Joshua, and all the days of the elders who outlived Joshua, who had known all the works of the Lord, that he had done for Israel.* But the very next generation shewed a different disposition. For we read Jud. ii. 10. *when that generation was gathered to their fathers, there arose another generation after them, which knew not the Lord, nor yet the works which he had done for Israel; and the children of Israel did evil in the sight of the Lord, and served Baalim, and they forsook the Lord god of their fathers, who brought them out of the land of Egypt, and followed other gods, of the gods of the people who were round about them, and bowed themselves unto them, and provoked the Lord to anger, and they forsook the Lord, and served Baal and Ashtaroth.*

The history of this people, till the time of Samuel, is nothing but a repetition of revolts, and punishments for them, by the invasion and oppression of some neighbouring

ing nation. *When they repented,* as we read Jud. ii. 16. *the Lord raised up judges, who delivered them out of the hand of those that spoiled them, and yet they would not hearken unto their judges; but they went a whoring after other gods, and bowed themselves unto them. They turned quickly out of the way which their fathers walked in, obeying the commandments of the Lord; but they did not so. And when the Lord raised them up judges, then was the Lord with the judge, and delivered them out of the hand of their enemies, all the days of the judge. And it came to pass when that judge was dead, that they returned and corrupted themselves more than their fathers, in following other gods, to serve them, and to bow down unto them. They ceased not from their own doings, and from their stubborn way. And the anger of the Lord was hot against Israel, and he said, Because this people has transgressed my covenant, which I commanded their fathers, and have not hearkened unto my voice, I also will not henceforth drive out any from before them, of the nations which Joshua left when he died, that through them I may prove Israel, whether they will keep the way of the Lord, to walk therein, as their fathers did keep it, or not.*

For

For thefe revolts they were reduced into fervitude, firft by Cuſhan-riſhathaim, king of Mefopotamia, from whofe power they were refcued by Othniel, then by the king of Moab, from whom they were delivered by Ehud; then by the Philiftines, when they were delivered by Shamgar. From Jabin king of Canaan, they were delivered by Deborah and Barak; from the Midianites by Gideon, from the Ammonites by Jephtha, from the Philiftines a fecond time, in part by Samfon, but more completely by Saul and David, under whom the worſhip of Jehovah was rendered triumphant; and in that ftate it continued till the latter end of the reign of Solomon, when he had the weaknefs not only to indulge his wives, taken from the neighbouring nations, in the worſhip of the gods of their refpective countries, but to join them in it.

Notwithſtanding the very flouriſhing ftate of the affairs of the Ifraelites in the reigns of David and Solomon, which was always in thofe days, and long afterwards, afcribed ascribed to the power of the gods that they worshipped, the ten tribes which revolted from the house of David, revolted also from the religion of Moses, at first indeed by only setting up images at Dan and Bethel, in honour of the true God, but afterwards, and especially in the reign of Ahab, worshipping Baal, and all the host of heaven. And though by the judgment of a three years drought, in which they found that the worship of Baal could give them no relief, and the seasonable miracle of Elijah at mount Carmel, they were recovered, at least for some time, from this species of idolatry, they continued to worship the calves at Dan and Bethel, till their captivity by the Assyrians; when they became so mixed and incorporated with other nations, as not to be distinguished; and whether they be now discovered or not, they are without any badge of their antient religion, to which it is evident they never discovered any attachment.

The

The kingdom of Judah having the temple within its limits, and other advantages, adhered better to the worſhip of the true God, but with ſeveral remarkable departures from it, as in the reign of Rehoboam the ſon of Solomon, who as we read, 2 Chron. xii. 1. *forſook the law of the Lord, and all Iſrael with him*; in that of Jehoram, the ſon of Jehoſaphat, of Ahaziah, of Joaſh, after the death of the pious high-prieſt Jehoiada, of Ahaz, of Manaſſeh, who made uſe of the temple itſelf, for the worſhip of other gods; and of Amon, Jehoiakim, and Zedekiah, whoſe reign was put an end to by Nebuchadnezzar taking Jeruſalem, deſtroying the temple, and carrying the people into captivity to Babylon.

If this hiſtory, of which I have only given a faint outline, do not ſupply ſufficient and redundant evidence of the diſlike which the Iſraelites had to the inſtitutions of Moſes, and conſequently of the reluctance with which they muſt have received, and conformed to them, nothing can

can be proved concerning the difpofition and turn of thinking of any people whatever. It cannot, therefore, be denied, that all the miracles wrought to eftablifh this religion, and confirm them in it, may be confidered as exhibited before enemies, perfons predifpofed not to receive, but to cavil at, and reject it. This is the more remarkable, as there is no other inftance in all hiftory, of any nation voluntarily abandoning the religion of their anceftors till the promulgation of Chriftianity, before which they all gradually difappeared, like clouds before the fun.

The Babylonifh captivity having been foretold, together with its exact duration, by the Hebrew prophets, and the overthrow of Babylon, famous for its addictednefs to idol worfhip, effectually cured thofe of the Jews who returned to their own country, and no doubt many others, of any difpofition to the worfhip of foreign gods, but they were not by this means the more, but in fact, the lefs difpofed to receive the miracles of Jefus. Indeed

Indeed it is evident that they had not been previously disposed to believe any miracles. For before the appearance of Jesus, there had been no pretensions to a power of working miracles in the country, a circumstance which by no means agrees with the charge commonly advanced against the Jews as a credulous people. It is well known, however, that when Jesus appeared, the nation in general, then in a state of subjection to the Romans, a situation which they ill brooked, were in anxious expectation of the appearance of the Messiah announced by their prophets, and who they took for granted, was immediately to assume the character of a temporal prince, rescue them from their subjection to the Romans, and give them the dominion of the whole world; and certainly to this character that of Jesus bore no resemblance.

Besides, Jesus's free censure of the priests, and leading men in the nation, soon made them his most bitter enemies. They, seeing, that whatever he was, *they* had

had nothing to expect from *him*, spared no pains to destroy him, and did not rest till they had actually compassed his death. All the miracles of Jesus, therefore, were exhibited before enemies. Even the most virtuous and best disposed of the Jews were as much attached to the idea of a temporal prince, for their Messiah, as any of their countrymen, so that even this part of the nation must have been exceedingly indisposed to receive Jesus in that character; and when they did it, it was with the idea that, though he did not assume it *then*, he would at some future time. Even after his resurrection, the apostles asked him whether he would *at that time restore the kingdom to Israel*, Acts i. 6. and their minds were not fully enlightened on this subject till after the descent of the Holy Spirit on the day of Pentecost.

The resurrection of Jesus, though the most pleasing event to all his disciples, was a thing of which, it it is evident, they had no expectation after his death, so that it was not without the greatest difficulty, and

and the most undeniable evidence, that of their own senses, that they were brought to believe it. The manner in which the apostle Thomas expressed his incredulity on the subject, is very remarkable. He was not present at the first appearance of Jesus, and when the others, as we read, John xx. 25, said unto him, *We have seen the Lord*, he said unto them, *Except I see in his hands the prints of his nails, and put my finger into the print of the nails, and thrust my hand into his side, I will not believe.* In this particular, however, Jesus, the next time that he appeared to his disciples, gave him the satisfaction that he demanded. For *he said to Thomas, Reach hither thy finger, and behold my hands, and reach hither thy hand, and thrust it into my side, and be not faithless, but believing.* No doubt all the rest of the apostles were at first, in the same state of mind with respect to this event. In this case, therefore, even the disciples of Christ, may be considered as prejudiced against the reception of this great miracle, and are by no means to be chargeable with credulity.

The apostles, and all the first preachers of christianity, were in the same situation with respect to the great body of the Jews, that Jesus had been in before them; and nothing could be more violent than the opposition they actually met with. One of the most remarkable conversions, was that of Paul, and in the history of it, we see, in the strongest light, the extreme prejudice which even the better kind of Jews, entertained against christianity. Nothing less than the appearance of Jesus himself, was able to effect his conversion. Of the miraculous circumstances attending this conversion, his chosen companions, men who, no doubt, were actuated with as much zeal as himself, against the new religion, and who probably continued enemies to it, were witnesses, and to them he afterwards appealed for what they saw and heard, viz. a light surpassing that of the sun at noon-day; and the sound of a voice, though they did not distinguish the words, that were directed to him.

As

As to the Gentiles, nothing can be imagined more unpromising than the mission of the apostles to them. The pride of the Jews, and the contempt with which they treated other nations, had given rise, as was natural, to an equal degree of hatred and contempt on their side; so that nothing coming from a *Jew*, was at all likely to be favourably attended to by them. The heathens in general, and the Greeks and Romans in particular, were most strongly attached to the rites of their religions, and thought the observance of them necessary to the prosperity of their several states. The gravest magistrates dreaded the discontinuance of them, and the profligate and licentious among the heathens, gave a loose, as I have shewn, under the sanction of religion, to their favourite vicious propensities, in the greatest latitude. The learned and philosophical among the heathens, looked with the greatest contempt on the plainness and want of eloquence, in the apostles, and other preachers of christianity. In this state of things, then, was it to be expected

expected that the heathen world in general, would be at all credulous, with respect to miracles wrought by such men. On the contrary, the preachers of christianity, had nothing to expect but the extreme of incredulity. In fact, great numbers could not be brought to give the least attention to any thing that was reported concerning them, or to look into any of their books. Dr. Lardner observes, that it is pretty evident that even Pliny, who gave the emperor Trajan an account of his proceedings against the Christians, and his examination of them, when they were brought before his tribunal, (and he was a man of letters) had not read any of the books of the New Testament, or any other writings of Christians, which were unquestionably extant. If, therefore, the new religion did make its way, it must have been against every possible disadvantage, and history shews that this was the case.

5. In order to secure credit to accounts of miracles, there must be both *opportunity*, and *motive*, for examining into the truth of

of the facts. Now, the miracles being numerous, a circumftance on which I have already enlarged, gives opportunity for examination; fo alfo does that of their continuance fome fpace of time, and this was the cafe with refpect to many, I may fay almoft all the miracles, which have been already mentioned, particularly the feveral plagues of Egypt, none of which were momentary appearances, but all were of fome days continuance. Such, alfo, was the paffage through the red fea, and the river Jordan, one of which took up a whole night, and the other a whole day. The fame was the cafe with refpect to the delivery of the ten commandments from mount Sinai, but more efpecially the miracle of the manna, and the pillar of cloud and fire, which conuued forty years.

The cures performed by Jefus, though inftantaneous, produced lafting effects, efpecially his raifing of the dead, as of Lazarus, which, as we read, excited much curiofity to fee him afterwards. Our Saviour's own appearance after his refurrection, was not like

like that of an apparition in the night, but always in the day time, and frequently repeated. His firſt appearance was when his diſciples had no expectation of any ſuch thing, ſo that they could not have been deceived by their imaginations, and afterwards by particular appointment, ſo that they had time to recollect themſelves, and to procure any kind of ſatisfaction that they wanted; and this continued the ſpace of forty days before his aſcenſion, which appears to have been leiſurely, ſo that they who were preſent ſtood gazing ſome time, while they ſaw him go above the clouds. He did not leave them in a private manner, and go they knew not whither.

But the beſt opportunity for examining the truth of any facts, is when ſome perſons aſſert, and others deny them, and when they are at the ſame time much intereſted in the event of the inquiry, as by having what is moſt dear to them depending upon it. And this was remarkably the caſe with reſpect to the reſurrection of Jeſus. With reſpect to his miracles, and alſo

also those of the apostles, there does not appear to have been any dispute about them, by those who were then in the country. They only ascribed them to a false cause. But Jesus not appearing to all persons after his resurrection, and especially not to his enemies, but only to his friends, though in numbers abundantly sufficient for the purpose, his enemies denied *that* fact.

The fact, however, was of so very important a nature, that we cannot doubt but that it must have been thoroughly investigated, much more so than any other fact in all history, because infinitely more depended upon it, than upon any other fact whatever. For in a very short time such was the rage of the rulers of the Jews against the rising sect, that not only were the peace, and the property, but the lives of the Christians at stake, and these they would not give up for an idle tale. At the same time their persecutors, who were the men in power, stimulated by hatred and opposition, would leave nothing untried to refute the story. This state of things began immediately after

after the refurrection of Jefus, and continued about three hundred years, during all which time the Chriftians, though expofed to grevious perfecution, kept increafing in number, till at the time that Conftantine was advanced to the empire, it was not only fafe, but advantageous to him to declare himfelf a Chriftian. We may therefore be fatisfied, that the great fact of the refurrection of Jefus, on which the truth of chriftianity more particularly depends, underwent a more thorough inveftigation than any other fact in hiftory.

This rigorous fcrutiny began while the event was recent, and when there was, accordingly, the beft opportunity of examining into its truth or falfehood. Paul, who fays that Jefus at one time appeared to more than five hundred perfons, fays that the greater part of them were then living, and of courfe liable to be interrogated on the fubject. Now, had Jefus appeared as publicly after his crucifixion as he did before, and of courfe the whole Jewifh nation had become Chriftians, we fhould should now have been without this most satisfactory argument for the truth of the fact.

It would, in this case, have been said, that the Jews, always a credulous nation, (though this has appeared to have been the reverse of the truth) had for some reason or other, which it is now impossible to ascertain, changed their religion, or rather made some addition to what they professed before, and that as no person objected to it at the time, there is no evidence now before us that the facts, or reasons, on which it was founded, were properly scrutinized; and that it is impossible to do it at this distance. And thus christianity might have spread no farther than Judaism.

6. To ensure the credibility of miracles, it must appear that the accounts of of them were written while the facts were recent, so that an appeal might be made to living witnesses, and this was never in antient times questioned with respect to the principal books of the Old or the New Testament.

Teftament. Befides, the internal evidence of the books afcribed to Mofes, having been written by him, or by fome perfon under his direction, which to every impartial reader of them, muft appear ftronger than the evidence of any other books having been written by any other perfons, whofe names they bear, the fact was never doubted by the Hebrew nation, the only proper witneffes in the cafe, from the earlieft times to the prefent; and nothing ftronger than this can be faid in favour of the authenticity of any writings whatever.

This argument is peculiarly ftrong with refpect to the writings of Mofes, on account of the reluctance with which thofe writings, and the whole hiftory of that nation, fhows, that they received his inftructions. If thofe of the Ifraelites who were addicted to the religious rites of the neighbouring nations, and who were frequently the majority of the people, could have fhewn that the books afcribed to Mofes, were not written by him, or by by his authority, would they not have done it, and thereby have had the beft reafon for continuing in the religion they preferred? And what motive could any man have to forge books which would be fure to give the greateft offence, and could not fail to be rejected with contempt and indignation?

The account of the death of Mofes in the laft chapter of the book of Deuteronomy, could not have been written by himfelf. But what was more natural, than for fome perfon of eminence, acquainted with the fact, perhaps Jofhua, or the high prieft at the time, adding this account to the writings of Mofes, and its being afterwards annexed to them. Alfo, notes by way of explanation of certain paffages, were, no doubt, firft inferted in the margin, as has been the cafe with many antient books, and afterwards added by tranfcribers, in the text. But fuch circumftances as thefe are never thought to affect the genuinenefs of any antient writings. Judicious criticifm eafily diftinguifhes the cafual additions, from the original text.

The

The internal evidence of the authenticity of the writings of Moses is peculiarly strong. No other than a person actually present at the transactions could have related them in the manner in which we find his narratives written, with so many particulars of persons, times, and places, and with so natural an account of the impression that was made on the minds of men by the events that he relates*.

---

* That additions may be made to books, and even such as the writers disapprove of, we have a remarkable instance of in the first part of Mr. *Paine's Age of Reason*. In the second part just published in this city, he says, p. 84. "The former part of the *Age of Reason* has not been published two years, and there is already an expression in it that is not mine. The expression is, *The book of Luke was carried by a majority of one vote only*. It may be true, but it is not I that have said it. Some person, who might know of that circumstance, has added it in a note at the bottom of the page of some of the editions, printed either in England or in America, and the printers, after that have erected it into the body of the work, and made me the author of it. If this has happened within such a short space of time, notwithstanding the aid of printing, which prevents the alteration of copies individually, what may not have happened in a much greater length of time, where there was no printing." He adds, "and when any man who would write, could make a written copy, and call it an original by Matthew, Mark, Luke, or John." But though this might easily happen with respect to slight circumstances, according with the rest of a book

It should also be considered, that books were not forged till men were practised in the art of writing, and many books had been written, so that considerable advances had been made in the art of composition and of criticism. We may therefore conclude with certainty, that the books ascribed to Moses, which are unquestionably of as great antiquity as any in the world, except perhaps the book of Job, and a very few others mentioned by Moses, are no forgeries. Otherwise, the art of forging historical writings, the most difficult of all others, was brought to the greatest perfection all at once, a supposition that cannot be admitted. Indeed, there does not appear to have been the

a book, well known to exist, the fabrication of *whole books*, which were not known to exist at all, and imposing them on the world, when the belief of their contents drew after it the sacrifice of every thing dear to a man in life, and often of life itself, was not so easy.

The insertion Mr. Paine complains of, being a recent thing, and all the editions of his book not very numerous, may be traced to its author, and it behoves him, or his friends, to do it; but this cannot be done with respect to books written two or three thousand years ago.

least

least suspicion of the forgery of any books till after the time in which all those of the Old Testament are well known to have been extant. There cannot, therefore, be any reasonable doubt but that the books ascribed not only to Moses, but those to the prophets Isaiah, Jeremiah, Ezekiel, and Daniel, are genuine, except so far as they may have suffered by transcribers.

The objection of Porphyry to the book of Daniel, that it was written after the time of Antiochus Epiphanes (for which it does not appear that he had any other evidence than the exact fulfilment of some part of his prophecies in the events) is certainly not to be regarded. It can derive no more weight from the time in which he wrote, than if it had been first advanced at this day, because it is only an argument from what appears on the face of the book itself, which is before us, as it was before him. And at that time the evidence of the whole Jewish nation, which had always recieved that book, and in fact that of the Samaritans too, who,

as

as far as appears, never objected to it, was againſt him.

In is moreover ſelf evident, and indeed never was denied, that the books of the Old Teſtament were written by different perſons, and at different times. That any number of them ſhould have been written by the ſame perſon, or a combination of perſons, and impoſed upon a whole nation as written in former times, and by different perſons in thoſe times (eſpecially conſidering the many ungrateful truths contained in theſe books) is an hypotheſis which no perſon will ſay is even poſſible. Conſequently, the references to particular books from others, may ſafely be admitted as an evidence of their genuineneſs, which is the principal argument for the age, and the genuineneſs, of all other antient writings. Now it appears from the books of Kings and Chronicles, that Iſaiah lived in the time of Hezekiah, and from the ſame that Jeremiah lived at the time of the ſiege of Jeruſalem by Nebuchadnezzar, which is abundantly evident from his own writings.

ings. The narrative part of the book of Jeremiah is remarkably circumstantial, so as to render its internal evidence unquestionable. I do not even think it possible for any person of the least degree of judgment in these matters, to entertain a suspicion of its being a forgery of a later time. Jeremiah is also mentioned in the book of Daniel. Such too is the internal evidence for the genuineness of the book of Ezekiel who makes mention of Daniel, of that of Daniel too, and of all the other prophetical books, in which there is any mention of or allusion to historical facts.

A circumstance which adds to the authenticity of the writings of Moses, is, that the solemn customs and religious rites of the Jews, such as their public festivals, and especially the observance of the passover, were coeval with them, so that they, as it were, vouch for each other. The passover was a solemn custom, expressly instituted, in commemoration of the deliverance of the Israelites from their bondage in Egypt, and began to be observed at the

the very time; fo that accompanied as it is with the written account of it, it is the moft authentic of all records. No other event in hiftory, is fo fully authenticated as this, except that of the death of Chrift, by a fimilar rite, viz. that of the Lord's Supper.

The early exiftence of the fect of the Samaritans affords a proof that the books of Mofes have not undergone any material alteration from before the time of the Babylonifh captivity. If Ezra, who collected the books after that event, had made any material alteration in them, the Samaritans, who were then extremely hoftile to him, and to all who refided and worfhipped at Jerufalem, would, no doubt, have expofed it. But in our Saviour's time, they had the fame refpect for the books of Mofes, that the Jews themfelves ever had; and this they have at this very day. It is probable too, that they had the fame refpect for the writings of the prophets, though they did not make ufe of them in their religious worfhip, and therefore had no copies of them; for they appear (John iv. 25.) to have expected a Messiah, of whom there is no account, but in the writings of the prophets.

There is similar evidence, internal and external, that the principal books of the New Testament, by which I mean the historical ones, and also that the epistles of Paul, were written while the events were recent, and that they were received as such, by those who were most interested in their contents. This was never questioned by any unbeliever, within several hundred years of the time of their publication. It was admitted by Celsus, and the emperor Julian, both of whom wrote against christianity, and did not even question the truth of the greater part of the miracles recorded in them. And yet Mr. Paine, ignorant of this, asserts in the second part of his *Age of Reason*, p. 83. that ' there is not the least shadow ' of evidence, who the persons were that ' wrote the books ascribed to Matthew, ' Mark, Luke or John, that none of the ' books of the New Testament, were written

' ten by the men called apoftles, and that
' there was no fuch book as the *New*
' *Teftament*, till more than three hundred
' years after the time that Chrift is faid to
' have lived,' that is about the time of
Conftantine. On this fuppofition how ftu-
pendous a miracle, muft have been the
overthrow of heathenifm, and the general
reception of Chriftianity, in the Roman
empire at that period. This would have
been far more extraordinary, than all the
miracles recorded in the fcriptures. But to
this obvious confequence of his hypothefis,
Mr. Paine had certainly given no attention.
In the fame manner, he alone, of all unbelievers, fays that none of the books of
the Old Teftament, were written before
the Babylonifh captivity. He might with
as much plaufibility, fay that the whole
Bible was a publication of the laft century.

Facts fo interefting to thoufands, recorded in this manner, in books univerfally
received as genuine, by thofe who muft
have known whether they were fo or not,
have the teftimony not of the writers only,

but

but of the age in which they were publiſhed. In reality, the authenticity of the facts recorded in the New Teſtament, does not at all depend on the authenticity of the books; for chriſtianity exiſted, and had made a conſiderable ſpread, long before any of the books were written. The books were not the *cauſe*, but the *effect*, of the belief of it. The authors of theſe books were not writers by profeſſion, but only wrote when neceſſity, in a manner, called for them, that is, when thoſe who were beſt acquainted with the facts, were about to quit the ſtage, and other perſons ſolicited their teſtimony to them; and this was not till about thirty years after the death of Chriſt, when there were Chriſtians in all parts of the Roman empire. The epiſtles of Paul were written before that time; and in them we find alluſions to the ſtate of things, at the time of his writing, and their exact correſpondence to the hiſtory, would be a ſtrong confirmation of it, if ſuch confirmation were wanting.

7. In the laſt place, the miracles recorded in the ſcriptures, produced a great and permanent effect, correſponding to their extraordinary nature; which abundantly proves that they were believed by thoſe before whom they were exhibited, or who had an opportunity of informing themſelves concerning them. Thoſe which were wrought in Egypt, effected the deliverance of the Iſraelites, from their ſtate of ſervitude in that country, though they were then the moſt unwarlike, and their maſters perhaps the moſt warlike people in the world, and exceedingly deſirous to detain them.

But what was much more than this, addicted as the Iſraelites were to the religious rites of the Egyptians, and fond of ſimilar rites, in the religions of all the neighbouring nations, ſuch an impreſſion was made upon them by the miracles wrought in their favour, and eſpecially the delivery of the law from mount Sinai, that they actually adopted a very complex ſyſtem of religion, the reverſe of any thing of
the

the kind, to which they had been accuſtomed, and which they were far from being prediſpoſed to like, or to receive; and in all their apoſtacies afterwards, it does not appear that they ever diſbelieved the facts. They only thought they might join the worſhip of other gods with that of their own, at leaſt with the acknowledgment of the truth of their own, which was then the prevailing ſentiment of all nations, who ſcrupled not to admit the pretenſions of other gods along with their own, and to join in their worſhip, eſpecially in the countries ſuppoſed to be under their immediate protection, which was the caſe with reſpect to the modes of worſhip, to which the Iſraelites ſo often revolted. On the other hand, it appears, that the neighbouring nations entertained the greateſt reſpect for the God, and the religion, of the Iſraelites, though they did not conform to it. This was the caſe with the Philiſtines, the Syrians, the Babylonians, and the Perſians; as it would be eaſy to ſhew by facts in their hiſtory.

The

The effect produced by the miracles recorded in the New Testament was still, more evident, because more extensive. Many thousands of the Jews became converts to christianity on its first promulgation, notwithstanding their extreme aversion to receive any scheme of the kind, from their attachment to their antient religion, which they thought to be incompatible with the new, especially after the admission of the Gentiles into the christian church. From this time, indeed, Jewish converts were much less numerous than before, this circumstance shocking their prejudices in a peculiar manner. Many of those who were already christians were exceedingly offended at it.

But the most extensive effect of the miracles wrought by Christ and the apostles was the reception of christianity by the Gentiles, attached as they were to the rites of their antient religions, which were enforced by the laws, and recommended by all the learning and philosophy of the age, and notwithstanding the preachers

preachers of the gospel laboured under the greatest disadvantages, being Jews, generally illiterate, and destitute of any talent of public speaking or writing, and having nothing to promise their converts but happiness in another world, with persecution in this. Yet with all these disadvantages, in a reasonable space of time, and exceedingly short, considering the magnitude of the event, a complete revolution was effected in all the Roman empire, which at that time comprehended almost all the civilized part of the world; the heathen religion which had prevailed from time immemorial, being every where discredited, and new rites and customs the reverse of them, adopted.

No revolution produced by force of arms can be compared to this, which was effected without arms, by the mere force of truth, the evidence of which must have been invincibly strong to have prevailed as it did. Incredulous as unbelievers now are, thousands, as incredulous as they, and more interested than they can be, be, to discredit christianity, became converts to it; and therefore, though they now give little attention to the evidence, which does not force itself upon them, as it did upon those who lived nearer to the time of the transactions, had they lived in those times, they might, with the same indisposition to this religion, have been unable to resist the evidence with which the publication of it was accompanied. To do themselves and the question justice, they should put themselves in the place of their predecessors, consider how the evidence stood in their time, what was then objected to christianity by men as quicksighted and as prejudiced as themselves, and say whether they would abide by their objections. They certainly would not, because they go upon quite different principles, and such as all modern unbelievers would reject, and even with more contempt, than they reject christianity. Will they now ascribe the miracles of Christ and his apostles to the power of magic?

The

The state of the argument very near to the promulgation of christianity is easily ascertained, and certainly ought to be particularly attended to. All that the antient unbelievers objected to christianity, has been carefully collected by Dr. Lardner, in his excellent work on *Jewish and Heathen Testimonies*, and a summary view of the whole may be seen in the second part of my *Letters to a Philosophical Unbeliever*. But *inattention*, joined to *aversion*, to any subject will account for any degree of incredulity with respect to it. Several among the most considerable unbelievers in France will not admit that there ever was any such person as Jesus Christ; when with more reason they might say there were never such persons as Alexander the Great, or Julius Cæsar.

But the greatest effect produced by the miracles recorded in the New Testament, an effect far more difficult to be accomplished than any change of *opinion*, or speculative principles, is from vice to virtue, which, however, was produced in thousands.

thousands. For this we have the testimony of all history. *Be not deceived*, says the apostle Paul, 1 Corin. vi. 9, *neither fornicators, nor idolaters, nor adulterers, nor effeminate, nor abusers of themselves with mankind, nor thieves, nor covetous, nor drunkards, nor revilers, nor extortioners, shall inherit the kingdom of God. And such were some of you. But ye are washed, but ye are sanctified, but ye are justified in the name of the Lord Jesus, and by the spirit of our God*, that is by the power of christianity and its evidences, commonly called the gift of the spirit.

If we compare the evidence of the miracles recorded in the scriptures with that of any that are mentioned by heathen writers, we shall soon be convinced of the superiority of that of the former. Mr. Hume says, that the cure of the blind and the lame man, said by Tacitus and Suetonius to have been performed by the emperor Vespasian, at Alexandria, is 'one of ' the best attested of any in profane history,' and he meant, I doubt not, in any history.
But

But this boasted miracle is not related by any person who was present. The oldest account we have of it being written about thirty years after the event. It was not exhibited before enemies. Such cures as these might easily have been pretended by persons prepared beforehand. The heathens were very credulous with respect to things of this kind, and the report of these might be very useful to procure credit to the new emperor. There was no scrutiny into the truth of the fact at the time. Indeed such scrutiny would have been discountenanced, and not have been very safe. And lastly, the pretended miracles do not appear to have produced any effect. It is even almost certain, that the historians themselves did not believe them. What then must have been the force of prejudice in a man who could think that these miracles were better attested than those of the scriptures?

Such, my brethren, is the outline, for it is nothing more, of the evidence of the credibility of the miracles recorded in the Old

Old and New Teftament. It is readily acknowledged, that the great truths to be proved by them, have nothing in them incredible, but on the contrary, are of fuch a nature as to be both defirable in themfelves, and probable, *a priori* (confidering the ftate of vice and igorance in which the world was involved, when deftitute of that light, and confidering the benevolence of our common parent, who indeed permits all evils, but only for a time, and makes them fubfervient to good) they yet require much ftronger evidence than ordinary facts, in proportion to their want of analogy to fuch events as fall under our daily obfervation. But notwithftanding this, the evidence for them is abundantly fufficient for the purpofe. The miracles, as I have fhewn, were fufficiently numerous, they were performed on the largeft fcale, they were, from their nature, free from any fufpicion of trick and impofition, they were exhibited in the prefence of perfons the leaft predifpofed to believe them, or to be influenced by them; they were

were subjected to the most rigorous examination at the time, and while they were recent, the written accounts of them were of the same age with the events themselves, and they actually produced the most extraordinary effects; which proves that they were fully assented to at the time, by those who had the best opportunity of inquiring into the truth, and the strongest motives for doing so.

More than this it is not in the power of any person to require, and therefore it is all that is necessary to the most complete satisfaction. I mean of the candid and attentive.

For there is a state of mind in which no evidence can have any effect, as we see every day, and we must not expect that miracles will now be wrought for the conviction of any persons, and least of all miraculous changes in the dispositions of men's minds. Indeed, such miracles as those do not appear ever to have been wrought. All miracles were external, and the reflection on them produced its natural effect.

effect, on the minds of those who gave due attention to them; and who were suitably impressed with them.

As to the proper time for working miracles, and making this or that age the witnesses of them, and of course the vouchers of their reality to others, it is a question which we must acknowledge we are not able to answer. But neither does it concern us to answer it, any more than to assign a reason why it pleased the Divine Being to create the world, or men and other animals, at one time rather than another, or why he did not make more or fewer planets to attend the sun, &c. &c. Of every thing of this nature, he alone is the proper judge. It is enough for us if we be satisfied, on sufficient evidence, that miracles have been wrought at any time, and if we have been informed of the purpose for which they were wrought. If they were actually seen by others, though at ever so great a distance of time, they ought, in reason, to have the same effect as if seen by ourselves, and we are as inexcusable excufable, if we be not as much influenced by them. And if God has fpoken, it cannot be a matter of indifference, whether we will attend to his voice or not. In this cafe I may fay, after our Saviour, *He that hath ears to hear, let him hear.*

DISCOURSE XI.

The proof of Revealed Religion from Prophecy.

I have even from the beginning declared it unto thee. Before it came to pafs I fhewed it thee, left thou fhouldeft fay mine idol has done them, and my graven image, and my molten image, have commanded them.

ISAIAH. xlviii. 5.

THERE is not, perhaps, any thing more exclufively within the province of the Supreme Being than the foreknowledge of future events, depending on the volitions of men. For though all things future may be faid to exift in their caufes, which are prefent, thofe caufes are not apparent, and their operations and combinations, are fuch as no human intellect can trace; fo that to us they are as contingent, and uncertain, as if the caufes did not exift. They who know mankind in general, and even particular perfons, the beft, can only *conjecture* how they will act in given circumftances, and are often miftaken; but how they will act in *future time*, when it cannot be known in what circumftances they will then be, is what no man will pretend to, and this ftill lefs with refpect to perfons then unborn. A prediction of a future and diftant event, depending on the voluntary actions of men, has therefore the effect of a miracle of the moft indifputable kind. Now many fuch are recorded in the fcriptures, and confequently ought to be enumerated among the cleareft proofs of their divine authority, and of the truth of the religion they contain. For this reafon I fhall make them the fubject of this difcourfe, fhewing, from the circumftances of the predictions, that they are not liable to any juft fufpicion of impofture, that in this refpect they were the reverfe of the oracles of the heathens, and that they have been clearly verified by the events.

There

There were two ways in which the knowledge of future events was communicated to the Hebrews. One was by confulting the *oracle*, as it may be called, when anfwers to particular queftions were given to the high-prieft; and the other by prophets, who were raifed up from time to time to fpeak to the people in the name of God. I fhall confider the circumftances of both.

1. The regular method of confulting the divine oracle, called *inquiring of the Lord*, was by the chief magiftrate attending in the fanctuary along with the high-prieft in his proper veftments, directing him what queftions to put; when the anfwers were equally heard by them both. Thus when Jofhua was appointed to fucceed Mofes, it is faid, Num. xxvii. 26. *And he fhall ftand by Eleazar the prieft, who fhall afk council for him, after the judgment of Urim, before the Lord.* From this it is obvious, that it was not in the power of the high-prieft to impofe upon the country what he thought proper, as a divine oracle.

cle. It does not even appear that he ever went of his own accord to confult the oracle, but only when required to do fo by the civil magiftrate, who attended along with him, and heard the anfwer as well as himfelf. Of this we have feveral examples in the courfe of the fcripture hiftory. Indeed, it is evident from the whole hiftory of the Hebrews, that neither by this, nor by any other means, was it in the power of the priefts to acquire any more authority than was given them in the original conftitution.

If this had been the cafe, they would always have preferved their fuperiority over any occafional prophet, whofe claim to refpect interfered with theirs. How, for example, could it be fuppofed that the old high-prieft Eli would eafily have acquiefced in the divine communications made to the child Samuel, which contained the heavieft denunciations againft himfelf and his family? But inftead of contradicting them, though delivered by a mere child, he, with the greateft refignation, replied,

replied, *It is the Lord, let him do what seemeth him good.* Surely here was no priestcraft. Neither under the judges, nor under the kings, did any high-priest acquire the smallest addition to his civil power, or to his emolument.

2. The Hebrew oracle appears to have been accessible at all times alike; which was not the case with the oracles of Greece. That at Delphi could only be consulted during one particular month in the year, which was in the spring; and, as it should seem, only on a few stated days in that month. At other times, as we are informed, the greatest princes could not by any means obtain an answer. This certainly gave the heathen priests a better opportunity of knowing what questions were likely to be proposed, and of being prepared with the answers.

3. No expence attended the consultation of the Hebrew oracle, so that the priests could not derive any emolument from it; whereas the consulting of the Grecian oracles was so very expensive, on account of

the

the sacrifices that were to be offered, and the presents that were expected on the occasion, that only the great and the wealthy could have access to them. The riches of which the temple of Delphi was possessed, from the donations of opulent princes, such as Cræsus king of Lydia, were immense; but it does not appear that either the tabernacle, or the temple, of the Israelites, gained any thing by this means.

4. Nothing was done to overawe the persons who consulted the Hebrew oracle; or to affect their imaginations, so as to prepare them to receive whatever answers the priest, who directed the oracle, might suggest; which was the case more or less, with all the Grecian oracles, but especially that of Trophonius. The person who consulted this oracle went into a cavern, and and not immediately, on his presenting himself, but after much solemn prepartion.*

---

* In this time all his food was the remains of sacrifices, and he was not permitted to bathe. After this he was washed by boys of thirteen years of age, and when this was done, he drank of two waters, one of oblivion, and the other of remembrance, and before he entered the cavern he was brought to

Such were the marks of terror and melancholy with which persons usually came out of this cavern, that when any person was unusually dejected, they said he looked as if he had been consulting the oracle of Trophonius.

5. The answer of the Hebrew oracle was always delivered in an articulate voice, which was not liable to misconstruction; whereas all the Grecian oracles, except that of Apollo, gave their answers in a different manner, as by dreams, the flight of

---

to a certain statue, before which he made some prayers. Being then conducted to the mouth of the cavern, he descended by a ladder, which he brought with him for the purpose. At the bottom of this descent he came to a narrow passage, through which he was required to thrust himself with his feet foremost; but during this he was forcibly dragged along till he came to the place where he was to wait for his answer, which was sometimes given in words, and sometimes only by appearances of various kinds. After this, which sometimes detained him more than a day, he returned through the narrow passage in the same manner as before, viz. with his feet foremost. The priests then placed him on a kind of throne, and inquired of him what he had heard or seen, and they made the report to others, who then carried him, commonly in a state of stupefaction, with terror and astonishment, to the chapel of good genius, and of

good

of birds, or the entrails of beasts, &c. &c. At Pheræ, a city of Achaia, there was an oracle of Mercury, where the person who consulted it, after making the proper sacrifices and offerings, proposed his question; and in order to get an answer to it, walked with his ears stopped by his hands, through the market-place, and then removing them, took the first words that he happened to hear for the answer of the oracle. At another oracle in Achaia, the answer was given by throwing dice, inscribed with particular characters, which the priests interpreted. At another place in

good fortune, where after some time he recovered his senses and cheerfulness. This account is given by Pausanias, an eminent Greek writer, who says that he had himself consulted this oracle.

Another person, of whom Plutarch gives an account, was detained two days and nights in this cavern, and when he came out he gave an account of many strange sights that he had seen, and frightful sounds that he had heard, resembling the yellings and howlings of wild beasts, as well as a discourse that was delivered to him. Who does not see that it was in the power of the priests to conduct all this machinery just as they pleased, taking advantage of the terror which was unavoidable in these circumstances?

in the same country, the answer of the oracle, which was only given to questions relating to sickness, was given by letting down a mirror into a fountain, and observing the figures and images on its surface.

6. There was no ambiguity in the answer given by the Hebrew oracle. It was always plain and direct, not capable of two constructions, of which the priests might avail themselves on comparing it with the event, as was remarkably the case with respect to many of the answers returned by the Grecian oracles, even that of Apollo at Delphi, which, however, was celebrated for the comparative perspicuity of its answers. Two of these answers are particularly mentioned by Herodotus.

When the Lacedemonians inquired of the oracle whether they should succeed in their attempt to conquer all Arcadia, they received for answer, they should not, but that he would give them *Tegea*, which

was

was very fruitful, and which they should measure with a line. On this they had no doubt but that they should gain the possession of it; but being defeated in battle, many of the Lacedemonians were made prisoners, and compelled to cultivate the ground for their conquerors; and in doing this, they made use of a line to measure it, which was deemed to be a fulfilment of the oracle. Again, when Cræsus consulted the same oracle, on his engaging in a war with Cyrus, he received for answer, that if he did, he should overturn a great empire, and that the Persians would not conquer him until they had a mule for their prince. Being conquered, and losing his empire, he sent to upbraid the oracle for deceiving him, but he was answered, that the empire that was to be overturned was his own, and that Cyrus being descended from a Persian father, and a Median mother, was the mule intended by the oracle.

The Hebrew oracle never returned such answers as these, but always such as were

were direct, and perfectly intelligible. The divine oracle subsisted, though in some different manner, before the time of Moses. For we read that Rebecca, when she found herself with child, and felt a violent motion in her womb, inquired of the Lord, and received the following answer, Gen. xxv. 23, *Two nations are in thy womb, and two manner of people shall be separated from thy bowels. The one shall be stronger than the other, and the elder shall serve the younger.*

When the oracle was consulted after the death of Joshua, we read, Jud. i. 1. *Then Israel asked the Lord, saying, Who shall go up, for us against the Canaanites first, to fight against them, Jehovah said Judah shall go up, behold I have delivered the land into his hand.* David, in the course of his life, received several answers from the oracle, one of which was very particular. The Philistines spreading themselves, as we read, 2 Sam. v. 23. in the valley of Rephaim, when David inquired of the Lord,

Lord, he said, *Thou shalt not go up, but fetch a compass behind them, and come upon them over against the mulberry trees; and let it be when thou hearest the sound of a marching in the top of the mulberry trees, that then thou shalt bestir thyself, for then shall the Lord go out before thee to smite the host of the Philistines.* We have no account of any other answer from this oracle, that was not equally plain, and free from ambiguity.

All the directions and predictions that were occasionally delivered by the God of Israel, or by angels commissioned by him, were equally clear and intelligible. Such was the original command given to Abraham, Gen. xii. 1. ' Get thee out of thy
' country, and from thy kindred, and from
' thy father's house, unto a land that I will
' shew thee, and I will make of thee a
' great nation, and thou shalt be a blessing.'
such was the message to Hagar when she fled from her mistress, Genesis. xvi. 11.
' And the angel of the Lord said unto her,
' Behold thou art with child, and shalt bear

'bear a fon, and call his name Ifhmael, 'and he will be a wild man; his hand will 'be againſt every man, and every man's 'hand againſt him, and he fhall dwell in 'the prefence of all his brethren.' A prediction which has been exactly verified in the general character, and hiſtory, of the Arabs, who are defcended from Ifhmael, to this very day. All the commands of God to Mofes were perfpicuous, and free from ambiguity; and fo were all the divine communications without any exception.

Sometimes communications were made in dreams, and by means of emblems; but the interpretations were given in the moſt intelligible language. Thus Jofeph in the interpretation of their refpective dreams, told Pharoah's baker, that after three days he would be hanged, and that the butler would at the fame time be reſtored to his office; and he told Pharoah that the next feven years would be years of unufual plenty, but would be followed by feven years of famine. The prophetic dreams of Nebuchadnezzar were interpreted

preted with the fame diftinctnefs by Daniel, and Daniel's own dreams by an angel.

Befides the regular *oracle*, to which the Ifraelites had accefs on particular emergencies, God was pleafed to fend to that nation a fucceffion of *prophets*, and they all delivered their meffages in the plaineft language, as became the meffengers of God. The greateft, and ftrictly fpeaking, the firft, of thefe prophets, was Mofes; and nothing could be more diftinct and intelligible than the manner in which he always fpake in the name of God, on a great variety of occafions; and he was informed that there would be a fucceffion of prophets, like himfelf, Deut. xviii. 18. ' I will raife them up a prophet
' among their brethren, like unto thee,
' and will put my words in his mouth,
' and he fhall fpeak unto them all that I
' command him.'

An example of this we have in the meffage which the prophet Ahijah was directed to deliver to Jerufalem, of which

we

we have an account 1 Kings, xi. 29. 'And
'it came to pass at that time, when Je-
'roboam went out of Jerusalem,' (which
was in the reign of Solomon,) 'that the
'prophet Ahijah the Shilonite found him
'in the way, and he clad himself in a new
'garment, and they two were alone in
'the field. And Ahijah caught the new
'garment that was on him, and rent it in
'twelve pieces. And he said to Jerobo-
'am, Take thee ten pieces. For thus
'saith the Lord, the God of Israel. Be-
'hold I will rend the kingdom out of the
'hand of Solomon, and will give ten
'tribes to thee, because they have for-
'saken me, and have worshipped Ashta-
'roth, the goddess of the Sidonians, Che-
'mosh the god of the Moabites, and Mil-
'com the god of the children of Ammon,
'and have not walked in my way, to do
'that which is right in mine eyes, to keep
'my statutes and my judgments, as did
'David his father. Howbeit, I will not
'take the whole kingdom out of his hand,
'but I will make him a prince all the
'days

'days of his life, for my servant David's
'sake, whom I chose, because he kept
'my commandments and my statutes:
'but I will take the kingdom out of his
'son's hand, and will give it unto thee,
'even ten tribes, &c.' In the same plain
and direct manner, did all the prophets
deliver themselves; as Elijah to Ahab,
Isaiah to Ahaz,* and Hezekiah, and Jeremiah to Zedekiah. With the same distinctness did our Saviour deliver his prophecy concerning the destruction of Jerusalem, the demolition of the temple, and
the desolation of Judea.

Let this be compared with the manner
in which the pretended prophets among
the

---

* Mr. Paine charges Isaiah with being a false prophet in what he announced to Ahaz, concerning the invasion of his kingdom by Rezin king of Syria, and Pekah king of Israel, which was as follows. Isaih vii. 1, 'And it came
'to pass in the days of Ahaz, the son of Jotham king of
'Judah, that Rezin the king of Syria, and Pekah the son of
'Remaliah, king of Israel, went up towards Jerusalem to war
'against it, but could not prevail against it. And it was told
'the house of David, saying, Syria is confederate with Ephraim; and his heart was moved as the trees of the wood
'are moved with the wind. Then said the Lord unto Isaiah,
'Go

the heathens delivered themselves. It was always in a kind of madness, or ecstasy, to give the appearance of some other being than themselves speaking from within them, or making use of their organs. When the pythoness at Delphi delivered the oracle, with which she was supposed to be inspired, she began to swell and foam at the mouth, tearing her hair, cutting her flesh, and

'Go forth now to meet Ahaz, thou and Shear-Jashub thy
' son, at the end of the conduit of the upper pool, in the
' high way of the Fullers field, and say unto him, Take heed
' and be quiet, fear not, neither be faint-hearted, for the two
' tails of these smoking firebrands, for the fierce anger of
' Rezin with Syria, and of the son of Remaliah, because
' Syria, Ephraim, and the son of Remaliah have taken evil
' council against thee, saying, Let us go up against Judah
' and vex it, and let us make a king in the midst of it, even
' the son of Tabeal. Thus saith the Lord God, it shall not
' stand, neither shall it come to pass.' He farther assured him that before a child that was soon to be born could distinguish between good and evil, the countries of his enemies would be 'forsaken of both their kings.'

On this Mr. Paine says, p. 47, 'To shew the imposition and
' falsehood of Isaiah, we have only to attend to the sequel of
' this story, which, though it is passed over in silence in the
' book of Isaiah, is related in the 20th chapter of 2 Chronicles,
' and which is, that, instead of these two kings failing in
'their attempt against Ahaz king of Judah, as Isaiah had
' pretended to foretel in the name of the Lord, they succeeded.

D d

and in all her behaviour appearing as if diftracted. One of them was at one time fo enraged, that fhe terrified not only thofe who confulted the oracle, but the priefts themfelves, fo that they ran away and left her, and foon after fhe died. Others, who were fuppofed to pry into futurity, lay like dead men, deprived of all fenfe and motion, and when they returned to themfelves,

'ceeded. Ahaz was defeated and deftroyed, an hundred
' and twenty thoufand of his people were flaughtered, Jeru-
' falem was plundered, and two hundred thoufand women,
' and fons and daughters, were carried into captivity. Thus
' much for this lying prophet and impoftor Ifaiah, and the
' book of falfehoods that bears his name.'

Such is the charge, but the defence is extremely eafy. The calamity which Mr. Paine, with much exaggeration defcribes, was in the beginning of the reign of Ahaz, before the prophecy was delivered. For it commenced about the death of Jotham his predeceffor. After reciting the events of the reign of Jotham, the hiftorian fays, 2 Kings, xv. 37, ' In thefe days the Lord began to fend againft Judah, Rezin ' the king of Syria, and Pekah the fon of Remaliah. And ' Jotham flept with his fathers, and Ahaz his fon reigned ' in his ftead.'

This calamity, great as it was, by no means extended fo far as Mr. Paine afferts. For Jerufalem was fo far from being plundered, that it is exprefsly faid, 2 Kings, xvi. 5. ' That thefe two kings came up to Jerufalem to war, and ' they befieged Ahaz, but they could not overcome him.'
Agreeably

themselves, they related what they had seen and heard. For it was their opinion that the soul might leave the body, wander up and down the world, visit the regions of the dead, and even converse with gods and heroes. Plutarch relates that while the soul of one Hermodorus of Clazomenæ was thus out of his body, a woman who had the custody of it, delivered it to his enemies, who burned it.

Agreeably to this, Isaiah says 'they went up towards Jerusalem, to war against it, but could not prevail against it.' And so far were they from being able to dethrone Ahaz, and set up another king, the son of Tabeal, that Ahaz reigned sixteen years, and in the fourth year of his reign Pekah king of Israel was slain in a conspiracy of his own subject, 1. Kings, xv. 30. and about the same time an end was put to the kingdom of Syria by Tiglath Pileser king of Assyria taking Damascus, whither Ahaz went to meet him.

Mr. Paine takes advantage of the figurative and no doubt hyperbolical language of the prophet Ezekiel, in his account of the desolation of Egypt during forty years after the conquest of the country by Nebuchadnezzar, chap. xxix. 11. ' that no foot of man or of beast should pass through it.' We have no particular account of the state of Egypt in this interval, but the civil war between Apries or Pharoah Hophra and Amasis, which followed the devastation made by Nebuchadnezzar, must have made travelling particularly hazardous.

The delivery of prophecies in a frantic manner, as if the prophet was poſſeſſed by ſome demon, is ſtill practiſed in ſeveral barbarous nations, as in Tartary, and among the Indians of ſome parts of America, of which travellers give amuſing accounts. In fact, when the Grecian oracles were inſtituted, that nation had as little knowledge as the Tartars, or Indians. At this day the random ſayings of ideots, and perſons diſordered in their ſenſes, are catched up in the Eaſt, as if they came from the inſpiration of ſome ſuperior being.

But the principal queſtion before us is, not in what manner prophecies were delivered, but whether predictions ſaid to come from God, and, as ſuch, recorded in ſcripture have been verified by the events. And to this the Divine Being himſelf appeals. When the ſucceſſion of prophets mentioned above was announced to Moſes, he ſays, Deut. xviii. 21, ‘ If thou ſhalt
‘ ſay in thine heart, how ſhall we know
‘ the word which the Lord hath not ſpoken?
‘ it

it is anfwered, ' When a prophet fpeaketh
' in the name of the Lord, if the thing
' follow not, nor come to pafs, this is
' the thing which the Lord hath not
' fpoken, but the prophet hath fpoken pre-
' fumptuoufly. Thou fhalt not be afraid
' of him.' And on this fubject it is that
Jehovah challenges the gods of the heathens, in Ifaiah xli. 21, ' Produce your
' caufe, faith the Lord, bring forth your
' ftrong reafons, faith the God of Jacob.
' Let them bring them forth, and fhew us
' what fhall happen. Let them fhew for-
' mer things what they be, that we may
' confider them, and know the latter end
' of them, or declare us things for to
' come. Shew the things that are to
' come hereafter, that we may know that
' ye are gods.' This is what no heathen
oracle or prophet could do. But the fcriptures abound with prophecies which have
indifputably been verified by the events,
and in fome cafes, at a great diftance from
the time of their delivery.

There

There are few prophecies more remarkable than thofe of Mofes, which extend even to the prefent times, and indeed far beyond them. When his nation was in a ftate little better than that of the wild Arabs, wandering in the wildernefs; he not only looked forward to their certainly taking poffeffion of the land of Canaan, then inhabited by a warlike people, who had horfes and chariots of iron, and whofe cities are faid to have been fenced up to heaven, and who had many years notice of the intended attack upon them, when none of the Ifraelites had feen war, when they were poorly provided with weapons, and could only fight on foot, and muft have been wholly unacquainted with the method of attacking fortified places; but he foretold their apoftacy from their religion, their confequent expulfion from the land of Canaan, their difperfion into all the moft diftant parts of the world, their cruel fufferings, and contemptuous treatment, in thofe countries, of which we near three thoufand years after the prediction, are now witneffes, witnesses, their subsisting, notwithstanding this, as a separate people, of which also we are witnesses, and likewise their final restoration, and resettlement in their own country, when they are to be the most distinguished of all nations. But I do not enlarge on this subject, because I have done it already, in a discourse which is before the public.

There is no nation bordering on the land of Canaan, whose future destiny was not foretold by some of the Hebrew prophets, and there is no pretence for saying that the predictions were written after the events. For the accomplishment of several of them is quite recent; whereas the books have been extant between two and three thousand years. I shall confine myself to those concerning Egypt, Babylon, and Tyre, with some observations on the prophecies of Daniel.

1. The Egyptians were the first nation that rose to any great degree of power, and they continued in the first rank of warlike people, till they were conquered by

by Nebuchadnezzar. But several years before that conquest, viz. in the tenth year of the captivity of Jehoiakim, three years before he undertook the siege of Tyre, and fourteen before his invasion of Egypt, *the word of the Lord came to Ezekiel,* as we read, Ez. xxix. 1. &c. *saying, Son of man, set thy face against Pharoah king of Egypt, and prophecy against him, and against all Egypt. Speak and say, Thus saith the Lord God, Behold I am against thee Pharaoh king of Egypt, the great dragon that lieth in the midst of his rivers, who has said, My river is my own, and I have made it for myself*. But I will put hooks in thy jaws, and I will bring thee up out of the midst of thy rivers. And I will leave thee thrown into the wilderness. I have given thee for meat to the beasts of the field, and to the fowls of heaven, and all the inhabitants of Egypt shall know that I am the Lord, because they have been a staff of reed to the house of Israel.*

* This king of Egypt Pharaoh Hophra (called Apries by Herodotus) was remarkable for his pride and impiety. According to this historian, he boasted that it was not in the power of the gods to dethrone him.

rael. Thus faith the Lord God, I will bring a sword upon thee, and cut off man and beast out of thee, and the land of Egypt shall be desolate and waste, and they shall know that I am the Lord. He then foretels a state of desolation, which was to continue in Egypt forty years, after which he says, v. 14. 15. *they shall be a base kingdom. It shall be the basest of the kingdoms, neither shall it exalt itself any more above the nations, for I will diminish them, that they shall no more rule over the nations.*

A short time before Nebuchadnezzar's expedition, Ezekiel again prophesied as follows, Chap. xxx. 10. *I will also make the multitude of Egypt to cease by the hand of Nebuchadnezzar king of Babylon, he and his people with him. The terrible of the nations shall be brought to destroy the land, and they shall draw their swords against Egypt, and fill the land with the slain, and I will make the river dry*, and sell the land into the hand of the wicked,*

---

* This is a figurative expression, denoting probably that the river, of which this king made so great a boast, should not avail him when he was invaded by his enemy. It should be as easily passed, as if its channel had been dry.

wicked, and I will make the land wafte, and all that is therein by the hand of ftrangers. I the Lord have fpoken it. Thus faith the Lord God, I will alfo deftroy the idols, and I will caufe their images to ceafe out of Noph, and there fhall be no more a prince of the land of Egypt, and I will put a fear in the land of Egypt.

The hiftory of Egypt from that time to the prefent, which is more than two thoufand years, correfponds in a remarkable manner to this prediction; that country having been ever fince under the dominion of foreigners, viz. the Babylonians, Perfians, Macedonians, Romans, Saracens, Mamluks, and Turks. And, judging from appearances, it is not at all probable that the Egyptians will ever recover their liberty, and have a king of their own. Indeed, Egypt has been fo often conquered and enflaved, fo many perfons of foreign extraction have fettled in it, that it muft be hard to fay who of the prefent inhabitants are of the ftock of the antient Egyptians. But it is not probable that any native of the

the country, of whatever stock, will ever have the sovereignty of it.

2. Isaiah lived in the reign of Uzziah, Jotham, Ahaz, and Hezekiah, kings of Judah, about one hundred and fifty years before the conquests of Nebuchadnezzar, and more than two hundred before those of Cyrus, while the kingdom of Babylon was inferior to that of the Assyrians, yet he foretold the fall of the Babylonian empire, in language peculiarly emphatical, and his predictions have been verified by the events in a most remarkable manner, some of the particulars not having taken place, till many ages had elapsed. Isaiah xiii. 9. *Babylon the glory of kingdoms, the beauty of the Chaldees excellency, shall be as when God overthrew Sodom and Gomorrah. It shall never be inhabited, neither shall it be dwelt in from generation to generation, neither shall the Arabian pitch his tent there; and their houses shall be full of doleful creatures, and owls shall dwell there, and satyrs shall dance there, and wild beasts of the islands* (that is foreign wild beasts) *shall cry in their desolate houses, and dragons*

dragons in their pleafant palaces, and the time is near to come, and her days fkall not be prolonged. He alfo fays, Chap. xiv. 22. *I will rife up againft them, faith the Lord of hofts, and cut off from Babylon the name and remnant, and fon, and nephew, faith the Lord. I will alfo make it a poffeffion for bitterns, and pools of water; and I will fweep it with the befom of deftruction, faith the Lord of hofts.* The prophet even mentioned the nations, then in their very infant ftate, by which Babylon would be conquered, when he faid, chap. xxi. 2. *Go up Elam,* (i. e. Perfia) *befiege, O Media,* for they were the Medes and Perfians in conjunction that overturned the Babylonian empire.

Jeremiah, who lived in the reign of Nebuchadnezzar, at the time when the Babylonian empire was in its greateft ftrength and glory, prophefied to the fame purport with Ifaiah, chap. 50. ' Lo, ' I will raife up, and caufe to come up ' againft Babylon, an affembly of great ' nations from the north country, and ' they fhall fet themfelves in array againft
' her.

'her. From thence she shall be taken.
'Because of the wrath of the Lord it shall
'not be inhabited, but it shall be wholly
'desolate. Every one that goeth by Ba-
'bylon shall be astonished, and hiss at all
'her plagues, for it is a land of graven
'images, and they are mad upon their
'idols. Therefore the wild beasts of the
'desert, and the wild beasts of the islands,
'shall dwell there, and the owls shall
'dwell therein, and it shall be no more
'inhabited for ever, neither shall it be
'dwelt in from generation to generation.'

This prophet also mentions the names of the future enemies of Babylon, chap. li. 11. 'The Lord shall raise up the spirit 'of the kings of the Medes; for his devise 'is against Babylon to destroy it.' The duration of the captivity of his countrymen by the Babylonians, Jeremiah exactly foretold. After mentioning the conquests of this nation, he proceeds thus, chap. xxv. 11, 'Those nations shall serve 'the king of Babylon seventy years, and 'it shall come to pass, that when seventy years

'years are accomplished, I will punish the
'king of Babylon, and that nation, faith
'the Lord.' Chap. xxix. 10, 'For thus
'faith the Lord, that after seventy years
'be accomplished at Babylon, I will visit
'you, and perform my good word to-
'wards you, in causing you to return to
'this place.'

The prophecies concerning the desolation of Babylon were not fulfilled in their full extent, till long after the time of our Saviour. Babylon was taken by Cyrus exactly seventy years after the conquest of Judea; but it was not reduced to the state mentioned in these prophecies but by slow degrees. Cyrus having taken the city by turning the river which flowed through it out of its channel, all the neighbourhood became marshy and unhealthy. Diodorus Siculus, who wrote a little before the time of our Saviour, says, that the buildings of Babylon were then decayed, that only a small part of it was inhabited, and that the rest of the inclosure was employed in tillage. Pliny, who wrote in the
first

first century after Christ, says that Babylon was then reduced to solitude, being exhausted by the neighbourhood of Seleucia, which was not far from it. Pausanias, who wrote about the middle of the second century, says, that " of Babylon the great-" est city that the sun ever saw, there was " nothing remaining but the walls;' and Lucian, who wrote about the same time, says, that very soon it would, like Nineveh, be sought for, and not be found. In the time of Jerom, who lived in the fourth century, the whole inclosure of the walls of Babylon was actually converted into a place for keeping wild beasts, and was used for that and no other purpose by many of the kings of Persia. At length, even the walls of this great city, so much celebrated for their height and thickness, were demolished, but by whom is not known. About seven hundred years ago, Benjamin a Jew, found some remains of the ruins of Babylon, but people were afraid to go among them on account of the serpents and scorpions with which it swarmed, ed, and at prefent it is not agreed among travellers, in what place the great city of Babylon ftood. In this cafe, furely, there cannot be any pretence for faying that the prediction was fubfequent to the event, and yet no event was ever more diftinctly defcribed.

What is perhaps, however, more remarkable ftill, Ifaiah mentions *Cyrus* by name, as the conqueror of Babylon, and the perfon who was deftined to favour the people of Ifrael, by ordering the rebuilding of Jerufalem and the temple, though in his time they were both ftanding. Ifa. lxiv. 22. ' Thus faith the Lord, thy re-
' deemer, and he that formed thee from
' the womb, I am the Lord that maketh
' all things, that ftretcheth forth the hea-
' vens above, that fpreadeth abroad the
' earth by myfelf; that faith to Jerufalem,
' Thou fhalt be inhabited, and to the cities
' of Judah, Ye fhall be built, and I will
' raife up the decayed places thereof; that
' faith to the deep, Be dry, and I will
' dry up their rivers, that faith to Cyrus,
' he

'he is my shepherd, and shall perform all
'my pleasure, even saying to Jerusalem,
'thou shalt be built, and to the temple,
'thy foundation shall be laid. Thus saith
'the Lord to his anointed, to Cyrus,
'whose right hand I have holden, to sub-
'due nations before him, and I will loose
'the loins of kings, to open before him
'the two-leaved gates. I will break in
'pieces the gates of brass, and cut in sun-
'der the bars of iron. And I will give thee
'the treasures of darkness, and hidden
'riches of secret places, that thou mayest
'know that I the Lord, who call thee by
'thy name, am the God of Israel. I
'have surnamed thee though thou hast
'not known me. I am the Lord, and
'there is none else. There is no god be-
'sides me. I girded thee though thou
'hast not known me; that they may know
'from the rising of the sun, and from
'the West, that there is none besides
'me. I am the Lord, and there is none
'else. I form the light, and create dark-
'ness:

'ness: I make peace, and create evil; I
'the Lord do all these things.'

3. Not less remarkably have the prophecies concerning Tyre, received their accomplishment. In the eleventh year after the captivity of the Jews, which was before the siege of Tyre by Nebuchadnezzar, Ezekiel says, Chap. xxvi. 1. 'The
'word of the Lord came unto me, saying,
'Son of man, because that Tyrus hath
'said against Jerusalem, Aha, she is bro-
'ken, that was the gate of the people,
'she is turned unto me, I shall be replenish-
'ed now she is laid waste. Therefore thus
'saith the Lord God, Behold I am against
'thee, O Tyrus, and will cause many na-
'tions to come up against thee, and they
'shall destroy the walls of Tyrus, and
'break down her towers. I will also
'scrape her dust from her, and make her
'like the top of a rock. It shall be a
'place for the spreading of nets in the
'midst of the sea, for I have spoken it
'saith the Lord God, and it shall become a
                                    'spoil

'spoil to the nations.' It is added v. 14. 'Thou shall be built no more.'

When this prophecy was delivered Tyre was in its glory, probably the most wealthy and the strongest city in the world. It was taken by Nebuchadnezzar, but not till it had sustained a siege of thirteen years. That city was never rebuilt, but another on an island, at the distance of half a mile from the shore, which in time became as flourishing, and as powerful, as the former. This, however, was taken by Alexander the Great, and it never recovered itself. It is now a heap of ruins, visited, not inhabited, by a few fishermen. A traveller, who, about a century ago gave an account of it, says that when he approached the ruins of Tyre, he found rocks stretched out into the sea, and great stones scattered up and down on the shore, made clean smooth by the sun, the waves, and the wind, and of no use but for the drying of fishermen's nets, many of which were at that time, spread upon them; so that the full completion of this prophecy, delivered above two thousand three hundred years ago, did not take place till within the last two or three centuries.

4. The prophecies of Daniel relate to the most distant times, even those which we have not yet reached; but some of the great events indicated in them by emblems, and afterwards explained in words, have so evidently come to pass, that for this, and no other reason, (which is merely taking the question for granted, against the strongest evidence, internal and external) it has been said, that they must have been written after them.

To Nebuchadnezzar, chap. iv. was revealed in a vision of a great image, consisting of different kinds of metal, overturned by a stone, which afterwards became a great mountain, filling the whole earth, the succession of four great monarchies, of which his own was declared to be the first, and of which the last can be no other than the Roman, terminating in ten kingdoms, which now exist, after which is to come what is called *the kingdom of of heaven*, which will continue for ever, and this, according to many other accounts of it, is to be the reign of peace and righteousness.

In another vision, seen by Daniel himself, chap. vii. four great empires, and no doubt the same with the former, are represented by four beasts, the last of which had ten horns, succeeded by the appearance of one like to the son of man, *to whom was given dominion, and glory, and a kingdom which should* be universal and everlasting. The first of these empires being the Babylonian, it is impossible not to interpret the succeeding ones to be the Persian, the Macedonian, and the Roman, divided at last into ten kingdoms as before.

Farther than this, another power is described as arising among the ten kingdoms, in which the last of the four empires terminates, and by this it is almost impossible not to understand, the papal. *I considered the ten horns*, says Daniel, chap. vii. 8. *and behold there came up among them another little*

little horn, before whom were three of the first horns plucked up by the roots, and behold in this horn were eyes like the eyes of a man, and a mouth speaking great things, v. 21. *I beheld, and the same horn made war with the saints, and prevailed against them, until the antient of days came, and judgment was given to the saints of the Most High, and the time came that the saints possessed the kingdom.* In the interpretation of this, the angel says, v. 24. *The ten horns out of this kingdom are ten kings that shall arise, and another shall arise after them, and he shall be diverse from the first, and he shall subdue three kings. And he shall speak great words against the Most High, and shall wear out the saints of the Most High, and think to change times and laws, and they shall be given into his hand until a time and times, and the dividing of time. But the judgment shall sit, and they shall take away his dominion, to consume and to destroy it unto the end.* The history of the popes, though I cannot now enter into the particulars, corresponds in a wonderful manner with this prediction, delivered unquestionably above a thousand years before the event.

In

In another vifion, chap. viii. a ram with two horns, the one higher than the other, of which the higheft came up laft, was deftroyed by a he-goat, with one great horn between his eyes, which being broken off four others came up in its place. And in the interpretation it is exprefsly faid, that the ram with two horns reprefented the empire of the Medes and Perfians, of which the latter was more powerful than the former, though it was not fo at the firft, and that the he-goat reprefented the kingdom of the Grecians, that the great horn was the firft king, and that after him four fhould ftand up out of the nation, but not in his power.

This vifion was in the reign of Belfhazzar, before the conqueft of Babylon by the Medes and Perfians, while the Medes were by much the more powerful nation, and therefore long before the conqueft of Perfia by Alexander, on whofe death his dominions were divided among four of his generals. The remainder of this vifion, and others, which probably relate to times that

that are yet future, have some difficulty in their interpretation, which time will probably clear up. But if Daniel described the empire of the Greeks or Macedonian, and much more that of the Romans, it cannot be questioned but that the events indicated in his writings, were subsequent to the prediction of them, and such as no human sagacity could at that time discover.

We find the clearest marks of a prophetic spirit in the New Testament, as well as in the Old. Jesus, besides foretelling his own death, and that by crucifixion, with all the circumstances of indignity attending it, also his resurrection and ascension, appears by his parables, to have had a clear foresight of the spread, and final prevalence, of his religion in the world, of the persecution of his followers, the dissention and mischief of which it would for some time be the occasion, and of the corruption of his doctrine. He also foretold in the clearest language, without any figure or parable, the destruction of Jerusalem, the

the total demolition of the temple, and the defolation of the country of Judea, with many figns of its near approach in that generation, when no other perfon of that nation, or any other, appears to have had the leaft apprehenfion of fuch events. The warning he gave his difciples to flee out of the country on the approach of thefe calamitous times, was well underftood by them, and was the means of faving them all; no Chriftians being in Jerufalem when it was befieged and taken by Titus.

The apoftle Paul forewarns Chriftians of the rife of a power in the Chriftian church, which would advance higher claims than thofe of any other earthly potentate, that he would gain his authority by artifice, and pretences to miracles, that he would recommend abftinence from certain meats, and difcourage marriage; but that it would be finally deftroyed at the fecond coming of Chrift, 2 Theff. ii. 3. *Let no man deceive you by any means, for there muft come a falling away*, or an apoftacy, *firft*, i. e. before the time of final judgment, *and that man*

man of sin must be revealed, the son of perdition, who opposeth and exalteth himself above all that is called God, or that is worshipped, so that he, as God, sitteth in the temple of God, shewing himself that he is God---*whom the Lord shall consume with the spirit of his mouth, and shall destroy with the brightness of his coming; even him whose coming is after the working of Satan, with all power, and signs, and lying wonders, and with all deceitfulness of unrighteousness.* 1 Tim. iv. 1. *The spirit speaketh expresly, that in the latter times some shall depart from the faith, giving heed to seducing spirits and doctrines of demons*---*forbidding to marry, and commanding to abstain from meats, which God has created to be received with thanksgiving.* A farther description of this same power, is given in the Revelation of John, with the steps by which it rose, and the shocking use that would be made of its power, in the persecution of the church. Certainly all these characters are to be found in the Pope, and the church of Rome, and what probability was there of the rise of any such power, at the time that the prophecies

cies were delivered? This apoftle alfo gives a fketch of the moft interefting events of every kind, from his own time to the end of the world. But as, for evident reafons, this prophecy is delivered in figurative language, and emblems, its correfpondence with the events cannot be expected to be apparent, till after they have taken place. And therefore it is not much for the purpofe of my prefent argument, though I think that till pretty near to the prefent times, the correfpondence will be fufficiently evident to the impartial and candid.

But without any regard to thefe predictions, which are acknowledged to be better calculated to confirm the faith of the believer, than to convert unbelievers, the prophecies I have enumerated, though few in comparifon of what might have been adduced, will fatisfy any reafonable perfon, that they muft have been dictated by a forefight more than human, and therefore that the Jewifh and Chriftian religions, having the fame author, muft be of divine authority.

DISCOURSE

DISCOURSE XII.

Internal Evidence of Jesus being no Impostor.

We are in him that is true, even in his Son Jesus Christ.

1 JOHN, v. 20.

BESIDES the evidence of *miracles*, including that of *prophecy*, which is the proper seal of God to any thing that is alleged to come from him, with which we become acquainted by history, or tradition, and which is usually called the *external evidence* of divine revelation, there is another kind of evidence properly denominated *internal*, which to those who have a sufficient knowledge of human nature and human life, is hardly less satisfactory. For knowing what men are, and what men have done, we readily judge what is probable or improbable, possible or impossible, fible, with refpect to the defigns and actions of men; and if any thing be afferted of a man, and efpecially of a number of men, which we well know could not be afferted with truth of any man, or any number of men, with whom we were ever acquainted, or concerning whom we have had any authentic information, we do not hefitate to pronounce it to be highly improbable, and perhaps abfolutely impoffible.

It is, therefore, of the greateft importance, that we apply the knowledge we have of human nature, and human life, in our ftudy of the evidences of divine revelation, to attend accurately to the characters and circumftances of Mofes and the prophets, of Chrift and the apoftles, that we may form a judgment whether what is related of them, on the fuppofition of their having had divine communications; or of their having been impoftors, be probable or otherwife. Having in a former fet of difcourfes confidered the circumftances of the hiftory of Mofes, I fhall in this confider the hiftory of Jefus;

sus; and I think it will appear, that, if what is, and must be, allowed concerning him be true, it was absolutely impossible that he should have been an impostor, every thing related of him being perfectly natural on the idea of his being conscious to himself, or fully persuaded in his own mind, of his having a divine mission, but in the highest degree unnatural, and even impossible, on the idea of his having been an impostor. That he was a mere *enthusiast,* and really imagined that he had a divine mission when he had none, is another question, which I shall consider only incidentally. This indeed was evidently impossible in such a case as this, and will not, I am persuaded, be supposed by any unbeliever; so that if Jesus was no impostor, and did not know that he was deceiving his followers and the world, his divine mission must be acknowledged.

1. If we consider the nature and extent of the undertaking of Jesus, it must appear highly improbable that it should have

have occurred to a perfon of his country, and of his low birth, and education. Had his views, whatever they were, extended no farther than his own country, is undertaking any thing that fhould bring him into notice, and advance him in life, (which is all that an impoftor can be fuppofed to aim at) muft have appeared very unlikely to fucceed, and confequently muft have been very unlikely to enter into his thoughts, and have been undertaken by him. With the Jews, the place of a man's birth was a circumftance of no fmall moment, and Jefus was of Nazarreth, efteemed a mean place, in a defpifed part of the country, fo that, on this account, he muft have lain under great difadvantage; and his occupation, which was that of a carpenter, without any advantage of education, fuch as his country afforded, muft have made his undertaking much more difficult. In thefe circumftances, ambition fo prepofterous as that of Jefus, muft have bordered on infanity or infatuation, which muft have appeared in his conduct.

conduct. But nothing of this kind *does* appear in him. Exclusive of the language suited to his undertaking, there was nothing like extravagance in his words or actions. On the contrary, his whole behaviour shewed a mind perfectly composed and rational, and what is more, there was not in him any thing of ostentation, but the most amiable humility and modesty, though accompanied with becoming dignity.

Whatever we may think of a Jewish education, and Jewish literature, they were highly valued by Jews, and must have been necessary to gain general esteem, especially with the higher classes of men, and for the purpose of acting any conspicuous part in that country. Jesus himself could not but have found, and have felt, this disadvantage; and if he had not been deterred by it from his undertaking, he must have had such an immoderate and absurd conceit of himself, as could not but have appeared in his general conduct, and must have exposed him to contempt. Such is always the case if any person in
similar

similar circumstances with us attempt any thing above his sphere of life. It frequently happens that men of no education, and, even of low occupations, step out of their sphere, and become preachers, but they are seldom attended to, except by persons like themselves, and they generally appear ridiculous in the eyes of others. But such was not the case with Jesus. He was revered and dreaded, by the chief persons of his nation; and the contempt they sometimes expressed for him was either affected, or conceived before they had sufficient knowledge of him. The manner in which they at length proceeded against him, shews that they were most seriously alarmed, and thought their own credit and safety depended on their destroying him.

Some persons destitute of the advantages of birth and education, have great natural talents, which supply their place, and give them great influence. But Jesus does not appear to have had any advantage of this kind. Like Moses, he was neither an orator, nor a warrior. He could, indeed, speak pertinently upon proper occasions, and he discovered great presence of mind in critical circumstances. But this is not very uncommon, and there was nothing in his manner of speaking to captivate an audience, by moving the passions. He never attempted any thing of the kind, and the admiration with which his discourses were heard, was excited not by any thing that we call *eloquence*, but by the importance of what he delivered, and and his authoritative manner of speaking, which a consciousness of a divine mission naturally gave him. It is evident that he avoided as much as possible all occasions of drawing a crowd after him, and when, from the fame of his miracles, this was unavoidable, he always withdrew as soon, and as privately, as he could.

2. If we consider what it was that Jesus undertook, we shall find that it was of a nature least of all calculated to strike and captivate the Jews. All that we know of them, of their general character and

and views, make it evident that the only perſon likely to gain their favourable attention was one who would perſonate their *Meſſiah*, who was then expected to make his appearance, to deliver them from the ſtate of ſubjection they were then under to the Romans, and to give them the empire of the world. Except Jeſus himſelf, and his forerunner John the Baptiſt, no other perſon ever gained any conſiderable number of followers among the Jews, who did not flatter their ambition, by advancing that pretention, or in ſome other form erected the ſtandard of liberty among them. But with theſe pretenſions they never failed to gain many followers in that nation. Jeſus, however, eſtabliſhed a permanent intereſt in the affections of thouſands of that country, all prepoſſeſſed with the idea of a temporal deliverer (at firſt, indeed, fondly hoping that *he* was the perſon) though he carefully diſclaimed all ſuch pretences. And what is more extraordinary, his diſciples and followers in-creaſed

creased after his death, when every idea of that kind must have been given up.

By setting himself alike against the Pharisees and Sadducees, Jesus not only rendered himself obnoxious to all the higher orders of persons in the country, but must have been less likely to succeed even with the common people, by whom the Pharisees were held in the highest esteem. Indeed, it cannot be said that there was any class or description of persons to whom he paid court, or was at all studious to recommend himself. One of his discourses to the people was of such a nature, that all his audience left him, except the twelve apostles, and yet he was not concerned or discouraged by it; but, turning to the twelve, he calmly said, *Will ye also go away?* Of what kind, then, must have been the ambition of Jesus, which was equally independent of the favour of the great, and of that of the commonality? What could he have expected but universal contempt?

A Jew,

A Jew, whose object had been to draw attention as a prophet, would naturally have assumed the habit and manner of the antient prophets of that nation, which had in them much of austerity. And by this means John the Baptist, who did not pretend to work miracles, was highly and generally respected. But Jesus, though with that example before him, adopted a very different manner. He appears to have dressed, and to have lived, like other persons, without any peculiarity whatever. Whenever he was invited, he did not decline being present at entertainments, and his presence does not appear to have been at any time a check upon their innocent festivity. This was so much the case, that his enemies said of him, that he was *a gluttonous man and a winebibber*, as well as a *friend of publicans and sinners*.

Besides, that, in a civil respect, the appearance and pretensions of Jesus were ill adapted to favour any ambitious views, he taught nothing with respect to religion that

that was likely to recommend him to his countrymen. He did not pretend to teach any doctrine that was properly new, but his expofing of the abfurd comments of the authorifed expounders of the law of Mofes, together with their perfonal vices, was certainly hazardous. The general object of his preaching was to inculcate the ftricteft and pureft morality, fuch as is found in the antient prophets. But he drew the attention of his hearers in a more particular manner to *a future ftate*, much more than had been done by any of the prophets who had preceded him.

The doctrine of a refurrection was at that time the general belief of the Jewifh nation, as it continues to be at this day. But what he afferted of himfelf being appointed to raife all the dead, and to judge the world, muft have appeared in the higheft degree extravagant, and revolting, without the moft evident teftimonials of a divine authority for fuch high pretenfions. What could an impoftor, who muft have known that he had no authority for fuch a claim,

claim, if such an idea could have been entertained by him (which, however must be confessed to be very improbable) have expected, but that, on the first hearing of such pretensions, his audience would have turned from him with derision. His pretending to a kingdom, and a kingdom not of this world, but in another, after he should be dead, was also more likely to expose him to contempt, than to procure him respect. And this declaration was made by Jesus when he was before a court of judicature, expecting immediate death. That, notwithstanding these circumstances, Jesus did not appear an object of contempt, but attracted the most respectful attention, and had many disciples while living, and many more after he was dead, has surely in it something very extraordinary, and well deserving to be enquired into; great effects always implying great causes. All these circumstances certainly shew that Jesus was conscious to himself of having advantages sufficient to counterbalance all the disadvantages he lay under, and his

success

succefs proves that he was really poffeffed of them.

3. Still more extraordinary was it that such a person as Jesus should have extended his views beyond his own country, as it is evident that he did when he directed his disciples *to proselyte and baptize all nations*, and when he foretold the universal spread of his religion, which, though inconsiderable in its rise, like a grain of mustard seed, or a small quantity of leaven, was destined to embrace the whole world. No other Jew, of any rank or character, had talked in this manner before; and considering the extreme contempt in which the Jews must have known that they were held by other nations, except by the few whom they had proselyted, any Jew must have known that a person of his nation undertaking any thing considerable, was likely to meet with the worst reception, and nothing more offensive, or more hazardous, could have been undertaken by any man.

The object of the religion of Jesus, was nothing less than to overturn all the established

established systems of religion then subsisting in the world, systems always most intimately connected with civil policy, and as such most vigilantly guarded by all the power of the respective states, and, as was then universally thought, with the greatest reason; it being taken for granted, that their temporal prosperity depended upon the observance of the rites transmitted to all nations by their remote ancestors. The philosophers, who despised these rites, never ventured to hint at the propriety, or the safety, of discontinuing them; and the few who incautiously spake with disrespect of them were charged with atheism, and had been put to death, or banished. We may, and justly do, laugh at the religion of the Greeks and Romans, and that of the rest of the heathen world, as systems of the most wretched superstition; but they were serious things with themselves; and besides their reputed sacredness, and the general dread of a neglect of them, they mixed with all their habits of life.

In all antient nations all occasions of joy or sorrow, and almost every transaction of a civil nature, partook of their religion; but more especially was every season of festivity, to which they were most passionately attached, a religious act. Even the theatrical exhibitions of the Greeks and Romans, calculated to entertain persons of the most refined taste, as well as the festivals of Bacchus and Venus, which gratified the lewdest and most debauched of the vulgar, were equally in honour of their gods. Also all their most admired poems were with them, as with other nations, tinctured with their religion; so that without a knowledge of their religion, it is not now possible to understand them. I cannot, indeed, give a just idea of the extreme difficulty of the undertaking, to overturn the religion of the several states of antiquity, without entering into a detail of particulars, too long for any discourse. Only persons well acquainted with antiquity, will ever conceive it.

This being the cafe, to change the religion of a people was, in a manner, to make them over again. To fubdue them by force of arms muft have appeared much more eafy. There is not, indeed, a fingle inftance in all antient hiftory, of a nation changing their religion from perfuafion or example. It is what the greateft calamities, and the approach of extermination has not been able to effect. The cafe of the Jews is the only exception on record. For they were ever ready to adopt the religion of the neighbouring nations. But then their remote anceftors in Mefopotamia, according to Jofhua, and themfelves in Egypt, had been addicted to them. Though the Egyptians faw the inability of their gods to fave them from a feries of the greateft calamities, and though the Canaanites found that theirs could not prevent their expulfion from their country, and their almoft extermination, both the Egyptians and the remains of the Canaanites, appear to have continued as much attached to their feveral religions

ligions as ever. They would rather suppose that their gods were angry with them, and had for that time deserted them, than imagine that they had not been *able* to defend them, or that the gods of other nations (whose power they never called in question) had in that particular prevailed over theirs. For no heathen nation in all antiquity excluded the agency of superior powers in any event, public or private. The events of battles, though most evidently depending on the conduct of the generals, and the valour of the combatants, were always ascribed to the secret interference of the gods.

The prophet Jeremiah, expresses in very emphatical language, the extraordinary case of the Israelites in revolting from their religion, Chap. ii. 10. *Pass over the isles of Chittim, and see, and send unto Kedar, and consider diligently, and see if there be such a thing. Hath a nation changed their gods, which are yet no gods; but my people have changed their glory for that which doth not profit.*

In those circumstances, such an undertaking as that of Jesus, of the magnitude of which it is not easy for us at this day to form an idea, must surely have appeared impossible to a Jewish carpenter. Or if, from ignorance, he had conceived such an idea, he, or his followers, would soon have found the impracticability of it, without divine aid. Jesus himself did not go beyond the bounds of his own country, but no sooner did the apostles begin to preach to other nations, and appeared to be something different from Jews (whose privileges and customs had been long tolerated, without any serious inconvenience arising from it) than they found, that if they persisted, it must be at the hazard of every thing dear to them in life, and of life itself. And with these difficulties the preachers of christianity actually struggled about three hundred years; when the whole system of heathenism, which had prevailed from time immemorial, in the whole extent of the Roman empire, having been gradually undermined, gave way on the converſion of Conſtantine; and from that time, nothing, as we may ſay, remained of it, but ruins, which alſo crumbled away and diſappeared in about three hundred years more. And now nothing more remains of the worſhip of Jupiter and Juno, Apollo or Bacchus, than if it had never exiſted. Theſe celebrated deities are gone into oblivion, together with Baal of the Canaanites, Iſis and Oriſis of the Egyptians, and Thor and Woden in Europe. It is only in hiſtory, and the books in which they are mentioned, that the memory of them, and of the horrid and abominable rites with which they were worſhipped, is preſerved. What could have accompliſhed ſo great a revolution, a revolution far more aſtoniſhing than any that has ever been effected by policy or by arms, but a power not leſs than divine, accompanying Jeſus and the apoſtles?

The revolution produced by Mahomet had nothing it in approaching to this. He did not queſtion the divine origin of the

the Jewish or Christian religions. He only pretended that his own was derived from the same source, so that he had no occasion to work any miracles. Idolaters, indeed (who, however, do not appear to have been very numerous) he subdued by force, but Jews and Christians, unable to treat them in the same manner, he tolerated. When the Mahometan power was fully established, and the caliphs of Bagdat had long made the greatest figure of any princes in the Eastern world, and their subjects had attained a high degree of civilization, some Tartar nations emerging from barbarism, adopted their religion; as the Tartars who conquered China, adopted the institutions of the Chinese, and the Romans the literature and philosophy of the Greeks. In this there is nothing at all extraordinary. But the Greeks and Romans changed their religion for the Christian when they were the most learned and civilized, and the Jews, in their opinion, the most ignorant, and the most despised of all nations, and the preachers

ers of chriftianity were at firft of the moft illiterate of that defpifed nation. This is a fact that cannot be contradicted; and having no parallel in the hiftory of mankind, is certainly deferving of particular attention.

3. With all thefe difficulties before him, from the nature of his undertaking, and the people whom he had to gain to his purpofe, Jefus promifed to his difciples nothing at all in this world, but only in another. On the contrary, he frequently apprized them, that if they adhered to him, they had nothing to expect in this life, but perfecution; and many of them that violent death to which he himfelf was deftined. This is a kind of conduct which muft certainly be deemed in the higheft degree prepofterous, and unaccountable, in an impoftor, who, whatever he gave out, could not have had a view to any thing but fome advantage in this life. It muft have been to facrifice himfelf and his followers, for whom it is evident he had the greateft affection, for no advantage

tage whatever, to himself or them, which is what any man must pronounce to be absolutely impossible.

That a great number of persons should deliberately abandon themselves to persecution and certain death, in order to establish a scheme which they conceived to be favourable to the happiness of mankind, is not to be admitted. That a single person should devote himself to present death, when immediate and great glory would certainly accrue to himself, and an ample recompence to his family, is possible, though examples of it are uncertain and rare. But that many persons should do this, when the prospect of fame to themselves, and of advantage to their families, was distant and uncertain, and when for the present, and an indefinite length of time, contempt would be joined to their other sufferings, is impossible while human nature is what we know it to be. Such conduct would be deemed to be nothing less than *infanity;* and that a number of persons should be insane in exactly the same way, and infect thousands with the same species of the disorder, would be most miraculous.

That Jesus *did* expect a violent death for himself, and that he apprized his followers that many of them must expect the same, appears from the whole course of his history. It was not a thought that occurred to him only just before his death, and which he had not time to reflect upon; but it appears that it was what he had steadily in view, so as to have had an opportunity of considering it in all its terrors, and all its consequences, from the very beginning of his ministry, and what he in good time informed his disciples of. Some time before his last journey to Jerusalem, it is said, Matt. xvi. 21. *From that time began Jesus to shew to his disciples how that he must go up to Jerusalem, and suffer many things of the elders, and chief priests, and the scribes, and be killed, and be raised again the third day.* This, as was natural, staggered his disciples, who at that time expected preferment in the kingdom which they believed he was about to erect, and Peter said unto him,
This

This be far from thee Lord. But Jesus, so far from palliating the matter, and endeavouring to soften it, and reconcile their minds to it, replied, *Get thee behind me satan, thou art an offence unto me. For thou favourest not the things that are of God, but those that be of men;* and turning to his disciples, he said, *If any man will come after me, let him take up his cross and follow me. For whosoever will save his life, shall lose it, and whosoever will lose his life for my sake shall find it.* On another occasion he said, Matt. x. 38. *He that taketh not his cross and followeth after me, is not worthy of me.* On all proper occasions he clearly apprized his disciples that in this world they had nothing better to expect than the treatment that he himself met with. For when the sons of Zebedee, James and John, applied to him for the chief seats in his kingdom, he said, Matt. xx. 22. *Ye know not what ye ask. Are ye able to drink of the cup that I shall drink of, and to be baptized with the baptism that I shall be baptised with?* And when they said, *we are able,* he said, *Ye shall indeed drink of my cup, and be baptized with the bap-*

tism that I am baptized with. When he foretold the destruction of Jerusalem, he said to the apostles, Matt. xxiv. 9. *Then shall they deliver you up to be afflicted, and shall kill you, and ye shall be hated of all men for my name's sake.* By way of encouragement to bear all this, he could only say, and this he did in his first public discourse from the mount, Matt. v. 10. *Blessed are they that are persecuted for righteousness sake, for theirs is the kingdom of heaven. Blessed are ye when men shall revile you, and persecute you, and say all manner of evil against you falsely for my sake. Rejoice and be exceedingly glad, for great is your reward in heaven.*

What could any man expect from this mode of address, from which Jesus never varied, but that his hearers, who looked for nothing but worldly advantage (which at first was the case of the apostles themselves) finding that he had nothing of that kind to offer them, would turn from him with indignation and contempt. Disappointed in their fond prospects, what could have kept them with him but a firm persuasion

suasion that he had a divine mission, and therefore that it was their duty to follow him implicitly, confident that, in some way or other, of which they had no idea, they would in the end find their account in it. Notwithstanding his persisting in disclaiming all pretensions of a temporal nature, they did not abandon the expectations they had entertained; still flattering themselves that though he did not acquaint them with it, he would at a proper time assume kingly power. But when he was apprehended as a malefactor, which did not at all surprize or disconcert *him*, they *all forsook him and fled*; while he with a painful and ignominous death before his eyes, met his dreadful fate with the greatest composure, and went through the whole of the trying scene without giving the least suspicion that he wished to avoid it. Naturally indeed he did, and therefore he prayed that *the bitter cup might pass from him.* But he immediately added, *but not as I will, but as thou wilt.* Surely this behaviour was very unlike that of an impostor.

This

This was far from being the conduct of Mahomet. Besides promising his followers the enjoyment of every luxury of life, and especially that of women (free, as he frequently repeats it, from impurity,) he did not fail to hold out to them something worth fighting for in this world. Neither himself, nor any of his immediate followers, were voluntary martyrs to their religion.

As Jesus did not fail to apprize his followers of the dangers, and the inconvenience, to which their adherence to him would expose them, he did not conceal the great evils which would attend the propogation of his religion, though it would ultimately be in the highest degree beneficial to the world, and would finally prevail in it. *Think not*, says he, Matt. x. 30, *that I am come to send peace on earth. I came not to send peace, but a sword. For I am come to set a man at variance against his father, and the daughter against her mother, and the daughter-in-law against her mother-in-law, and a man's foes shall be they of his own household,*
V. 21.

v. 21. *The brother shall deliver up the brother to death, and the father the child; and children shall rise up against their parents and cause them to be put to death, and ye shall be hated of all men for my name's sake.* Surely such discourses as this was not likely to recommend his religion, or invite followers.

4. An artful impostor, would probably have *secrets* and confidental friends, to whom he would intrust what he did not choose to communicate to others, though this is not necessary to every impostor. But Jesus had no secrets, nor does there appear to have been any persons to whom he communicated what he concealed from others. When his audience discovered great perverseness, and a disposition to cavil, he spake to them in parables, but he afterwards explained the meaning of them to his apostles, one of whom was Judas, who, as he betrayed him, would, no doubt, have divulged whatever he had known to his prejudice. In the general instructions which Jesus gave his apostles, he directed them to publish to the world every thing that

that they had heard from him without exception. Matt. x. 27. *What I tell you in darkness, that speak ye in the light ; and what ye hear in the ear, that preach ye on the house tops.*

The only secret that Jesus had, was not his pretensions to a divine mission (for this he always openly asserted, and appealed to his miracles for the evidence of it) but to his being the Messiah, announced in the antient prophets. But this was only for fear of exciting an alarm which would have done no good, and at a proper time he declared this to all the apostles, and to Judas among them. After his resurrection and ascension, this was no secret to any person. He also avowed it in the most solemn manner at his trial before the highpriest.

5. Jesus discovered no anxiety about the evidence of his divine mission, which would have been natural to a person who had been conscious to himself that he was unable to produce any that was satisfactory. This anxiety appears through the whole of the

the Koran. Mahomet's affertion of his divine miffion, of the chapters in the Koran being fent to him from heaven, his denunciations of the wrath of God, and of hell-fire to the unbelievers, are repeated without end, fo as to be tirefome in the extreme. What he wanted in evidence he endeavoured to fupply by confident affertions, and this, together with the fuccefs of the battles that he fought fufficiently anfwered his purpofe. To thefe he appealed, and his followers, no doubt, thought that God would not give fuch fuccefs to a mere impoftor.

On the contrary, Jefus never, of his own accord, faid any thing about his miffion, leaving it to thofe who faw his miracles to make the neceffary inference from them. He contented himfelf with anfwering objections as they were made to him; and as his miracles were never queftioned, he eafily fhewed the abfurdity of every thing that was objected to them, efpecially that of his cafting out demons by Beelzebub. With great dignity he obferved ed, on one of these occasions, John x. 25. that *the works which his father gave him to do, bare witness of him*; and in answer to the clamorous demand of a sign from heaven, he referred them Matt. xii. 39. to the sign of the prophet Jonas, saying that as Jonas had been three days in the belly of a fish, he should remain so long in the state of the dead, and rise again on the third day; which it appears that his enemies well understood, by the precautions they took to prevent any imposition with respect to it.

How natural was this conduct on the supposition of Jesus having been conscious to himself that he had a commission from God, and that the evidence of it, which was constantly before the world, was sufficient to satisfy any unprejudiced person. Had he been conscious that his pretensions were destitute of any solid proof, he would naturally have made the most of any fallacious appearance of evidence that he could produce, as Mahomet did of his victory of Beder, and the excellence of the composition of the Koran.

6. The

6. The piety obfervable in the character of Jefus is alone a proof, to thofe who give due attention to the human character, that he was no impoftor. That he was actuated by the genuine fentiments of piety, appeared in all his difcourfes, and the whole of his conduct. He not only always declared that *he came to do the will of God who fent him,* and (John viv. 10.) that *the father within him did the works,* which evidenced his divine miffion; but it is evident that, as the Pfalmift faid, *God was in all his thoughts,* and that to his will he was at all times refigned. It was, as we read, John iv. 34, *his meat and drink to do the will of him that fent him.* He was frequent and earneft in *prayer,* and taught his difciples to pray, to avoid oftentation in prayer, Matt. vi. 6. to *go into their clofets,* and *fhutting the doors,* pray *to their father, who,* he faid, *faw in fecret.* Such a reverence for God, and devotednefs to his will, in life and in death, as Jefus difcovered, is abfolutely incompatible with falfe pretenfions to a miffion from him, whatever might be his object in the impofture. It muft have appeared

to him as the extreme of arrogance and impiety, such as could not fail to draw after it the divine displeasure, and the heaviest judgments.

No person can read the New Testament, and imagine that Jesus was an atheist, or an unbeliever in a future state of righteous retribution. Indeed, it is not probable that there were any proper unbelievers among the Jews in his time. Even the Sadducees were believers in the being and moral government of God, and in the divine mission of Moses. But Jesus was not a Sadducee. He was, without all question, a sincere believer in the doctrine that he taught. And that he was such an enthusiast as to imagine that he had those supernatural communications to which he pretended without having them, is even more improbable than the supposition of his having been an impostor. If ever man was in his *right mind*, and knew what he was about, it was Jesus. All his discourses and actions discover the greatest calmness and composure, and favour nothing of extravagance, which so egregious
an

an enthufiaft could not always have concealed. All his difcourfes are perfectly rational, and his whole conduct was of a piece with them; fo that, if he had no divine miffion, he muft have been not an *enthufiaft*, who had impofed upon himfelf, but properly an *impoftor*, who endeavoured to impofe upon the world; and whether this fuppofition be at all tenable, let any perfon, at all acquainted with human nature, now judge.

Befides the piety of Jefus, he was evidently a man of great benevolence, and had a ftrong fentiment of friendfhip for his apoftles and others. And it cannot be fuppofed that fuch a perfon would purpofely deceive and miflead his countrymen and friends. Impoftors have callous hearts. Intent upon their fchemes, they are deaf to ever other confideration.

Jefus gave many proofs of the ftrongeft and tendereft affection. When he came within fight of Jerufalem, he *wept over it*, in the profpect of the calamities that awaited it. He wept at the grave of Lazarus,

zarus, and his difcourfes to his apoftles a little before his death difcover the moft amiable fympathy, and concern, without the leaft regard to his own approaching fufferings. He was only occupied with the idea of what they would feel when he was removed from them. We fee nothing like this in the conduct of Mahomet.

Though Jefus affected no aufterity, he was free from all fenfual indulgence, which was by no means the cafe of Mahomet; and he certainly did not aim at temporal power, but refolutely declined feveral propofals of the multitude to make him a king. What, then, could an impoftor, without ambition, or perfonal indulgence, aim at? Jefus, being a man, muft have had fome fuch objects as other men have; but there was nothing that other men moft covet that his conduct was at all adapted to gain. He muft, therefore, have had views of a higher nature. On any other hypothefis his conduct is abfolutely unaccountable; but on the fuppofition of his being confcious of having a divine miffion, and of a ftation of of honour and power destined for him in a future world, all his discourses, and his whole conduct, are perfectly natural. *For the joy that was set before him* (Heb. xii. 2.) *he endured the cross, despising the shame* of that ignominous death; but that he should have done this without having had in view any thing that any other man ever thought worth pursuing, is not to be supposed of him, or of any man.

Let all these circumstances be duly considered, the obscure birth, and mean occupation of Jesus, in a distant and despised country, his high pretensions to be the Jewish Messiah, without any assumption of kingly power, universally deemed to be most essential to that character, his claim to a kingdom though not of this world, and to the power of raising the dead and judging the world, when he had nothing but the certain prospect of a violent death before him; his undertaking to overthrow all the religions of the heathen world, firmly attached as the several nations were to them, religions which had kept their
ground

ground from time immemorial, notwithstanding a long period now boasted of as the most enlightened of any till the present; when there had not been from the beginning of the world an example of any nation voluntarily changing their religion; his holding out to his disciples nothing but persecution in this world, and happiness in another; his having no secrets; his discovering no anxiety about the evidences of his divine mission, joined with his calm good sense, his exalted piety, his general benevolence, and the strong affection he always shewed to his friends and followers; let all these circumstances, I say, be considered and, without attending to his miracles, and his success, it must surely be thought impossible that this man could have been an impostor, and meant to deceive the world. This *internal* evidence added to the *external*, on which I have already enlarged, viz. from *miracles*, and *prophecy*, must be abundantly sufficient to satisfy any reasonable and candid inquirer, with respect to the truth of christianity, and of revealed religion in general.

DISCOURSE XIII.

The moral influence of Christian Principles.

If ye know these things, happy are ye if ye do them.
JOHN. xiii. 17.

IN the Discourses which I have already delivered, on the subject of *the evidences of revealed religion*, I first endeavoured to shew the value of *religion in general*, then the superior value of *revealed* religion, compared with that which is called *natural*. After this I gave you a view of the state of the heathen world with respect to religion, and to philosophy also as connected with religion; and the great superiority of the system of Moses, which has been most objected to by unbelievers, in both those respects. I then proceeded to explain the direct, or *external*, evidence of the Jewish and christian religions, from *miracles*, and from *prophecy*; and in the last place, as a part of the *internal* evidence, I shewed, from the circumstances of the history of Jesus, the impossibility of his having been an impostor.

Having thus finished the *argumentative* part of my undertaking, I now proceed to conclude the whole with some observations of a *practical* nature.

1. If revealed religion be *true*, it must be of great *importance*, and demand our closest attention. It may well, indeed, be presumed, that if the divine Being, the great author of universal nature, has interposed in so extraordinary a manner as has been represented, in a scheme commencing with our first parents, carried on through the dispensation of Moses, continued by Jesus Christ, and to be resumed at his second coming, the object must be something of the greatest importance to the duty and the happiness of man; and it cannot be without hazard to ourselves if we neglect, and reject it.

The

The most interesting article in the scheme of revelation is the doctrine of a *future state*. And surely, if there really be a future state for man, if it be of much longer continuance than the present, especially if it is to last for ever, and if our well being in that state will depend on our behaviour in this, it behoves us to pay much more attention to it, than to any thing in this short and transitory life. Did any person now living in this country certainly know that he must soon leave it, and go to another, for example to France, where he had the prospect of succeeding to a large estate, would he not be thinking of his voyage, and making preparations for it? Would he not be learning the French language, and endeavouring in every other way to provide for his enjoyment of life in that distant country? And would a man be commended for his prudence in this case, and blamed for superstition and folly in another case exactly similar to it? Or would you not think a man insane who should forget a journey he was upon, and take up with his inn; and not think it reasonable that a man who believes he is travelling towards an eternal world, should have his attention fixed upon *it*, and make light of any inconvenience he met with in his way thither?

Surely, then, it becomes Christians, who profess themselves to be *pilgrims and strangers* here, and *citizens of heaven*, to be thinking of their proper country, and preparing for their remove to it.

Men of the world naturally say, *let us eat and drink for to-morrow we die*. This is the great burden of the song with all the heathen poets. But the Christian as naturally says with the apostle Paul, Phil. iv. 5. *Let your moderation be known unto all men, the Lord is at hand.*

To use one example more. If you knew that any particular child would die at a certain age, as at ten or twelve, you would adapt his education, and your whole treatment of him accordingly, and not trouble him with making him learn things which he would have no occasion for till he he was a man. But hoping and expecting that your children will grow to man's estate, you reasonably endeavour to qualify them for it, and would be universally blamed if you did not.

Let us, then, believing that we are born for immortality, overlook the transitory enjoyments and pursuits of this uncertain life, and, instead of laying up (Matt. vi. 19) *treasures on earth, where moth and rust corrupt, and where thieves break through and steal,* lay up *treasures in heaven,* where none of these inconveniences happen, and *where our treasure is, there let our hearts be also.*

2. If a life of virtue will alone ensure our happiness hereafter, and vice our misery, it certainly follows, that virtue is our greatest good, and vice our greatest evil. Consequently, our principal endeavour through life, should be the improvement of our moral character, to restrain every propensity to the irregular indulgence of our appetites and passions, to cultivate every generous sentiment of equity and humanity to our fellow-creatures, and habitual

habitual piety to God. Every thing elfe fhould in reafon be made fubfervient to this one great end of human life. To be rich, or to be poor, to be mafter, or to be fervant, to be healthy or difeafed, are mere trifles, and wholly infignificant, compared with acting our part in life well, whatever that part be, that of a king or of a beggar, becaufe it is upon our acting the part affigned us *well*, and not at all upon the nature or comparative dignity of it, that our future well-being will depend.

3. In fuch a world as this, in which it has pleafed divine providence, and, no doubt, with the greateft wifdom, to place us, a ftate of trial and of difcipline, a ftate in which temptations to vice and excefs of every kind are continually before us, conftant vigilance, and the moft ftrenuous exertion, are abfolutely neceffary. In youth the love of pleafure, in more advanced years objects of ambition and avarice, have ftrong charms for men; and the love of thefe things cannot be kept within

within due bounds without the moſt unremitted attention, till a habit of moderation and ſelf government be acquired and confirmed. This habit once formed not only takes away all pain of reſtraint, but converts our duty into pleaſure. But, then, ſuch powerful habits as theſe, are not acquired without much reflection and exerciſe. Reſtraint of any kind (and all virtue, at firſt, is ſuch) is neceſſarily painful, and therefore will not be ſubmitted to without ſome ſtrong counteracting principle, without a principle of ſubmiſſion to ſome *authority*, as that of a parent, of a magiſtrate, of conſcience, or of God. This, as I ſhewed you, is the moſt certain and the moſt powerful of all, and it is no where ſo clearly aſcertained as in revelation. There we learn in the moſt intelligible language, what it is that the Lord our God requires of us, in order to live and to die in his favour, ſo as to ſecure a happy immortality.

Do not deceive yourſelves by imagining that this great prize, of *eternal life*, is to be attained without exertion and labour.

Ad-

Advantages far inferior to this are never secured without them; and can we expect that the greatest of all good, should be obtained so easily? Christianity is, no doubt, the same thing now that it was in the time of Christ and the apostles: and he said, (Matt. x. 37.) *He that loveth father or mother, son or daughter, wife or friend, more than me is not worthy of me, and he that taketh not up his cross and followeth me is not worthy of me.* The apostle Paul frequently compares the life of a Christian to a state of *warfare,* as when he exhorts Christians Tim. vi. 12. *to fight the good fight of faith,* and Eph. vi. 11. *to put on the whole armour of God.* He also compares it to a *race,* as when he says, 1 Cor. ix. 14. *so run that ye may obtain,* viz. what he calls (Phil. iii. 14.) *the prize of the high calling of God in Christ Jesus.* Now both the state of warfare, and the exercises of running and wrestling, as practised in the Grecian games, to which the apostle alludes, required great preparation before the contest, and great exertion in the course of it.

If

If we be christians in earnest, we must have the advantages of Christianity, and the prospect of its rewards in a future state, so much at heart, that we shall prefer them to every other consideration, to every thing in life, and to life itself. I do not say that they who cannot do this are no Christians, or are to be numbered with the *wicked*, and consigned to future punishment; but they cannot have any just claim to those distinguished rewards of Christianity, which are promised to those who are said to have *overcome the world*, which implies a contending with great difficulties, and of whom it is said (Rev. iii. 21.) that *they shall sit down with Christ on his throne, as he also overcame, and is sat down with his father on his throne.* In the house of God the kingdom of heaven, there are *many mansions*, and the choicest are reserved for those who (Acts iv. 22) *through much tribulation enter into the kingdom of God.* But as we do not content ourselves with low attainments in this world when higher are within our reach, let the same ambition animate

animate us with respect to things of still more value, in another world.

As there are all varieties of characters in men, and all gradations in every character, in this world, there will, no doubt, be a corresponding distribution of rewards and punishments in a future state, though in a general way of speaking, and in the scriptures, men are usually divided into two classes, the righteous and the wicked. For the Judge of all the earth will, no doubt, do that which is *right*; and if so, there must be as great a variety of situations in the future world, as there are of characters and deserts of men in this, though we may not be able to form any idea, or conjecture, in what manner this will, or can, be effected.

It may, indeed, be said, and with truth, that if we love virtue at all, so as to be justly intitled to the character of *virtuous and conscientious men*, we shall set no bounds to our love of it. For if, in any case, we give other objects and pursuits a preference to it, it is only in some cases, and

and not universally, that we are disposed to act the conscientious and upright part; whereas God requires that we should give him our whole hearts, we must (Matt. xxii. 37.) *love the Lord our God, with all the heart, with all the soul, and all the mind*, that is, we must be wholly devoted to his will, in doing and in suffering, in life and in death. The apostle James observes (chap. ii. 10.) that *he who keeps the whole law, but offends in one point, is guilty of all*. If there be any case in which a man wilfully and habitually offends, he certainly wants the proper *principle of obedience*, that is, a just respect for the divine authority, which would lead to an uniform and invariable regard to the laws of God. This is a proof that there is some vicious propensity, to which, in his mind, every thing else will give way; and that, had he had as strong a propensity to any other gratification or pursuit, he would have been equally regardless of the authority of God in that case also. For he only obeys the laws of God, and the dictates of conscience,

science, when he feels no strong temptation to transgress them.

In this case no person can properly be said to be *a servant of God*, or of *righteousness*, but only a slave to his own favourite appetite or passion. But we cannot serve God and mammon.

In the present state of things, such as we cannot doubt is the best for a state of trial and discipline, a theatre on which to form great and excellent characters, a proper Christian temper is necessarily a difficult attainment. To form a truly great character there must be many difficulties to struggle with, evils of all kinds, moral as well as natural. For how could the greater virtues of forbearance, doing good against evil, resignation, and trust in God, be formed, but in a world in which men should be exposed to injuries of every kind. Not only could not real virtue be *tried*, and consequently *known*, but it could not even be *formed*, or exist, in other circumstances. And surely the character in which the virtues above mentioned exist is greatly superior

superior to that of the generality of the world; who not comprehending its nature or value, will under-rate and despise it. With them what is commonly called a high spirit, and a promptness to revenge injuries, will be more admired and cultivated than a disposition to pity and befriend the injurious person, which will be reckoned tame, and despicable; though certainly it must appear, on a little consideration, that the latter is more truly magnanimous, implying a greater command of passion, and superior reflection. It is no less evident that it is this prevailing *spirit of the world* which fills private life with quarrels, and which, entering into courts, fills the world with wars, the source of unspeakable misery; whereas a truly Christian temper, a humble, meek, and benevolent disposition would make the intercourse of individuals, and of nations, the source of peace and of happiness.

It is, however, no small attainment to get above the censure and contempt of persons whose minds are in a lower and more degraded state than our own, when they

they are the great majority of the world we live in, and are likely to continue fo. In this ftate of things great exertion of mind is requifite fo far to overcome the world, as to poffefs our own minds in peace and joy. It can only be done by looking habitually towards a ftate in which a truer judgment of characters will be formed, and in which thofe who are really fuperior here will be advanced to that ftate of confideration and refpect to which they are intitled.

The real difference between a merely nominal believer, and an unbeliever is very fmall, and of little confequence, compared to the difference between the merely nominal and the real Chriftian. What are the generality of Chriftians, in what are called chriftian countries? They are, in fact, perfons who mind nothing but their bufinefs, or their pleafure, without giving any attention to the principles of chriftianity at all. It is by no means the fubject of their daily thoughts, it fupplies no motives to their actions, it contributes nothing to moderate

moderate their joys, or to alleviate their sorrows. It neither enables them to bear the troubles of life, nor does it give them any solid hope in death. Whereas the real Christian, as the apostle says, Rom. xii. 15. *rejoices as though he rejoiced not, and weeps as though he wept not, because the fashion of this world passeth away*, and *the Lord is at hand.* He is ever *looking*, Tit. ii. 13. *to that blessed hope, even the glorious appearing of the great God, and his Saviour Christ*, and has peace and joy in believing.

4. Christianity is less to be considered as a system of opinions, than a rule of life. But of what signification is a *rule*, if it be not be complied with? All the doctrines of christianity have for their object christian morals, which are no other than the well known duties of life; and the advantage we derive from this religion is that the principles of it assist us in maintaining that steady regard to the providence and moral government of God, and to a future state, which facilitates and ensures the practice of those duties; inspiring greater piety

piety towards God, greater benevolence to man, and that heavenly mindedneſs which raiſes the heart and affections above thoſe mean and low purſuits which are the ſource of almoſt all vices. But chriſtian principles not reflected upon, or attended to, cannot be accompanied with any advantage of this kind; and better, ſurely, were it to make no profeſſion of any principles, than to live without a due regard to them. Better, therefore, were it for any perſon to be an unbeliever in chriſtianity, than to be a Chriſtian, and live as if he had not been one. He deprives himſelf of all apology or excuſe, for his bad conduct. And it would, I fear, be happy for thouſands of profeſſing Chriſtians, if they had been born and lived among heathens.

We cannot too much impreſs upon our minds, that religion of any kind, is only a *means* to a certain *end*, and that this end is good conduct in life. Conſequently, if this end be not attained, we not only loſe the advantage of the means, or inſtrument, of which we were poſſeſſed, but

but are chargeable with the guilt of such neglect, are guilty of an ungrateful contempt of the means that were afforded us for the greatest and best of purposes; and can we expect that this will go unpunished?

The guilt of *unbelief* does not consist in mere disbelieving. For *opinions* of any kind, as such, bear no relation to *criminality*, but in refusing to consider with due seriousness and impartiality the evidence of christianity that is laid before men; that refusal arising from, and implying, some vicious prejudice, or improper bias. And if, in any particular case (and I doubt not there are such) this refusal does not arise from any vicious prejudice, there is nothing to blame in such refusal. If, for example, any person had no access to the scriptures, by which he might have had the means of better information, and he was required to believe, as what was contained in them, things that he found it absolutely impossible for him to believe, as that bread and wine were flesh and blood, or any thing elfe that appeared to him equally impoffible, he muft of neceffity either be an unbeliever, or give up all pretence to common fenfe.

No perfon, however, can be wholly innocent who does not weigh the difficulties of believing with thofe of unbelief. Whatever difficulties any perfon finds, or are thrown in his way, he fhould confider the general evidence of the great facts on which chriftianity is founded; and if that be fufficient, he may be fatisfied that, though he cannot for the prefent account for fome particular appearances, or reprefentations, the difficulties occafioned by this circumftance cannot be infuperable; fince all truths are confiftent with one another. If it appear, from indifputable hiftorical evidence, that Chrift wrought real miracles, if he died, and rofe from the dead, his religion is unqueftionably from God, and then all the abfurdities charged upon his doctrine muft have arifen from fome mifconception, or mifreprefentation, though we may not be able to trace it. But it is no uncommon thing for a difficulty which

appears

appears insuperable to day, to be cleared up to-morrow, as we see in many cases.

The principles of christianity, however, may be, and no doubt are, of great use when they are not explicitly attended to. They have been the means of establishing such maxims and habits in parents, as are afterwards communicated to their posterity, more by the natural and silent operation of example, than by direct instruction; so that unbelievers, born of Christian parents, and living in a christian country, may be, in a manner, half Christians, without their knowing it. Also mere nominal Christians are, no doubt, often restrained from vices and irregularities forbidden by christianity, without their being aware that the restraint comes originally from that quarter; having acquired habits of decent and proper conduct, which operate mechanically, and without any explicit regard to christian principles, though originally derived from them.

There are also, all degrees of the influence of christian principles, from the exalted character of Christ and the apostles, and many others in every age, who had no other object of attention, and all whose thoughts, sentiments, words, and actions, were under the constant influence of them, who lived as the apostle said, as if *constantly seeing things invisible,* Heb. xi. 27. by *faith and not by sight,* 2 Cor. v. 7. as if the great scenes of the future world were present to them; there is a great difference, I say, between such christians as these, and those of the lowest order, who may, indeed, have read the scriptures, or part of them, and who retain some knowledge of them, and who entertain no doubt of their truth, but in their general conduct they give no explicit attention to them. Nevertheless the knowledge they have acquired has left some favourable impressions on their minds, some latent fear of God, and respect to his providence, and a world to come, which prevents the commission of great crimes, and leads to an uniformly better conduct than they would otherwise have been capable of.

5. If

5. If we have any value for our religion, thinking it to be an useful inftitution, and wifh well to our fellow creatures, to whom we are therefore *defirous* to recommend it, we fhould be particularly careful to exhibit it to proper advantage, in our own difpofitions and conduct. It is to *this* that the generality of mankind, inatentive to reafoning, will look, and not unjuftly. Our Saviour himfelf faid of pretenders to prophecy, and of men in general, Matt. vii. 6. *By their fruits ye fhall know them.* Indeed, as the only end of good principles is good practice, if the latter be not apparent, the former will not be inferred. On this account we muft not confine our religion to our clofets, but carry it with us into life, and in the bufinefs and buftle of it, difcover that fuperior meeknefs, benevolence, and difinterestednefs, which chriftian principles tend to infpire. We fhould, in all refpects, fhew a greater command of our paffions, and a greater freedom from the influence of a love of fenfual pleafure, of ambition, and

avarice

avarice, and from all thofe vices which arife from an exceffive love of the world, and the things of it, to which a regard to heaven and heavenly things, (on which alone our beft affections ought to be fet) naturally leads.

When this is done, but not before, the world in general will have an opportunity of perceiving the real effect of chriftian principles; and if they be not properly influenced by it, the blame will not be ours. There can be no doubt but that, though on fome the faireft and moft advantageous exhibition of chriftian conduct may have an unfavourable effect, fince as our Saviour obferved, there are thofe who (John. iii. 19.) *love darknefs rather than light,* and that the *world,* which *loves its own* (xv. 9.) will hate his difciples *becaufe they are not of the world,* this will be the cafe only with thofe whofe hearts are greatly corrupted. On others the effect muft be favourable. As he fays, (Matt. v. 6.) that *when our light fhines before men they would fee the good works of his difciples, and glorify his father who is in heaven*

heaven. What he meant by *glorifying God,* we clearly see from his saying on another occasion (John xv. 8.) *then is my father glorified when ye bring forth much fruit,* that is, *fruits of righteousness,* which the apostle also says, (Phil. i. 11.) are *to the praise and glory of God.*

But, on the other hand, if, in the whole tenor of men's lives, there does not appear to be any difference between the Christian and the man of the world, how can those who have no other means of judging, or who will not have recourse to any other, suppose that there is any advantage in the principles of the one more than in those of the other? If the nominal Christian behave just like other men, if he puts as little restraint upon himself in indulgences of any kind; if he be as ambitious, as avaricious, and as revengeful, when provoked; if he appear to have no greater regard to God, or love to mankind; shewing itself, as it natually will, in acts of kindness, generosity, and mercy; if the Christian appear to be in all respects, as much

much attached to the world, and the things of it, as other men are, they will naturally fay, that all his pretences to a belief in a future world, a world prepared for the righteous only, are vain, when it is evident from his conduct, that this world has as full poffeffion of his heart as it has of thofe of other men.

By this conduct, not becoming, and adorning, but difgracing, his profeffion, the nominal Chriftian incurs the *woe* pronounced by our Saviour, (Matt. xviii. 7.) *It muft needs be that offences come, but woe to the man by whom they come.* By this means we not only lofe the benefit of chriftian principles ourfelves, but, by giving others an unfavourable opinion of chriftianity, we indifpofe them to the reception of it, and confequently deprive them of the benefit of it. Inftead of being preachers of the gofpel, as every Chriftian in fome fenfe or other ought to be, and which every chriftian may be, at leaft by his example, a perfon who is only a nominal Chriftian, but a vicious man, is in fact a preacher of infidelity,

and

and does every thing that is in his power to unchriftianize the world. On this account there was great ufe in the ftrict difcipline of the primitive church, which rejected all fuch perfons from their communion. Vicious men were to them as *heathen men and publicans.* Being excluded from all connection with Chriftians, and being known to be fo, the caufe of chriftinity did not fuffer by their mifconduct*.

It

---

* It has been unfortunate for the caufe of chriftianity, that ecclefiaftical hiftory, like the civil, is, in a great meafure, an exhibition of vices, and of mifery. For thefe things are always moft prominent, and catch the attention of the generality of obfervers; while the beneficial effects of religious, as well as of civil inftitutions, are much lefs confpicuous. The meek, the humble, and the heavenly minded, though the benevolent among Chriftians, attract little attention, and therefore make no figure in the eye of an hiftorian. Befides, in all cafes, virtue is more common than vice; and on this account the latter attracts more attention. The former is like the gentle rain, or dew, which though it does infinite good, yet, becaufe it is common, is not fo much noticed, as the deftructive ftorm or hurricane, which tears up every thing before it, and lays a whole country wafte.

Wealth and power will corrupt the hearts of men. It cannot, therefore, be thought extraordinary, if this was the effect of wealth and power in the bifhops of the greater fees, and it is the conduct of thefe men about which ecclefiaftical

6 It will be enquired by what means the influence of the world can be counteracted, or by what means a due attention to

clefiaftical hiftory is moft converfant; while the poor, the humble, and laborious teachers of chriftianity, and their hearers in lower life, who were really influenced by its fpirit, and laid themfelves out to do good, hoping for no reward but in heaven, paffed unnoticed.

Occafions, however, have frequently occurred, which drew out thefe men, and their principles, into public view. I mean feafons of perfecution; and then it might be feen what the power of chriftian principles really is. And when it is confidered what numbers of Chriftians have fuffered for their religion, in the heathen, the Papal, and even proteftant, perfecutions, what torture many of them endured, and, what is much more trying, of how long continuance were the fufferings of many of them, in prifons and dungeons, where they lingered out their lives deftitute of every comfort, when liberty, life, honour, and wealth, would have been the reward of a fimple renunciation of their faith, it will be evident that there is in chriftianity fomething that has great power over the hearts and lives of men.

But the principal circumftance to be attended to in the hiftories of perfecutions is not the greatnefs, or the duration of the fufferings of the martyrs, but the temper of mind with which they fuffered; their piety, their patience, their meeknefs, their benevolence, their freedom from the fpirit of revenge, and the good will which they fhewed even to their enemies and perfecutors. This is an attainment of a truly extraordinary nature, which it is in vain that we look for among the heathens. This is not the difpofition with which the North American Indian bears his torture.

Should

to chriſtian principles can be beſt ſecured. I anſwer, the principal means to effect this great purpoſe, and one that will naturally lead to every other, is a familiar acquaintance with the ſcriptures. The zealous chriſtian will make theſe books his conſtant companions. With the pious Pſalmiſt (Pſalm i. 2.) *his delight will be in the law of the Lord, and in his law will he meditate day and night.*

Be aſſured that in reading the ſcriptures ever ſo often, you will always find ſomething new and intereſting. Many

---

Should perſecution again ariſe, chriſtian principles being the ſame that they ever were, would, I doubt not, produce as great and as extenſive effects. But I am far from wiſhing for an experiment of this kind. We are directed not to court, but to ſhun perſecution, if we can do it with integrity and honour, from which, however, we are never to ſwerve. And perhaps chriſtian principles undergo a trial no leſs ſevere in proſperity than in adverſity. It is commonly ſaid, and with truth, that if adverſity has ſlain its thouſands, proſperity has ſlain its ten thouſands. A ſeaſon of perſecution forces an attention to chriſtian principles, and unites numbers in the ſame cauſe; but in proſperity we muſt of our own accord, and without any external impulſe, give attention to chriſtian principles; and this the obtruſion of worldly objects too often prevents.

difficulties

difficulties you will, no doubt, meet with, as may be expected in books of such great antiquity, written many of them in a language which is but imperfectly understood, and abounding with allusions to customs with which we in this part of the world are unacquainted, and, which being in many respects the reverse of ours, will of course appear unnatural. But new light is thrown upon things of this nature every day. Many difficulties are already cleared up in the most satisfactory manner, and in the mean time every thing of this nature may be safely neglected, or referred to farther consideration, especially if you read for the purpose of moral improvement, the greatest part of the Bible being perfectly intelligible to every capacity, and in the highest degree useful and edifying.

A familiar acquaintance with the scriptures will preserve upon the mind a lively sense of God and his moral government. It will continually bring into view, and give you an habit of contemplating, the great plan of providence, respecting the design designs of God in the creation of man, and his ultimate destination. You will by this means have a clearer view of the divine wisdom and goodness in the government of the world, even in the most calamitous events, as in the corruption of true religion, as well as in the reformation of it. You will perceive signs of order in the present seemingly disordered state of things, and will rejoice in the prospect of the glorious completion of the scheme, in universal virtue and universal happiness. Such views of things as these, which will be perpetually suggested by the reading of the scriptures, have the greatest tendency to ennoble and enlarge the mind, to raise our thoughts and affections above the low pursuits which wholly occupy and distract the minds of the bulk of mankind, they will inspire a most delightful serenity in the midst of the cares and troubles of life, and impart *a joy which the world can neither give nor take away.*

By the frequent reading of the scriptures we shall be unavoidably led to the exercises of meditation, constant watchfulness

fulness, and prayer, and every other means of virtuous improvement, whatever has any tendency to repress what is vicious and defective, and promote what is most excellent in the human character.

The study of the scriptures, which contain the history of the transactions of God with men, and which furnish topics of discussion proper for the exercise of the greatest genius, is equally interesting to the lowest and the most improved of the human race. Sir Isaac Newton, whose reputation as a philosopher stands higher than that of any other man, devoted almost the whole of his time after he was turned forty (and he lived to the age of eighty-four) to theology; and from my personal knowledge I can say that some persons now living, and lately living in England, who had greatly distinguished themselves, in mathematical and philosophical pursuits, declared that, as they advanced in life, they had the most satisfaction in theological ones. Nor can this be thought extraordinary, when it is considered that these

these are subjects of infinitely more moment than any others to rational beings, born for immortality.

Let us then, my christian brethren, whatever be our situation or employment in life, whether our pursuits relate to agriculture, manufactures, commerce, natural philosophy, or any of the learned professions; though we should be employed in the more immediate service of the public, in any civil, or military capacity, let us not forget that we are *men* and *Christians*, and without neglecting the immediate and necessary business of this life, attend chiefly to what is of infinitely more importance, viz. our destination to *another;* and, accordingly be solicitous to act such a part, and to cultivate such habits, as will be our best preparation for it; that whenever we come to die, the great business of life may be done, and we may be like servants constantly looking for the return of their lord, that *when he shall return, and take an account of his servants, we may be found of him,* as the apostle says, 2 Pet. iii. 14. *without spot*

spot and blameless, and not be ashamed before him at his coming: but at the *great day,* emphatically so called, before the consideration of which every thing else should vanish like a shadow, we may hear the joyful sentence, Matt. xxv. 21. *well done good and faithful servants, enter ye into the joy of your lord.*

www.ingramcontent.com/pod-product-compliance
Lightning Source LLC
Chambersburg PA
CBHW022143300426
44115CB00006B/318